D1006408

MATURE MONEY

Marketing Financial Services to the Booming Maturity Market

MATURE MONEY

Marketing Financial Services to the Booming Maturity Market

JOAN M. GRUBER

The Irwin/IAFP Series in Financial Planning

IAFP

INTERNATIONAL ASSOCIATION
FOR FINANCIAL PLANNING

IRWIN
Professional Publishing®
Chicago • London • Singapore

Times Mirror
Higher Education Group

Library of Congress Cataloging-in-Publication Data

Gruber, Joan M., (date)
 Mature money : marketing financial services to the booming
maturity market / by Joan M. Gruber.
  p. cm.
 Includes bibliographical references and index.
 ISBN 0-7863-0971-7
 1. Aged—Finance, Personal. 2. Retirement. 3. Postemployment
benefits. I. Title.
HG179.G794 1997
332.1'068'8—dc20   96–31817

Printed in the United States of America

1 2 3 4 5 6 7 8 9 0 DO 3 2 1 0 9 8 7 6

Ten percent of the author's profits from this book will be donated to The National Coalition for the Homeless.

This book is dedicated to all my teachers

PREFACE: THE MATURITY MARKET: WHY ALL THE FUSS?

I was teaching a Chartered Life Underwriters (CLU) course, "Planning for Retirement Needs," in the spring of 1992 to several veteran insurance agents. The first half of the course was about planning *for* retirement. It was a detailed study about qualified and nonqualified plans. The agents loved it. Working with business owners was exciting to them. They did their homework faithfully and never missed a class. I'm glad they loved it because I didn't. This was *not* my area. My expertise was working with the already retired, or the about-to-be-retired. I call it the *post-retirement* market. The issues for that group are very unique.

When we finally arrived at the second half of the course, which dealt with the post-retirement issues, I noticed a marked decrease in the agents' enthusiasm. "This is boring. We don't have any interest in learning about clients' needs once they are retired," they said. "How will you serve your clients when they retire if you don't start learning about the issues now?" I asked them. They responded, "We'll call you for help!" They weren't kidding. That really was their plan.

That was the first time I realized how ill prepared my colleagues are to serve the maturity market. There is a whole body of knowledge the basics of which the financial service professional needs to know to be successful in this market. The issues range from being familiar with the basic health care, legal, tax, housing, and financial issues, special financial products, changing public policy, marketing and sales, to an ability to deal with death and multigenerational issues. This book is about how to market to the most experienced generation. Hopefully you will know where to get help with the other areas when the need arises. We will take a practical approach so that you can immediately apply what you learn. However, if you wish to learn more, see Further Reading in the rear of the book, which includes references about demographics, theories of aging, and changing consumer behavior.

The book provides information for any financial service professional who aspires to work successfully with the maturity market. Chances are that your company or product manufacturers (mutual funds, insurance companies, etc.) are already working with a maturity market consultant to develop product, marketing strategies, advertising campaigns, sales materials, and point-of-sale brochures.

If you work for a large financial service company, your "home office" product and marketing strategists are probably already aware of the concepts in this book, but they might not be sharing this information with you. My contention is that you need these tools to facilitate your success in the marketplace. If you are a salesperson or advisor, you are in front of clients every day—where the rubber meets the road. The challenge is to take some of the theories that are driving the development of products and services and translate them into a system that you can use to enhance your success with this vast and rapidly growing market. More "systems" will be available to you as the market evolves, but the information in this book will get you started.

CONTENTS

Chapter 3

How Salespeople and Marketers Can Attract the Maturity Market   41

Chapter 4

Successful Client Interaction   77

Chapter 5

Keys to Client Loyalty   93

MATURE MONEY

Marketing Financial Services to the Booming Maturity Market

CHAPTER

The Maturity Market Defined

CHARLOTTE: THE SOUTHERN LADY

Charlotte had experienced many heartaches in her life, but they never seemed to affect her outlook on the world, except perhaps to strengthen her faith. Meetings with Charlotte were always a good time thanks to her bright, cheerful smile and buoyant laughter. She was 70 when I met her, a widow with three living adult children and several grandchildren. Charlotte was a beautiful woman—tall, dignified, and full of life. Although she was a lady of means, money had no meaning for her. I remember complimenting her once on her handbag. I recognized it since I had just purchased one. It was made by a well-known manufacturer of quality, expensive leather goods. She just giggled like a naughty schoolgirl with a secret. "I'm embarrassed to tell you where I bought it and what I paid for it. But I'll tell you if you won't tell anybody. I took a pile of clothes to donate to the church secondhand clothing store yesterday. While I was there I spotted this bag that someone else had brought in. It was only $10! It looks like it's never been used, don't you think? So I bought it. I felt so silly taking clothing in to give away and walking out with a purchase." Charlotte knew value, and the fact that she had bought the bag at a secondhand store didn't phase her. The real joke was on me. I had just paid $225 for the identical bag. So we had a good laugh.

Charlotte: The Southern Lady (continued)

She was playful and had a terrific sense of humor. One time she brought in a book she had purchased years ago for her children called *Jumping Joanie*. That had become her nickname for me, inspired by my high energy level. To prove that such a cartoon character existed, she brought me the book. After that I was known in the office as "Jumping Joanie" thanks to Charlotte's playfulness.

Charlotte was a very compassionate, caring lady. A few years after I met her she was introduced to a very handsome man and started to date for the first time in years. She would ask her attorney and me for advice about how to entertain him and what to wear on dates. The special thing about her gentleman was that he was totally blind. But that didn't bother Charlotte. I always made it a point to tell him how beautiful she was, to which he would respond, "Yes, I know." What I remember most about Charlotte was her dedication to her church. When she wasn't painting landscapes, or caring for her flower beds, she would spend hours a day at her church arranging flowers for the altar and doing whatever else needed to be done. Charlotte passed away nearly five years ago as a result of a heart attack. She was a wonderful example of many characteristics of the maturity market.

To help you gain a perspective on the maturity market and why it is so important to develop a good working definition consider its size. By the year 2020, nearly 40 percent of the U.S. population will be age 50 and over.[1] Any product or service provider who does not accurately define and target this enormous group will be missing out on a major opportunity, if not fighting for survival.

Professionals who work with the mature market define it in several very different ways. Often as we age our outlook on life, our values, and our needs go through enormous changes. This alone is responsible for much of the confusion surrounding the pursuit of a useful definition. It is no wonder that although this market is aggressively pursued, it is rarely understood. A better understanding of it might result in greater success not only in reaching mature consumers but also in capturing and retaining their business.

We can examine the mature market from three separate viewpoints: chronological age, physiological status, and psychological profile. Within these segments, we can further define it to include other variables such as net worth or needs.

Chronological Age

Defined by chronological age, this market includes:

- The older baby boomers born between 1946 and 1950.
- The silent (or IKE) generation born between 1932 and 1945.
- The World War II, Great Depression, and other generations born before 1932.

By most standards, this definition is overly broad, except for some specific product and service providers. Although most advertising efforts have defined the market by age alone, it is important to note that no one ever bought anything because of his age.

Physiological Characteristics

We can also define the mature market by the physiological characteristics of its members, since physical changes occur as we age. However, due to improved health care, diet, exercise, medical technology, and cosmetic surgery, any attempt to define this group according to physical characteristics is useless.

Psychological Profile

A third way to define it is by psychological characteristics. If we use this method, theoretically anyone of any age who exhibits characteristics of the mature individual could be considered a mature consumer. However, as a practical matter, that rarely happens since the psychological characteristics of the mature person result from life experiences that typically take place over several decades.

A Vague Correlation between Age and Psychological Development

Generally speaking, the characteristics of most mature individuals begin to become apparent somewhere in their 40s and are very apparent by the time they reach their 60s. This gradual transition creates a challenge for the product developer and marketer. And, as we will discuss later, some who are chronologically older never quite make it to a more mature level of psychological development. Trying to create and market products and services for the mature market is like trying to hit a moving target. This idea of transitioning into maturity is a critical point for the salesman and marketer to grasp. To further complicate the situation, people have different transitions styles. Some change suddenly, some slowly, while others take two steps forward and one step back. What works with a client today might fall flat tomorrow. If you are still relating to him after he has begun his transition the same way you did before he began to change, you might lose him as a client.

CHARACTERISTICS OF THE MATURE MARKET

In the early years of my career as a financial planner, like most planners, I worked with all sorts of people, accepting anyone who walked in the door. But I eventually became bored. There were days when I loved what I did and days when I was ready to leave the profession. I suspected that the reason for my ambivalence lay in the type of clients with whom I was working. To discover what determined my attitude of the day, I pulled client files out of the drawer and separated them into two piles: those I enjoyed working with, and those I did not. The pile with the clients I enjoyed comprised almost entirely those over 60 years of age; the other pile was made up almost entirely of those under age 60.

I wondered what made the over-60 somethings more enjoyable for me. I discovered that they had certain characteristics that I found appealing and easier to be with professionally. Here is a list of those characteristics, as well as other characteristics I have discovered over the years as I have continued to work with older individuals.

People in the later years tend to be:

1. *Independent:* They gather information and make their own decisions, resisting manipulation, coercion, and control.
2. *Realistic:* They are honest with themselves and with others.
3. *Discriminating:* They simply will not associate with anyone or anything that does not represent honesty, integrity, and value.
4. *Unpretentious:* They are not materialistic and not easily impressed.
5. *Content:* They accept their station in life.
6. *Spontaneous:* They respond to the moment untethered by baggage from the past.
7. *Fun loving:* They enjoy humor and can be very playful.

8. *Grateful:* They appreciate what life and people have taught them.

9. *Self-reliant:* They keep their own counsel and take responsibility for themselves.

10. *Caring:* They are aware and responsive to the needs of others.

11. *Compassionate:* They are empathetic about others and nature, and are nonjudgmental.

12. *Altruistic:* They recognize the needs of others and give willingly of their time and money.

13. *Genuine:* They are uninhibited in expressing their thoughts and feelings.

14. *Appreciative:* They enjoy nature, beauty, the arts, and other cultures.

15. *Balanced:* They strive to balance body, mind, and spirit, which includes balancing the commonly accepted male and female sides of themselves.

16. *Spiritual:* They connect with their spiritual side through their love of the arts, nature, travel, people, and religious practices.

17. *Connected:* They are relationship oriented toward people and nature.

18. *Peaceful:* They accept themselves and others.

19. *Responsible:* They take responsibility for society and for themselves by getting involved.

20. *Private:* They insist on keeping their personal and business affairs confidential.

21. *Wise:* They have grown through their experiences, which they no longer judge.

22. *Intuitive:* They have a keen ability to discern vital information about people and things. This includes knowing who they can and cannot trust.

23. *Accepting:* Their integrated personalities allow them to accept the ambiguities of life.

24. *Beneficent:* Because it is important to them that they leave their mark on the world, they express their values through charitable works and bequests to family and others.

25. *Humble:* Humility is the natural result of their appreciation of themselves and others, and the vital role each of us plays.

26. *Timeless:* Their view of life and death and their priorities are the result of their ageless and expansive vantage point regarding time.

Some Real-Life Examples of Mature Individuals

A few examples might help us to better understand some of the characteristics listed above and other important concepts. Throughout the book you will find scenarios about current or past clients. I would not be sharing this information about their personal lives except that they have given me explicit permission to do so, except of course, for those who have passed on. Maybe you will recognize qualities that you have observed in your clients. I will point out the most salient characteristics from the above list that apply in each case, although most of the individuals discussed will possess nearly all of them.

Recognizing the Road to Maturity

The process of transitioning to a higher level of development usually begins sometime in the 40s, although for others it can begin as early as in the mid-30s. This is the point in life when we begin to raise serious issues such as "Why am I here?" "What is my purpose in my life?" "What is the meaning of various events in my life?" As maturity market consultant David Wolfe has pointed out, the "psychological center of gravity"[2] of this country is shifting, and it will continue to do so dramatically as an enormous segment of our population enters this phase of life when metaphysical questions become a focal point. This shifting of consciousness will have a profound effect on every aspect of our society, including how we view money and its purpose in our lives, how we arrange our priorities, and how we develop and present products and services.

MATURITY IN SHADES OF GRAY

Not all of our clients are at the same place on the maturity continuum, and it is important for us to recognize that. I do not wish to represent that all of my clients possess all of the qualities mentioned above nor that all have grown into mature individuals. Some never quite make it to full maturity. You will discover many, as I have, who seem to be at a different level of psychological development. I sometimes accept those who exhibit few of the characteristics of more mature individuals for a number of reasons:

1. They need competent professional advice.
2. I recognize an opportunity to enhance my own personal growth.
3. I recognize an opportunity to develop my professional expertise.

However, I never accept, nor would I continue to work with, a client who is verbally abusive, who makes unreasonable demands on my time and services, and is neither appreciative nor willing to adequately compensate me for my time and expertise.

Some I include in the mature market have not fully moved into the mature stage of development, and perhaps they never will. Most are still stuck in the first two or three levels. They retain a self-image that was given to them, attempting to live out someone else's blueprint of what they ought to be. They are out of focus, not congruent with themselves, not their true selves. Because they look outside themselves for satisfaction of their needs, they are often described as needy or codependent.

During the later years, this group is lumped together with the developmentally mature group by virtue of their age. However, the extremes of the two groups bear little resemblance to one another, except for the sharing of their chronological age. Nor is their approach to products and services the same. It is important for the marketer and the salesperson to be able to identify which category of person he is dealing with, and with what level of maturity.

Some common characteristics of the needy or codependent group are fear, insecurity, blame, judgment, lack of self-reliance, controlling or rigid behavior, powerlessness, magical thinking, low self-esteem, and victimization that sometimes verges on paranoia. They often feel overwhelmed, are rarely genuinely joyous, and are fearful of nearly everything. Many have no clue as to how to get their adult needs met. They violate the boundaries of others and allow themselves to be violated. They rarely take responsibility for themselves, and they experience life as a series of extremes, overreacting to everyday events. Many are depressed, as indicated by either agitation or a low energy level. Those at the extreme of codependency are the most challenging to work with. Unlike those at the other end of the maturity spectrum, who seem to come from a position of faith and love, they react with fear. But the reality is that many of them need our products and services and they can afford to pay us. In short, they are likely clients and customers and we need to learn how to work effectively with them.

The Human Maturity Continuum

Combining all of this information about the psychology of aging can be a daunting task, but an important one if we are to relate effectively to the maturing person. While you might not recognize the characteristics I am using here to describe the mature individual, keep in mind that many of your clients are continuing to mature. To relate to them as they age and mature, it will be helpful for you to be able to recognize these changes and be flexible enough to relate to them as they change. Carl Rogers stated eloquently the idea that individuals are always maturing. They are multifaceted, and to be able to relate to them we must be aware of all their components: "Whether the stimulus arises from within or without, whether the environment is favorable or unfavorable, the behaviors of an organism can be counted on to be in the direction of maintaining, enhancing and reproducing itself. This is the very nature of the process we call life."[3] "The psychologically mature person exhibits a trust in the direction of inner organismic processes which, with consciousness participating in a coordinated rather than a competitive fashion, carry one forward in a total unified integrated, adaptive, and changing encounter with life and its challenges."[4]

I developed the Human Maturity Continuum, Figure 1–1, to help you see in a snapshot the stages we go through as we mature. I include the entire life in the continuum even though I realize that the subject at hand is not infants, teenagers, or young adults. I include the early years for a reason. As discussed earlier, many in their later years still operate psychologically from the perspective of a much chronologically younger person. They can fool you since they are in a grown-up body. Also, some in a young body have the maturity level of those who are older. The Human Maturity Continuum will help you visualize the various parts of ourselves that converge to make us who we are. The continuum includes psychological characteristics that are all pegged to an age group. However, these age groupings are general, referring to the average age at which certain events occur. In Figure 1–2, Characteristics of Human Behavior, I have listed the basic characteristics of adults in two extreme stages of maturity and how you might relate to them.

MASLOW'S HIERARCHY OF NEEDS

No discussion of maturity would be complete without at least a brief overview of the theories of noted psychologist Abraham Maslow. According to Maslow, the human has a natural tendency to grow and

Human Maturity Continuum: Psychological Aspects

	Birth	Childhood	Teen Years	Adult	Later Years
NEEDS:	**Physiological** ■ Food ■ Clothing ■ Shelter ■ Hygiene ■ Touch	**Safety and Security** ■ Nuturing ■ Modeling: Moral values ■ Modeling: Social skills ■ Modeling: Boundaries	**Love and Belonging** ■ Peer acceptance ■ Modeling: Self-care ■ Modeling: Life skills ■ Sexual exploration	**Self-esteem and Esteem of Others** ■ Esteem:Colleagues ■ Esteem: Mate ■ Esteem: Friends ■ Career achievement	**Self-Actualization** ■ Connectedness ■ Creative expression ■ Spiritual experience ■ Peace
Approximate Age:	0–2	3–10	11–19	20–59	60 +
VALUES:	Physical comfort	Toys and Playmates	Physical attractiveness	■ Family ■ Material acquisitions ■ Status ■ Luxury ■ Convenience	■ Family ■ Experiences ■ Independence ■ Dignity ■ Comfort
PERSONALITY Characteristics:	■ Dependent ■ Playful ■ Spontaneous ■ Curious	■ Spontaneous ■ Curious ■ Unpretentious ■ Genuine	■ Competitive ■ Hopeful ■ Ego-driven ■ Sex conscious ■ Outer-directed	■ Ambitious ■ Controlling ■ Ego-driven ■ Denial ■ Outer-directed	■ Accepting/peaceful ■ Inner-directed ■ Independent ■ Balanced ■ Spirit-driven
GOAL:	SURVIVAL				➤ CREATION
MOTIVATOR:	FEAR				➤ LOVE

FIGURE 1–2

Characteristics of Human Behavior

	Undeveloped Adult	Highly Developed Adult
BASE MOTIVATOR	Fear	Love
BASE PERSONALITY	Low self-esteem	High self-esteem
CHARACTERISTICS	Victim mentality	Powerful
	Anger	Joy
	Disconnected between body, mind, spirit	Balanced between body, mind, spirit
	Unbalanced male-female energy	Balanced male-female energy
	Dependence	Independence
	Obsession with bodily functions	Sees body as instrument for expression
	Obsessed with safety	Feels safe and secure
	No sense of humor	Laughs easily
	Controlling, manipulative	Accepting
	Unreasonably demanding	Realistic
	Low tolerance level for frustration	Patient
	Abusive of themselves and others	Respectful of themselves and others
GOAL	To survive	To create
HOW TO RELATE TO THEM	Be empathic: provide much support, direction, guarantees, and firm recommendations	Be empathic: provide lots of information; allow them to express and decide for themselves

develop both psychologically and physiologically. As he grows from one level of development to another, his values and needs change. Maslow's levels of human needs, culminating in the highest level, self-actualization, include:

Self-actualization.

Self-esteem and esteem of others.

Love and belonging.

Safety and security.

Physiological needs.

According to Maslow, as our needs at one level are met, we grow to the next level. The lower levels of human needs correspond with infancy, childhood, our teen years, and our working years. As our physiological needs for food, clothing, shelter, and touch are met, we can then move to the next level of maturation, safety and security. If we feel safe, free from bodily harm and emotional or verbal assault, for example, we can then move on to the need to be loved and to feel a sense of connectedness to the group. The teenager's need to feel accepted by his peer group is an example of this stage of development. Once this need to be accepted is met we can move upward to the need for self-esteem and the esteem of others. This is usually experienced during the working years as we strive to achieve in our careers. Once all these needs are met, we are then ready to achieve self-actualization. Those who are well entrenched in the self-actualizing stage have a highly developed spirituality—not to be confused with religion, which is more important to those still in the first four levels of development.[5]

Self-Actualization: The Pinnacle of Maturity

Self-actualization is the term Maslow assigned to the pinnacle of the maturation process to which we all aspire, but which very few actually achieve. Notice that the first three or four levels of needs are deficit-driven or fear-based. Fear, or lack, is no longer a reality for the self-actualizing individual. A detached love (my words) is the basis for every thought, feeling, and behavior of the fully mature, self-actualized person. This love might be totally unrecognizable to those in the other three or four levels, since it is both creative and detached, but not without feeling.

In reality, few ever achieve full self-actualization, at least not permanently. Self-actualization is to a greater or lesser degree the recognition of the possibility of reconciliation of such dualities as spirituality and materialism, boldness and humility, and detachment and compassion. It occurs when we begin to realize the true nature of man and his mission.

According to Maslow, the self-actualizing person has the ability to achieve "peak experiences." During a peak experience, he can view an object in the environment in a way that is totally detached from his ego. He sees the object in its entirety and as being whole, perfect, and complete, totally unrelated to the environment and the viewer, existing only for itself, free of a foreground or background. He views the object with unconditional love (my words) and total acceptance of the object in its essence as it is, merely allowing it to be. Typically, feelings of extreme well-being and positive emotional responses result from such experiences. The objects of the experiences are usually works of art, nature, or the presence of a lover, child, or other loved one. During the experience, the viewer is free of all judgment, and is therefore not comparing the viewed object to anything in the environment. For the viewer, time and space are suspended.

Alan Watts, the great contemporary philosopher, described the spiritual experience (or "cosmic consciousness," as some have called it) eloquently in *This Is It and Other Essays on Zen and Spiritual Experience:* "The central core of the experience seems to be the conviction, or insight, that the immediate now whatever its nature, is the goal and fulfillment of all living. Surrounding and flowing from this insight is an emotional ecstasy, a sense of intense relief, freedom, and lightness, and is often of almost unbearable love for the world, which is, however, secondary."[6]

Maslow defines self-actualization experienced during a peak experience, which he claims "some rare people enter at the age of 60," as "an episode, or a spurt in which the powers of the person come together in a particularly efficient and intensely enjoyable way, and in which he is more integrated and less split, more open for experience, more idiosyncratic, more perfectly expressive or spontaneous, more fully functioning, more creative, more humorous, more ego-transcending, more independent of his lower needs, etc. He becomes in these intense episodes more truly himself, more perfectly actualizing his potentialities, closer to the core of his Being, more fully human."[7]

Clearly understanding and appreciating this concept of self-actualization are important for anyone who works with the mature market. A lack of understanding results in ageism in product and service design, marketing and advertising, and during face-to-face interaction with the client. Conversely, those who keep this phenomenon in mind as they design products, services, and marketing campaigns will be poised for success.

Needs of the Mature Individual

The needs and values of the more mature individual can be summarized as follows:

1. *The need to create through expression of his own uniqueness within the context of other people.* He recognizes that each person is unique and is a deliberate expression of the whole

of the universe. He has discovered what makes him unique and that it is his responsibility, his life's mission, to express that uniqueness as a necessary part of the whole.

2. *The need to experience and appreciate the beauty of the world as demonstrated in nature, people, and events.* He often enjoys traveling and soaking up other cultures. When he returns from a trip he will probably talk about the people he met and how they lived. He will probably be quick to point out the similarities between people of the world. If he buys anything, it will probably be something for his grandchildren, or maybe a work of art for himself. He buys art because of its beauty, or the richness of its history, and not because it is a symbol of his wealth. Experiences are often more important than things. The mature person loves to sample foreign flavors, and takes delight in a beautiful display of food. Epicurianism is a common interest of this group. This "gateway to experience," as David Wolfe calls it, is the basis for the message in successful advertising.

3. *The need to express gratitude for the gift of life and for all that he encounters, including all beings and nature, whom he views as his teachers.* He has come to love life with all its challenges and hurdles because each day is an opportunity to learn something new.

4. *The need to express love, fun, and humor.* He sees the seeming incongruities in life and takes pleasure in laughing along with them. He has grown from childish to childlike and delights in the simple joys. Humor and laughter are used to bring people together, not to demean or to set them apart through ridicule. He can also laugh at himself.

5. *The need to continue to grow both spiritually and intellectually.* Spirituality is an important part of the life of the mature individual. It is often quiet and unspoken. While some express spirituality within the walls of a church or temple, many turn to nature as their place of worship. They find listening to a symphony, a walk in the woods, an intimate moment with a loved one, or touring an art gallery to be a spiritual experience. Many sharpen their intellect by reading and taking on intellectually stimulating hobbies.

6. *The need to share the benefit of his bounty, including his experience, with others.* Many mature people are altruisitic. Giving is a natural extension of who they are. They give money

and time to charity. They share their expertise by mentoring younger people. They develop estate plans to share their material wealth with their progeny.

7. *The need to remain a detached observer of others and of life's events.* They remain at peace by being detached from their surroundings. While they have intentions and desires, they remain detached from the results.

8. *The need to express his connection to others and to nature.* He knows that separation destroys, while connection creates. He also knows that fear is the basis of all separation and that love is the connecting force that always seeks expression.

9. *The need to be self-reliant and to maintain his dignity and self-respect.* Because he recognizes that he is a whole, functioning organism within the context of a larger one, he sees his self-reliance as a way to maintain harmony in the world.

10. *The need for solitude and contemplation.* He has become comfortable with himself and recognizes that inner peace for each person is the key to maintaining peace in the world. He finds joy in going within and knows that inner peace is the key to contentment and health.

11. *The need to experience joy.* The mature person knows that he can be joyous no matter what the situation.

12. *The need to maintain balance between body, mind, and spirit, including optimum functioning of the body.* He has learned how to balance the body, mind, and spirit. This takes practice to observe proper habits including a healthy diet, proper exercise, intellectual stimulation, and honoring the cues his body is giving him.

13. *The need to be in charge of his own decisions about his life.* He gathers information and makes up his own mind. He is not easily swayed or influenced about anything.

The Needs of the Less Mature

Those in the fear-based group are still, even in the later adult years, fixated on meeting the needs Maslow placed at the lower level on the human needs list. These needs are:

1. *The need for food, clothing, and shelter.* Some in this group are truly obsessed with food and health care. Some are terrified that they will be out on the street. This is the group that poses the greatest challenge for our legislators and policy advisers as they attempt to sell block

grants and reduced Medicare and Social Security benefits to the older public. They often cannot see creative solutions because their fear is so blinding. They see doctor's visits and other traditional health care as the only solution to their health challenges, rather than healthier mental, spiritual, dietary, and exercise habits.

2. *The need to be cared for.* The extremes in this group are not self-reliant. It would not occur to many of them that it is not the job of others to be their caregivers. Many are emotionally dependent and unable to sort through issues and come up with solutions. This group often expects the government and family members to take care of them financially and emotionally.

3. *The need for attention from others.* The urgency to have their needs met is so great that they are often demanding and expect to be the center of attention, even competing with the younger members of the family for attention.

4. *The need to feel safe and secure.* This group has a difficult time dealing with unknowns. Because they never learned to trust themselves, they must depend on others, which is very frightening to them. They are often controlling and manipulative in an effort to feel secure. Money, or their perception of a lack of it, is prominent.

The members of this group seem to live in fear that their needs will not be met, in direct contrast to the members of the more mature group who have total confidence in their ability to accept and to handle whatever life experiences they encounter. The fear-based group lacks the ability for creative expression. They are still trying to survive. They live in fear, while the more mature group is love-based. The fear-based group's focus is on lack and all that they seemingly do not have. Those in the fear-based group have little to truly give since they are not whole within themselves, whereas the gift of the love-based group is merely an extension of love itself, which is overflowing.

Aspirations of Mature Individuals

The aspirations as well as the needs of older adults should be considered as an important influencing factor on the older person's value system and needs. In her dissertation, *Aspirations in the Later Years: the Inner Experience of Aging*,[8] Rachelle Dorfman wrote of wishes, desires, and interests shared with her by older residents, aged 67 to 102, in a continuing care retirement community in the Delaware Valley. She reported the aspirations of the residents as represented by how frequently they made statements that reveal certain goals, wishes, and desires. The statements made most often were about issues in these areas: spiritual, epicurean, health, learning, relationships, goals beyond death, euthanasia, not being a burden, being of service, and others.

How My Clients View Death

You will notice that in sharing stories about a few of my clients throughout the book, the subject of death comes up more than once. This is no coincidence. If you work with older people, death and illness are common. For that reason, it is not only helpful but necessary to be comfortable with the subject of death and illness and all the feelings that surround it. In fact, I have found that many clients who exhibit the characteristics of the mature individual are very comfortable discussing this issue.

It is important to understand the older persons' view of aging, illness, and death if you are to work with them successfully. I have never once met an older person who was afraid of death, although many are afraid of, or would not choose to suffer, a painful or prolonged death. Every older person with whom I have worked agrees, often volunteers, that he should have the right to terminate his own life rather than to suffer a prolonged painful death, loss of dignity, or to be a burden to his family or to society.

According to Barbara J. Logue in her book *Last Rights*,[9] the public's view of physician-assisted death has changed since early surveys on the subject in the 1930s. In a Roper poll (1991) respondents were asked, "As you know, lethal drugs are drugs which can be taken by mouth or by injection, that can end a person's life peacefully and quickly. Should doctors be allowed to prescribe lethal drugs to terminally ill patients who request them so that the patients can end their lives, if and when they decide to?" Sixty percent responded "yes" and 32 percent responded "no." This affirmative response is up from 37 percent to a similar question asked in a Gallup poll in 1947. I find clients are very willing to speak openly, often jokingly, about death. Their younger family members, however, rarely take such a lighthearted approach. Illness, terminal illness, suffering, and death, including sudden death, are very important issues for the older person. Since your client's money is a very important part of his life, even if money in and of itself has no meaning, how the client views money and his use of it are often connected not only with his view of death but also with his proximity to the end of his life. In short, his view of illness and death can have a profound effect on his priorities and how he spends his money.

There are many ways to view and cope with death. Some see it as a religious issue, while some view it from a spiritual, ethical, medical, or legal standpoint. Some see death as something to dread, fear, or mourn, while others see it as a cause for celebration. If we aspire to serve the mature market and win their trust and confidence, we need to keep an open mind and to embrace each client's viewpoint of his own aging and death. This might be a challenge if the client's viewpoint and ours clash, but our goal needs to be to honor and respect his viewpoint.

Elisabeth Kübler-Ross, M.D., has worked with the ill and dying for many years and has written extensively on the subject. I refer you to her works for a better understanding of the process of dying. In her book *On Death and Dying,* Kübler-Ross discusses the five basic steps a person goes through when he is terminally ill.

THE FIVE BASIC STEPS OF TERMINAL ILLNESS

First Stage: Denial

Second Stage: Anger

Third Stage: Bargaining

Fourth Stage: Depression

Fifth Stage: Acceptance

About death Kübler-Ross says, "It might be more helpful if more people would talk about death and dying as an intrinsic part of life just as they do not hesitate to mention when someone is expecting a baby. If this were done more often, we would not have to ask ourselves if we ought to bring this topic up with a patient, or if we should wait for the last admission. Since we are not infallible and can never be sure which is the last admission, it may just be another rationalization which allows us to avoid the issue."[10]

Many people have a difficult time dealing with the issues of death and dying and anything related to it for a number of reasons. Sometimes those who have not thoroughly grieved a loss have difficulty working successfully with older individuals. Perhaps there are unresolved issues surrounding the loss of a loved one in their past, a lost love, a lost job, or perhaps they have not come to terms with their own mortality or the prospect of the loss of their own youth. Many baby boomers tell me, usually in seminar settings, that they fear the illness and death of their parents and other elders because when they pass away, they, the adult children, will be "it." Some voice concern that they are not ready to step into the shoes of the elders of society and of the family. Perhaps they feel lacking in wisdom, which often results from years of conscious living.

More Ways to Define the Mature Market

Even if you define the maturity market by one or all of the three ways listed above, you can further refine your definition by including such things as net worth, needs, and product or service preferences. Since the highest income-earning years occur in the mid-40s to mid-50s, you could define the mature market by wealth or accumulated discretionary earnings. You could also define this market by needs. People have certain needs at different stages in life. For example, older people have different health care, estate-planning, and investment-planning needs than younger people. If you focus on sales, your definition might include only those who have need of your products or services.

A Practical Definition of the Maturity Market

The most practical definition of the maturity market involves a combination of the above categories. This will work for most product and service developers and marketers in financial services, with some variations. Geriatric care managers probably need to focus more on the physiological aspects, while public policy developers need to focus more on chronological age in order to include the majority of the older age segment when targeting their message. For most financial services, it is best to start with a definition based on the psychological aspects. You will need to add variations within that definition to be compatible with your purpose, such as net worth, earnings, needs, and preferences. This becomes a matter of who qualifies not only from a psychological, physiological, or chronological age standpoint for your service or product, but who qualifies financially as well.

Although my goal here is to keep our discussion as practical as possible, I admit that for my own purposes, I have approached this issue of defining the mature market from both a philosophical and a practical standpoint, relying heavily on a definition based first on psychological characteristics, then on needs. My priorities are to have fun with and to enjoy my clients, and to learn. I tend to accept nearly anyone who fits within my definition of the mature individual, adapting the depth of my services to what the individual can afford to pay. Whatever your approach, it is important to give serious thought to how you would define this market before investing time and money in product and service development and marketing efforts. I call your attention to Further Reading in the back of the book for a list of references to help you draw your own conclusions.

My Own Definition of the Maturity Market

The maturity market is a group of individuals who know who they are and are at peace with their purpose or mission in life, no matter how grand or humble. They view the purpose of every individual as vitally important to society as a whole, and because of this they have a clear sense of their own value and responsibilities, and those of others. They live their purpose and express their personal truth every day with total acceptance, regardless of their physical condition or environment. They are real people because they have become truly themselves, recognizing that no one is special and everyone is unique. They are totally comfortable with who they are, making no apologies and offering no pretense. Generally, the members of this market are approximately 60 years of age or greater.

WHAT'S IN A NAME

Just as important as defining the maturity market is deciding what to call its members. It is not unusual to see groups of older Americans referred to by age, color, perceived physical condition, mental state, or their outlook on life. Here are some examples:

- 50 Plus
- Silver Hairs
- Golden-Agers
- Prime-Timers
- Geriatrics
- Elderly
- Seniors
- Old
- Greedy Geezers

While these terms might not be offensive to some who are in their later years, many more find these labels demeaning, inaccurate, and not at all consistent with their self-image. Others find these terms totally acceptable. Even those who do find some of these terms offensive tend to ignore them as long as discounts and special programs are offered.

(Although these terms are not recommended for use in marketing, many are appropriate to use for the sake of convenience when referring to them in professional communications.)

I have had more success by referring to this group of people in terms of the level of psychological development achieved by a majority of its members. While some do not seem to care what we call them, the name "mature" seems to be the least offensive to most older adults with whom I come in contact. And, to me, it seems to be the most consistent with the characteristics of most of the members of this enormous market segment.

Even many professionals who work closely with the mature market (used interchangeably throughout the text with "maturity market") differ over what is acceptable terminology. My suggestion is that you take a broader view now of this market, since a narrow definition might work for the present but soon will be outdated as the baby boomers mature. The upscale baby boomers in general will probably be offended by all of the above terminology as they age. I contend that a greater percentage of the boomers will reach the higher levels of maturation than did previous generations due to their access to self-help programs and their tendency to strive for goals and self-improvement. It would be wise for advisors and salespeople to position ourselves now to appeal to the boomer market rather than to back ourselves into a corner only to find that we have lost a large segment of the market seemingly overnight.

CHAPTER 1 ENDNOTES

1. Jeff Ostroff, *Successful Marketing to the 50+ Consumer* (Englewood Cliffs, NJ: Prentice Hall, 1989), p. 300.
2. David B. Wolfe, Wolfe Resources Group, interviews with author, from June 1992 to April 1996.
3. Carl Rogers, *On Personal Power* (New York: Dell Publishing Co., 1977), p. 239.
4. Ibid., p. 249.
5. Abraham H. Maslow, *Motivation and Personality* (New York: Harper & Brothers, 1954), pp. 146–54.
6. Alan Watts, *This Is It and Other Essays on Zen and Spiritual Experience* (New York: Vintage Books, 1973), p. 18.
7. Abraham H. Maslow, *Toward a Psychology of Being* (New York: D. Van Nostrand Company, 1968), p. 97.
8. Rachelle A. Dorfman, Ph.D., "Aspirations in the later years: the inner experience of aging" (Temple University, 1990), p. 119.
9. Barbara J. Logue, *Last Rights* (New York: Lexington Books, 1993), pp. 81–82.
10. Elisabeth Kübler-Ross, M.D., *On Death and Dying* (New York: Collier Books, 1969), pp. 141–42.

CHAPTER 1 REFERENCES

Nielson, John, principal, The Sandcastle Group, interview by author, Minneapolis, Minnesota, February 20, 1996.

Rogers, Carl R. *On Becoming a Person*. Boston: Houghton Mifflin, 1961, pp. 115–22.

Wolfe, David B., principal, Wolfe Resources Group, interview by author, Reston, Virginia, February 13, 1996.

2 CHAPTER

How Aging Affects Marketing and Sales

BUD: THE OILMAN AND HIS DEVOTED WIFE

Bud seems to have discovered the secret to happiness: Focus on the things and the people you love, the rest will take care of itself. Although the pursuit of money does not interest him, he always seems to have what he needs when he needs it. Having been in the oil business all his life, now more than 80 years, he continues to run his modest oil production company. His office is filled with personal memorabilia, including dozens of pictures of children and grandchildren. Bud stays in shape by playing three rounds of golf weekly, weight training, and walking three miles every morning with his wife, Danna. A lover of the arts, he has been a fund-raiser for opera, theater, the ballet, and is an avid sports fan.

One of Bud's passions is big band music. He has an enormous collection of the original recordings of "the Greats," as he calls them, such as Glenn Miller, Benny Goodman, Doris Day, and Hoagy Carmichael, as well as some of the lesser known artists. He has actually seen many of them perform in person and loves to share stories about their lives and how they came to create their music.

I have come to know Bud through Danna, who is one of my clients and has been married to Bud for five years. I had the good fortune to meet Bud for the first time at his office recently. The purpose of the

---

Bud: The Oilman and His Devoted Wife (continued)

meeting was to introduce myself, as is my custom, to Bud, since he is one of Danna's closest living relatives. Knowing that I share his love of big band music, he brought along tapes to give me from his private collection. Bud puts together collections of recordings, 400 to date, with his personal commentary on each recording and its history, which he labels "Bud's Favorites." He gives the tapes away to his friends who also enjoy music from that era. They love to receive Bud's Favorites as much as Bud loves to put them together and give them away. Says Danna, "Bud is the most emotionally healthy and the most highly evolved person I have ever known. He loves life and people. I admire how he nurtures relationships such as those he has maintained for over 60 years with his "Aggie buddies" from his college days at Texas A&M."

    I have observed that balancing relationships with personal growth are Danna's priorities. She owned her own business, which she sold after marrying Bud in order make time to create a home life for them. Her pursuit of self-awareness includes a healthy diet, regular exercise, taking care of her finances, and personal reading. Danna has shared with me that "to become a whole, complete, and self-actualizing person you need to balance introspection with relationships. Being available to nurture my relationship with my husband, my family, and my friends is a priority."

THE NEED TO UNDERSTAND THE CHANGING BODY

Understanding how the body changes as we age will help you communicate more effectively with your client. Many of us have never stopped to think what it must be like to try to have a conversation when we cannot clearly see the other person or the printed material to which he is referring; when the words are garbled or totally inaudible; and when the method he uses to present material is foreign to our way of thinking and remembering. Having to participate in a social conversation under such circumstances might be challenge enough, but consider how the level of frustration must escalate when you are being asked to make an important decision that will impact your financial security. Is it any wonder that the mature generations, who experience these challenges every day, are so cautious and often wary of those with whom they do business?

    Hopefully our discussion about changing body functioning will help you better understand what our clients are experiencing and some things we can do to increase their comfort level. My goal is to create a level of awareness that results in your use of methods of communication more conducive to a productive relationship. We will concentrate only on those aspects of physical aging relevant to the client's comfort level, and his ability to receive and process information when he is making a decision about whether to purchase your product or service. Let's take a short quiz to see how much of the basics you know about the physiological aspects of aging. The word "older" here refers to those age 65 and over.

A Pop Quiz (True/False)

1. _____ The majority of older people are senile, have defective memory, are disoriented, or demented.
2. _____ The five senses—hearing, vision, taste, touch, and smell—all tend to weaken beginning at about age 55 to 60.
3. _____ Older people tend to take longer to learn something new.
4. _____ Older people tend to react more slowly than younger people.
5. _____ More older persons have chronic illnesses than do younger persons.
6. _____ Older persons have more acute (short-term) illnesses than do younger persons.

If you answered true to numbers 3, 4, and 5 and false to numbers 1, 2, and 6, you answered correctly. Number 1 is incorrect because fewer than 10 percent of older people have significant or severe mental illness; 10 to 32 percent have a mild to moderate impairment; but the majority are without impairment. Number 2 is incorrect because the senses begin to weaken long before age 55. In fact, hearing begins to decline for men beginning at age 19. Number 6, with regard to illness, is false because even though 46 percent of all older people, compared to 12 percent of younger people, have a chronic illness that limits their activities, older people do tend to have fewer acute illnesses than do younger people.[1]

When I was younger I felt sorry for older people who were physically impaired, viewing them as somehow handicapped or short-changed. Like most younger people, I viewed any loss of sensory functioning as a loss of mental capacity. It was all the same to me. I now know that a person can *appear* to have a cognitive impairment when in reality he simply cannot hear or see me. In addition, over the years I have observed that there seems to be a correlation in many people between reduced sensory functioning, such as vision or hearing, and the development of other abilities. It is almost as though the reduced functioning of the outer senses presents an opportunity to develop the inner senses, such as a more highly developed intuition, greater insight into situations and human nature, and wisdom, the hallmark of the more mature individual. This insight has changed my outlook and increased my respect for the older generations. It would be helpful if we could view changing bodily functions as a normal part of the aging process rather than as senility, sickness, or frailty. With a basic awareness of normal physical changes, I have been able to be more patient and more empathetic. This has resulted in more rewarding relationships with my clients.

Vision

As we age we experience the need for more light; less tolerance for glare; difficulty in seeing objects at close range (presbyopia); a decrease in the ability to discern different visual patterns and detail; and a slowing of the ability to adapt to changes in light and darkness. In addition, the neurons in the eye and the brain might become unable to properly process the impulses they receive due to the effects of injury or illness, such as a stroke. Although many of us often experience changes in these areas at a younger age, most of the effects of the aging of the eye become apparent for both men and women at about age 40.

If visual impairment is the result of a cognitive impairment, such as the effects of a stroke, special visual communication techniques, including cognitive techniques, might be necessary. In most cases, however, our ability to communicate visually with the customer or client can be improved by observing some simple guidelines. These can be applied to our written communications and presentation visuals.

Printed material needs to be on noncoated paper (stock), not glossy paper. Nor should the print be shiny. Anything that reflects light, such as white or metallic, can produce a glare. A deluster finish that coats the paper is ideal for brochures and other marketing pieces, since it reduces glare. The ideal printed material is on noncoated, off-white paper, such as ivory or light gray, with print (copy) in a contrasting color, such as black, very dark blue, or very dark gray. Avoid copy and stock of lower contrast, such as blue print on green paper, or gray print on gray paper. Avoid printing that has visuals as a background. It might be difficult for the aging eye to focus on your written message.

Type size, style, and spacing are very important. The minimum recommended type size is 12 point, although 14 point is ideal, and 18 is necessary for the seriously visually impaired. The type style needs to be simple and without flourishes (sans serif). The easiest to read fonts are Univers, Arial, Arrus, Times Roman, CG Times, and Courier. The letters themselves need to be thick with adequate spacing between the letters. Use italicized, all capitals, and bold or slanted letters infrequently and only when necessary. Thicker characters, which are far enough apart so as not to run together, are acceptable. Use mono-spaced fonts, that is, nonproportional spaced fonts. Margins should be at least one to one and one-half inches so that the printed line does not exceed six inches. Do not justify the right margins. This creates a need for proportional letters, with uneven spaces between them. Use 1.25 line spacing, or create lines that have space between them that is 25 to 30 percent of the point size. Always provide ample lighting in the room.

I have found it very challenging to impress younger administrative staff members and advertising designers with the need to produce printed material according to these guidelines. They usually insist on using a variety of type styles and sizes, right margin justification, shading around letters, multiple borders, distracting graphics, and noncontrasting colors. While all this high-tech desktop publishing might be beautiful and impressive, your message might never be read. In fact, some clients respond with anger and frustration if they receive illegible correspondence or other written material. The Securities and Exchange Commission's ADV Part II is one good example of difficult-to-read material that almost always evokes client's indignation. Double-check the readability of your written material, brochures, and so on, by asking an older person to read them. If they squint, look for more light, or exhibit any difficulty at all, ask them how you could make it easier to read. Handwritten notes add a personal touch, but observe these guidelines and take extra care to produce readable script. See Figure 2–1 for an example of readable text.

Hearing

Those who have lost a significant ability to hear are said to have presbycusis, which is the third most frequent chronic condition in those over age 65. According to Martha Bagley, Specialist to Older Adults at the Helen Keller National Center for Deaf-Blind Youth and Adults, 60 percent of all those over age 65 experience some hearing impairment. The common types of hearing loss are the diminishing ability to hear some pitches; and to sense all sounds; leading to difficulty in understanding speech. Since aging does not necessarily affect both ears equally, a person might be able to hear better with one ear than with the other. Another common hearing challange is tinnitus, which is the perception

FIGURE 2-1
_____
Univers 12 Point with No Justification

> I like my stockbroker very much. I particularly
> appreciate the fact that he drops me notes in
> the mail from time to time. Because the notes
> are easy for me to read, I study everything he
> sends me, taking to heart what he has to say,
> and considering his points very carefully. I
> usually respond by calling him to obtain more
> information. I trust him and would not make a
> decision about my finances without calling him
> first for his thoughts.

that there is a sound when there is none. This condition often affects the person's ability to sleep, although in extreme cases it can be quite a distraction even during waking hours. These effects of aging usually become apparent in our mid-40s for men and women, although men often begin to experience gradual hearing loss at about age 19. For the current older person this is believed to be caused by his early, and often lifetime, exposure to the loud noises of the factory, and to the sounds of war. Learning how to communicate verbally with older customers can be very challenging. Unlike with written material, it requires that we be spontaneous and that we "think on our feet." With a little practice, we can master these techniques.

The first thing to remember when speaking to someone with a hearing challenge is to look directly at him. Many people who have difficulty hearing will read lips. When speaking with two people at a time it is advisable to seat them so that you will not need to turn your face away from one to speak to the other. The one you are turning away from might not be able to hear what you are saying. Older clients will be more likely to hear what we are saying if we lower the pitch of our voice, speak slowly, enunciate very carefully, and lower the volume of our voice. Our natural inclination when communicating with an older person whose ability to hear is diminished is to speak louder when in fact volume is rarely the problem. Speaking louder rarely increases the chances that our customer will hear what we are saying. In fact, it only draws attention to him, often resulting in confusion, embarrassment, anger, and disruption of his train of thought. However, if he is having difficulty hearing us, we might ask if he would prefer that we speak louder. Sometimes it is appropriate to ask the listener if he has a good ear, and then speak closer to that ear. Sometimes the client will deliberately seat himself right next to you in a meeting. For those of us who were trained to always seat a couple at a table directly across from us so as not to miss their eye contact between each other, this can be somewhat unnerving. Perhaps that problem can be solved by seating the clients at a round table with the one with the greater hearing impairment closest to you and the other seated right next to him so that you can easily observe any nonverbal communcation between them.

The most important and the most challenging technique is to avoid using high-pitched sounds such as the soft *c*'s and the *s*'s. This takes practice and a great deal of concentration. If you work with a number of hearing-impaired clients you might wish to retain a speech or audio therapist to coach you in these skills. Another possibility is to purchase a mechanical device to keep on hand that the client can use during meetings to improve his ability to hear you. Please refer to Further Reading for some excellent basic reading material about the different types of hearing devices available. Many older people resist wearing a hearing aid, so you might need to work on your skills in this area to improve communication with the hearing impaired. Always avoid meeting with clients in environments with background noise such as restaurants. They only add to your challenge.

If your practice or business requires that you communicate by telephone, you will need to observe these rules even more carefully, since the listener will not have the advantage of seeing your face as you speak. He will need to depend entirely on his ability to hear you. Turn off the radio and eliminate other noise, such as conversations in the background, when speaking with clients on the telephone. The typical "bullpen" where several salespeople share office space is generally not an atmosphere conducive to productive telephone conversations. Typically in these settings, other conversations make it very difficult for your client to hear you. Cold calling might become less effective as a larger proportion of our potential clients move into this age category where audio communication becomes a challenge.

Equilibrium

Although maintaining our balance is a function of the ear, I am addressing it separately merely to call attention to it, since it is so important in understanding how we can communicate more effectively with the client. As we age, the ear loses its ability to recognize and respond to gravity, changes in speed, and rotation of the head. Sometimes the result is dizziness, the sensation that the body is moving or spinning, or vertigo, the sensation that the room is spinning. These have an effect on our ability to maintain our equilibrium and our body posture. These sensations can be stressful for the client. We can reduce his anxiety by moving more slowly when walking to or from the meeting area, offering to take his arm as he moves about or when getting in and out of a chair, and by offering to carry his beverages or belongings. In some instances it might be advisable to accompany him to his car.

Muscular Challenges

As we age we lose muscular strength, although much of this can be delayed by regular exercise, resistance weight training, and a healthy diet. As communicators we need to be aware that aging usually results in loss of hand-grip strength. A man's hand-grip strength will rise steadily from age 10 to approximately age 35, then steeply decline. A woman's hand-grip strength will remain relatively the same until about age 35, at which time it will begin a slow decline. When shaking the client's hand we need to let the client determine the strength of the grip and learn to automatically match his strength. The quality of the handshake is very important, especially since it is often a part of the client's first and lasting impression. It often communicates our level of trustworthiness. This loss of the ability to grip and to hold things is another reason for us to offer to carry items for the client.

Incontinence

It is common for both men and women to experience bladder conditions such as incontinence in the mid-60s. A larger percentage of women (11 to 50 percent over age 65) than men (5 to 16 percent over age 65) experience this condition at least temporarily. To improve the client's comfort level during meetings, offer to take breaks for whatever reason. The client will let you know if a break is not welcome or necessary. If you meet with clients in your office, rest room facilities need to be private, comfortable, and easy to get to.

Sleep Patterns

As we age our nightime sleep patterns change. Depression, side effects of medication, and less need for nighttime sleep because of daytime naps all contribute to these changes. Older people generally have more difficulty getting to sleep, and they tend to wake up frequently during the night. The result is a tendency to nap during the day. When scheduling meetings, resist encouraging the client to meet with you other than at a time convenient for him. There are probably times during the day when he tends to be less alert. Meeting during those times should be avoided, since the client needs to be alert in order to interact effectively with you. In addition, he might not be alert enough to drive during certain times of the day. I find that most older clients prefer, or insist on, meeting with me in midmorning or early afternoon. Most will schedule meetings so as to avoid rush hour traffic and to avoid missing meals.

A Word about Medication

Many clients will be taking or experimenting with one or more kinds of medication. This can create side effects such as thirst, headaches, fatigue, drowsiness, changes in energy level, shortened attention span, hunger, fluid retention, mood changes, and the need to eat at regular intervals. There is not much we can do to improve the client's comfort level in these instances. However, just being aware that an older client is likely to be on some sort of medication helps to remind us that the situation might call for more empathy and patience.

CHANGES IN COGNITIVE FUNCTIONING

This area poses the greatest challenge for the marketing and sales professional. The information available about changes in cognitive functioning is replete with ambiguity, numerous variables, and not surprisingly, conflicting research results. Cognitive functioning includes physiological changes in how we think, including changes in sensory input, the neurological functioning of the brain in terms of what the brain does with the data it receives, and the effects on thinking exerted by our feelings and emotions. Cognitive functioning is also affected by values, experiences, intellectual level, our general state of health, and our level of education.

For the sake of simplicity, we will take a look at the more widely accepted information about changes in brain functioning as we age. I emphasize that this discussion is far from comprehensive and is meant only to call your attention to useful information and to raise your level of awareness. Also, the mature market varies widely in terms of cognitive ability, so any statement made will not apply to everyone. An abundance of information is available if you wish to study this issue in depth. Please refer to Further Reading for references regarding changes in cognitive functioning as a result of aging.

Physiological Changes in the Brain

The average weight of the human brain decreases by as much as 10 to 20 percent during a person's lifetime. The female brain begins to decrease in weight as early as age 60, a decade earlier than the male. The physiological aspects of cognitive aging in the individual tend to be related to that person's educational level and lifestyle. Highly educated individuals tend to maintain their intellectual ability with little diminished capacity compared to those of a lower educational level. Evidence also suggests that those of higher intelligence and educational level live longer. A dramatic decrease in mental ability as a normal part of aging is a myth. In fact, fewer than half of all older people experience cognitive impairment from psychological or physiological causes.

Thanks to modern technology and behavioral studies, the mysteries of the brain are now being addressed and solved. We know that as we age, neurons, which transmit information in the brain, grow both in size and complexity but they do not regenerate. Some neurons cease to function and ultimately die throughout the later years. We also know that some neurons develop neurofibrallary tangles, which is the twisting of the fibers of the axon portion of the neuron. This twisting is part of the normal aging of the brain, except in cases of excessive tangling, which is present in behavior abnormalities and Alzheimer's disease. Despite researchers' ability to correlate certain brain cell abnormalities with various diseases such as Alzheimer's and Parkinson's, they have not determined that these cellular abberations actually cause the diseases.

Visual

Older people are slower than younger people at picking up information and putting it together from printed and other visual material, unless they know exactly where to look for the desired information within a field of irrelevant information. I often hear clients complain that they have difficulty finding information on their mutual fund statements, such as the account number and the year-to-date dividends and capital gains distributions. They also have more difficulty than the younger person when attempting to pick out important information from insurance illustrations. Recall that the various mutual fund families have different statement designs so that this information appears in different places on statements for the various fund families. It takes more time for the older person to sort through the information on the page to locate the desired information than it does for a younger person. Any unnecessary information makes it difficult if not impossible for the older person to feret out the desired information.

Knowing this, present the most relevant information in short bullets surrounded by ample white space. This format is especially helpful when presenting details about long term care insurance, financial plans, estate plans, and other complex concepts and strategies that might be unfamiliar. A simple presentation is best. Offer more complex backup analysis or information for the client to read at his discretion, at his leisure, and at his own pace.

Attention

Older people tend to be able to perform more than one task at a time as well as a younger person as long as the tasks are simple. As the complexity of the tasks increases, our ability to perform them tends to decrease. An example of this is the atmosphere of client meetings. I find a quiet setting with few distractions more conducive to productive client meetings, although I know of several successful financial service professionals who conduct business over a meal in a restaurant. I prefer to focus on business in an office setting where there are fewer distractions such as meal selection, waitress's interruptions, passing of food, comments about the food, and cutting and eating of food. Also, by meeting in your office, you can control other factors such as lighting, noise level, the time it takes to get seated, and the start and the end of the meeting.

Response Time

According to Salthouse and Somberg (1982), older persons tend to take longer to respond to questions or requests for information, especially if the information is ambiguous, complex, or requires that they search mentally for information. This is due in part to changes in the senses, such as sight and the ability to hear. It is also due to the ability to keep information in the working memory. The exception is if the activity is based on very familiar, previous experience, and if the client is generally healthy. If you are sharing important information with the client, and will then need to ask questions or ask for a decision, speak slowly and present the information very clearly, avoiding irrelevant information.

In addition, avoid asking the client a question point-blank that would require a quick answer. Give him time to process and respond to what you are saying. I recall an incident during a meeting with a client who was 72 and her 27-year-old grandson. The grandson very bluntly asked her to make a decision. When she did not respond as quickly as he thought she should, he asked her why it was taking her so long to make up her mind. She replied, "I have 72 years of experience to sort through before I can give you an answer."

Language Comprehension

Our ability to comprehend what is being said depends on several things, including our ability to receive information through hearing and sight, and our ability to store information in the working memory. The context in which information is presented seems to be of particular importance to older people's ability to understand what is being said. Older people can often comprehend what we are saying even if we speak rapidly, as long as the information is presented within a meaningful context. As we age, we look for ways to relate incoming information to exisiting knowledge about the subject. The more information we already have stored in memory to which we can relate the new information, the more likely we are to remember it.

One theory about cognitive aging is that our ability to retrieve information through memory depends on the extent to which we can encode incoming information. There is evidence that the capacity of older people to store information in the working memory is reduced. This might be due to the overall slowing rate of their ability to process information and to make the necessary connections between the new information and the information already held in memory. Or it could be due to a reduced ability to receive information as a result of decreased hearing and vision. However, as anyone who has worked with older clients knows, unless a serious cognitive impairment exists, they are often able to recall minute details from many years ago while remembering newer information often presents a challenge. Older adults tend to have more difficulty in retrieving information from the working memory, unless retrieval cues are provided. This is thought to be due to their diminishing ability to eliminate irrelevant information from the working memory. Longer study time is an advantage.

Often older people will ask the salesperson to "send me some information." Since the older person cannot assimilate the information as quickly as a younger person during a personal interview, he might merely be asking for an opportunity to review the information at his own pace. The average reading speed for younger adults is 144 words per minute, but 121 words per minute for older adults. When older adults are allowed to pace themselves, age differences are eliminated. Instead of viewing the request for written information as a stall tactic or rejection of a product or service, the salesperson needs to see it as a possible indication of interest.

Older adults are more cautious in their decision making than younger adults for several possible reasons: increased information processing time; reduced confidence in sensory-input accuracy and speed; increased experience in decision making; and lack of urgency due to a matured time awareness and changing values. As a result, the salesman's and marketer's tendency to attempt to create urgency might actually repel the older customer, who usually deliberately slows down the sales process unless he feels totally in charge. On the other hand, if he has done considerable research about your product or service, knows exactly what he wants, and knows exactly what he is willing to spend, he might want you to speed up the presentation. That does not necessarily mean that the salesman should speak more quickly, but you might need to bypass steps that you think you need to cover to make the sale. The salesman who insists on sticking with a canned presentation will probably turn the customer off and lose the sale because he went too slowly, sharing information that was of no interest to the client. The important thing to remember is to let the customer set the pace at which the information is presented, and the level of detail. Ask several times if there is anything he wishes to have repeated, explained in more detail, or explained in a different way.

Older adults are more likely than younger adults to recall that they performed a task that in fact they only observed. On the other hand, I have observed that older adults sometimes omit important facts about events that actually happened. This sometimes occurs when asking about their health history during the interview for insurance. I recently recommended long term care insurance to an older couple. Both husband and wife indicated that aside from her asthma, they were a picture of health. During a meeting with the insurance broker, they said the same thing, even after extensive questioning. It wasn't until the third meeting, as the insurance broker was taking the insurance application, that the clients revealed that the wife had had a mastectomy two years before and that the husband had had a triple bypass the previous year. The original oversight might have been due to a memory loss, or denial, or their view of their illnesses as irrelevant.

Memory loss can result from any number of things, including the effects of alcohol, prescription and over-the-counter drugs, depression, and the early stages of Alzheimer's. Sometimes it is not advisable to continue your work with someone who exhibits memory loss or confusion, since he might not have the mental capacity to work with you. In those instances, it is prudent to seek the advice of a professional who has the credentials to test the individual's capacity before proceeding. Continuing to interact with someone whose mental capacity is in question can result in a loss of confidence by the client, and by his family members, if and when you finally meet them. Worse yet, working with a client who is mentally incapacitated can have serious legal ramifications.

Wide Variations in Cognitive Aging

Researchers continue to explore how cognitive abilities change as we age. The results of studies depend greatly on several factors, including the methodology of the studies. For instance, some studies are performed using the same subjects over time (longitudinal), while others use subjects of various ages at a given point in time (cross-sectional). Schaie and others have done considerable research in the area of primary mental abilities and how they are affected by aging. There are 23 primary mental abilities, including number, word fluency, verbal meaning, associative memory, reasoning, spatial orientation, and perceptual speed. Cross-sectional data gives a more pessimistic view of the decline of primary abilities, while the longitudinal data produces a more optimistic view. One study done by Schaie and Hertzog (1983) demonstrated that the amount of variance in performance of primary mental abilities due to age alone did not exceed 9 percent, suggesting that the differences are due to factors other than age. The Labouvie-Vief cross-sectional studies (1985) demonstrate a decrement in intellectual performance with age, while longitudinal studies show no decrement, and often an increase in intellectual abilities. These and other studies seem to suggest that a decline with age in performance is due to differences between generations rather than age differences.

The secondary mental abilities include fluid and crystallized intelligence. Crystallized intelligence is related to experience and education, or intentional learning. Fluid intelligence reflects unintentional ability such as inductive reasoning. Crystallized intelligence does not decline with age, and often increases. Fluid intelligence can and often does decline with age, especially in our ability to organize information, to ignore irrelevant information, to focus and divide our attention, and to keep information in our working memory.

The limitations of research are demonstrated when we observe that the older subjects used in the past often had less education than today's older adult, and dietary and exercise habits were not nearly as healthy as today's and future older adults. Some studies have demonstrated various educational levels and health factors can account for some of the age differences in intellectual functioning.

How older individuals organize and store information is greatly affected by their educational level and their verbal skills. For instance, older women who have spent most of their adult years performing household duties that gave them little opportunity to develop their analytical skills might need some assistance in grasping concepts related to personal finances. However, it would be helpful before attempting a presentation to find out what her hobbies and interests are. You can use this information to develop a sales presentaton. We will look at examples of this technique, which I call Story Selling, in a later chapter.

If it is true that older adults process information within the context of their own feelings, it is important for us to incorporate our knowledge of their values and motivations into our understanding of their cognitive functioning. David Wolfe has synthesized much of the research on the functioning of the brain, how it changes in the later years, the effects of the personality on brain functioning, and the effect brain functioning has on the consumer and his decision to purchase your product or service. Wolfe, in his book *Serving the Ageless Market,* describes his Seven Principals for Maturity Markets. The Sixth Principal has to do with the functioning of the brain:[2]

Sixth Principal for Maturity Markets: The Cognitive Processing Principal
Discretionary purchase decisions of mature consumers tend to originate in the more "instinctive" right brain processes (B-cognition), and conclude with the left brain processes (D-cognition) in order to provide a rational validation of initial feelings.

The right brain deals with abstractions, as opposed to the concrete left brain, which takes in information and processes it digitally in a logical, ordered fashion. Left brain processing is slower than the right brain. According to cognitive psychologists the concrete left brain processes information in an ordered manner, converting it to symbols that can be manipulated. The right brain receives information in an abstract, undifferentiated state. Unlike the left brain, it does not analyze, judge, or compare, but perceives reality in its totality. In his description of the "healthy human specimen" Maslow included the "ability to fuse concreteness and abstractness."[3] I have observed that the mature individual has a highly developed ability both to think concretely and to use his ability to be creative, intuitive, and feeling.

While most veteran salespeople would readily agree that the customer's values are an important part of the sales process, many need to be reminded from time to time about the need to first understand the client's motivations and needs. I was a residential real estate agent in the 1970s. We were trained to sell by appealing to the emotions and then "rationalizing the sale" by reciting the facts about the property. "Lead with the emotions appealing to the customer's values and needs and then sell with the facts" or "justify the sale," we were told by every sales trainer. The technique was called "rationalizing the sale." But at that time we were taught that our customers had a small repertoire of emotions and needs such as greed, status, and comfort. So this concept of appealing to the right brain, or to the feelings and emotions, and then to the left brain by presenting facts and a logical reason to purchase is not entirely new. What is new is a preponderence of non-fear-based feelings and emotions to which to appeal in the first place. At the time, there were far more younger customers than older customers, so we were largely unaware of the distinctions between the motivations of customers based on their level of psychological development. We now know that the needs and motivations of the more mature person are far different, and far less materialistic and less status-conscious, than those of younger people.

Whether we tend to operate more from our right brain than from our left as we age is still open for discussion. It would seem that as we mature, we integrate the functioning of the two areas of the brain, calling upon a more reasoned approach when appropriate, and a more intuitive, feeling approach when appropriate, but integrating the two so that behavior is more fluid and less extreme. We will look at some examples of this right brain–left brain approach to selling later on since it can be effective when applied to the mature client.

The Human Maturity Continuum: Psychological and Physiological Aspects

Figure 2–2 combines the psychological aspects of aging we reviewed in Chapter 1 with the added dimension of the physiological changes that occur with aging we just discussed. This will help you to see all the changes our aging clients are experiencing.

FIGURE 2-2

Human Maturity Continuum: Psychological and Physiological Aspects

	Birth	Childhood	Teen Years	Adult	Later Years
NEEDS:	**Physiological** ■ Food ■ Clothing ■ Shelter ■ Hygiene ■ Touch	**Safety and Security** ■ Nuturing ■ Modeling: Moral values ■ Modeling: Social skills ■ Modeling: Boundaries	**Love and Belonging** ■ Peer acceptance ■ Modeling: Self-care ■ Modeling: Life skills ■ Sexual exploration	**Self-esteem and Esteem of Others** ■ Esteem:Colleagues ■ Esteem: Mate ■ Esteem: Friends ■ Career achievement	**Self-Actualization** ■ Connectedness ■ Creative expression ■ Spiritual experience ■ Peace
Approximate Age:	0–2	3–10	11–19	20–59	60 +
VALUES:	Physical comfort	Toys and Playmates	Physical attractiveness	■ Family ■ Material acquisitions ■ Status ■ Luxury ■ Convenience	■ Family ■ Experiences ■ Independence ■ Dignity ■ Comfort
PHYSIOLOGICAL Characteristics:	Development of all systems of the body	■ Sexual development ■ Hearing loss begins: 19—men	■ Visual acuity reduces 40—men and women ■ Hand grip reduces 30—men and women ■ Menopause beings 45—women ■ Hearing reduces: 45—men and women	■ Sexual functioning reduces: 55—men ■ Reproductive capability reduces: 70s—men ■ Incontinence occurs: 65—men and women	
PERSONALITY Characteristics:	■ Dependent ■ Playful ■ Spontaneous ■ Curious	■ Spontaneous ■ Curious ■ Unpretentious ■ Genuine	■ Competitive ■ Hopeful ■ Ego-driven ■ Sex conscious ■ Outer-directed	■ Ambitious ■ Controlling ■ Ego-driven ■ Denial ■ Outer-directed	■ Accepting/peaceful ■ Inner-directed ■ Independent ■ Balanced ■ Spirit-driven
GOAL:	SURVIVAL				CREATION
MOTIVATOR:	FEAR				LOVE

CHAPTER 2 ENDNOTES

1. Erdman B. Palmore, "The Facts on Aging Quiz," *A Handbook on Uses and Results* (New York: Springer Publishing Company, 1988).
2. David B. Wolfe, *Serving the Ageless Market: Strategies for Selling to the Fifty-Plus Market* (New York: McGraw-Hill, 1990), p. 182.
3. Abraham H. Maslow, *Toward a Psychology of Being* (New York: D. Van Nostrand Company, 1968), p. 157.

CHAPTER 2 REFERENCES

Bagley, Martha, specialist to older adults who are deaf or blind, Helen Keller National Center, interview by author, Dallas, Texas, February 8, 1996.

Botwinick, J. *Cognitive Processes in Maturity and Old Age*, New York: Springer Publishing Company, 1967, as quoted in *The Facts on Aging Quiz*, Erdman B. Palmore, New York: Springer Publishing Company, 1988, p. 5.

Botwinick, Jack. "Cautiousness with Advanced Age." *Journal of Gerontology* 21 (1966), pp. 347–53 as quoted in Sheila M. Chown. *Human Ageing.* Baltimore: Penguin Books, 1972, p. 219.

Braus, Patricia. "Vision in An Aging America." *American Demographics* 17, no. 6 (June 1995), pp. 34–38.

Cavanaugh, John C. *Adult Development and Aging.* Pacific Grove, CA: Brooks/Cole Publishing Co., 1993, Chapters 3, 5, 6 and 7.

DiGiovanna, Augustine Gasper. *Human Aging—Biological Perspectives.* New York: McGraw-Hill, 1994, p. 145.

Ellis, D. (1988). *Decision making behavior in the elderly: Wisdom as an explanation.* Unpublished doctoral dissertation, Indiana University of Pennsylvania, Indiana, Pennsylvania, quoted in Loretta Martin-Halpine, *Decision-Making and Older Adults: Accurate Decision-Making as a Demonstration of Practical Wisdom,* ii and 13.

Governmental Relations Department, American Foundation for the Blind, 1615 M Street, N.W., Suite 250, Washington, DC 20036.

Lamb, Marion J. *Biology of Ageing.* New York: John Wiley and Sons, 1977, p. 12.

Rockstein, Morris, and Marvin Sussman. *Biology of Aging.* Belmont: Wadsworth Publishing Company, 1979, pp. 58–59.

Salthouse, Timothy A. *Advances in Psychology in a Theory of Cognitive Aging.* The Netherlands: Elsevier Science Publishers B.V., 1985, pp. 179–189.

West, Sandy, director of marketing and policy research, Investment Company Institute, interview by author, Washington, D.C., January 15, 1996.

3
CHAPTER

How Salespeople and Marketers Can Attract the Maturity Market

THE LITIGATION ATTORNEY TURNED MINISTER AND HIS BEAUTIFUL WIFE

I began working with Walter and his beautiful wife Sarah a few years ago. They are a very exciting couple. The first thing you notice about Sarah is her beauty: the perfect skin, piercing green eyes, and perfectly coiffed silver hair. The next thing that becomes apparent is her keen intuition, intelligence, and thirst for knowledge. She is an accomplished musician who teaches music at a local university. In her spare time she surfs the Internet for information about investments and anything else that piques her curiosity. She also writes music on the computer. Walter is one of the warmest and most compassionate people I have ever met. At one time he was a very successful litigator. I am certain he was very effective, given his extraordinary speaking and communication skills. He left the legal profession many years ago after witnessing the cold-blooded murder of his client in the courtroom. He then became the minister of one of the largest and most prestigious Methodist congregations in Texas. Walter is a born orator. My only regret is that he retired from the ministry before I met him, so I never had an opportunity to hear him speak publicly. Walter is full of vitality and has a remarkable zest for life. Often when I meet with Walter and Sarah, he has already played a game of

---

The Litigation Attorney Turned Minister and His Beautiful Wife (continued)

tennis and motored around the lake, before our noontime meeting. By the way, Walter is 82 years of age.

Sarah takes care of the finances, faithfully maintaining all their data on the computer and carefully managing their investment portfolio. She loves to gather and evaluate information. She is very astute when it comes to investing and is a challenge for any financial advisor. They are both very caring and compassionate people dedicated to making this world a better place. Sarah has been involved in establishing the Texas Music Teacher's Association Education Foundation. It provides financial aid to talented young musicians who could not otherwise afford the necessary instruction to develop their skills. Several years ago Walter established a nonprofit foundation called the National Youth Foundation to help young people develop life skills through wholesome activities. He worked with two governors of Texas on this project and it remains his passion even today as he continues to fund and run the program. I always plan to spend extra time when meeting with Walter and Sarah because I know he will want to share with me about this project. Walter has a big heart that bursts wide open whenever he talks about the things he loves. His eyes sometimes fill with tears as he shares stories about things in his life that are important to him. Sarah, of course, is one of his treasures. But I also see his compassionate side when he speaks of the less fortunate.

There are countless ways to attract the attention of the mature market. We will take a look at several strategies that have worked for me as well as others. It is important to distinguish between marketing and sales. Marketing creates visibility and awareness in the target market that a particular service or product exists. Selling, on the other hand, is directed toward a particular, clearly identified customer or client in hopes that he will purchase from the person soliciting his business. This is a very basic concept that needs to be understood before any money or time is spent promoting your product or service. Without a clear understanding of the distinction between these two activities and their purpose, marketing results are often a disappointment. Marketing requires an investment of time and money, and the results are usually intangible since, unlike sales, they cannot be directly measured. In this chapter we will explore the opportunities to market our products and services, including visibility in the media, advertising, seminars, cold calling, networking, prospect networking, cause marketing, direct mail, and other strategies. In Chapter 4 we will take a look at specific techniques that have resulted directly in the sale of products or services.

The financial service professional needs to do five major things to attract the business of the mature consumer:

1. Be visible in key places.
2. Exude sincerity and integrity.
3. Project an image of expertise.
4. Offer products and services that appeal to the mature consumer.
5. Ask for the business.

BE VISIBLE

No matter how wonderful your services and products are, without effective marketing you are just winking in the dark. One way to create visibility is to be frequently quoted or to appear in the print, visual, and radio media. Working with the media attracts the attention of the older consumer, who often has an insatiable appetite for information. Although it will require a considerable investment of time on your part, there are many benefits to be derived from your commitment and effort. Not only will you attract potential clients and customers, but you will sharpen your communication skills, increase your knowledge base, and develop new networking contacts. If you lack the time, expertise, and patience to become an active resource to the media, consider hiring a public relations professional to help position you with reporters, editors, and producers.

My personal experience is that if you work for a larger company or firm, its presence in the marketplace through effective advertising and the like is helpful, but the older, savvy consumer is more interested in who you are. Creating visibility, like any marketing, does not produce quick sales, but it is an effective way to attract either potential clients who might eventually buy or their advisers who can refer prospects to you.

When I have asked clients over the years how they became aware of me and why they chose to work with me, their reply almost without exception has been because they liked what I had to say on the radio, in the newspaper, in a magazine, or as a guest speaker, even though they might have previously been referred to me by another professional. It was not until they saw me quoted somewhere or heard me speak that they picked up the phone and called me.

Boston elder law attorney Harley Gordon is a case in point. Starting with a radio talk show in the 1980s he has built one of the most successful elder law practices by understanding that things don't just happen. According to Harley, "The idea of specializing in long-term care planning was pretty straightforward. The problem was getting my name out. I started by canvassing all the organizations that catered to the elderly such as AARP, the local Council on Aging, Parkinson's, and Alzheimer's support groups. I did my own press releases understanding that the more controversial the subject matter was the more people would attend and that local media would pick up on it.

"What created the controversy was that I was teaching middle class families how they could qualify for welfare-based programs to pay for nursing homes. But I did not stop there. I built on the concept by writing a book *How to Protect Your Life's Savings from Catastrophic Illness and Nursing Homes*. However, I knew that the book would not be successful without aggressive marketing. Without it the book was DOA." Gordon hired public relations experts in Boston and Planned Television Arts in New York. "These guys were first rate. They understood the controversy surrounding middle class using benefits and sold it nationally."

The results have been impressive. He has been quoted in just about every publication, spoken at nearly every conference, and has appeared on major network TV such as "Larry King Live," "Today Show," "Front Line," and public television. "I zeroed in on a message and stayed with it." Harley sees public speaking as entertainment, theater. He delivers a very convincing impassioned message about the devastating effects of the costs of long term care on families, and then lets the audience know that he has the solutions. Harley is a good example of how the media will flock to you if you have timely information and if you can entertain and excite an audience.

Tips on How to Work Effectively with the Media

Working effectively with the media requires some skills that you can acquire. Since the mature market is hungry for information, they take advantage of every opportunity to learn from educational or newsworthy television programming, newspapers, radio, and on-line educational services. Because of this, it would be wise to become skilled at communicating effectively with members of the media. They can help you develop a public image that attracts the attention of the mature market. One important thing to remember about the media is its goal: to inform and entertain, not necessarily in that order. To tell a story or to inform is not enough. The news piece must evoke a reaction and engage the listener, viewer, or reader. To accomplish this, the reporter is always looking for a hook, or an edge. Please refer to Chapter 3 Appendix A for tips on how to work effectively with the media.

It would be a mistake to think of being quoted in the print media as free advertising, since you cannot control what actually appears in print, nor when it will appear, but it can help to establish you as an expert in a particular area. Keep in mind that the reporter's job is to present the story as he sees it. It is considered very poor form to tell the reporter what to say about you or your firm or to insist that you be referenced as a resource. In most cases, the editor, not the reporter, makes these decisions. It is not in your best interest to put the reporter on the spot.

I have found that reporters often already know what information they wish to include in their articles and the spin they wish to put on it. They are merely looking for someone who is credible to help them tell their story. So be careful; they will often give a different spin on what you are trying to communicate.

Many financial service professionals see little or no value in working with the media. It is time-consuming and inconvenient, the reporter cannot promise that you will be cited as a resource in the article, and it rarely results in immediate business. However, reporters are the megaphone for our profession, and it is important that they receive quality information. Offering information to members of the press is one of the best ways I know to disseminate quality information about serious topics that might otherwise go unaddressed. I see media coverage of a topic as an efficient way to educate the public and to attract attention to your product or service. Once reporters know that you are willing to make yourself available to provide information, they will call you often and consider you an invaluable resource. And it is one of the best ways to establish yourself as an expert. This is especially true if you are an expert in an area considered a "hot topic."

At this time the media is searching for expert resources to address issues pertaining to older people and their money, and the effect it has on their families. If you have a knack for communication and are willing to invest the time, it will be relatively easy for you to be quoted or featured in the media.

Print Media

If you are trying to attract business from local clients, concentrate on getting quoted in local newspapers or magazines. On the other hand if you are more likely to be retained by a family member of your mature client who lives at a distance, concentrate on the national media. Geriatric care manager Rona Bartelstone in Ft. Lauderdale, like many care managers, is often retained by the adult child who lives in another state. She has found exposure in the national print media to be far more effective in attracting out-of-state business. She also seeks out the media to interview her when she attends conferences in those areas where the adult child of the Florida resident might live.

Visual Media

Appearing on television can be more challenging. You need to have the ability to communicate effectively, and you need to "look" good as well as sound good. It requires networking with TV producers and the shows' hosts. But since your information is so timely and your message so urgent and credible, getting on shows can be relatively easy. To attract their attention you need to be knowledgeable, if not downright passionate about the topic. Always be willing to share information. And always be ready, period. TV show hosts and news reporters need information on a very timely basis, just as newspaper reporters do. So be up on the topics, and be prepared with quick sound bites that can translate to headlines, assuring you a spot or credit for your statements. Never turn down an opportunity to appear on TV, even cable TV if you are just getting started in the media. Look upon every effort as a step in the right direction, if only to gain experience.

When a Reporter Says "Jump"

Reporters often call at the most inconvenient times. For instance, I was rushing to leave my office one morning to get to the United We Stand conference in downtown Dallas. Just then a TV reporter called who wanted to interview a financial planner about the future of Social Security. He would also be interviewing U.S. Social Security Commissioner Shirley Chater. He insisted that I come to the TV studio within the hour. It was at least a 30-minute drive, plus parking time. My first thought was to see if someone else from my professional society would be willing to go. I quickly decided that there was not enough time to locate a willing, knowledgeable stand-in. Besides, this was my responsibility as the Public Relations Director for the Dallas–Ft. Worth Society of The Institute of Certified Financial Planners. I somehow arrived at the studio on time. The interview went well, and thankfully did not land on the cutting room floor. It turned out to be good public relations for our profession as well as for me personally, even if I did blatantly disagree with Commissioner Chater on the evening news for all to hear. I am certain that the reporter came away with a good feeling about financial service professionals as a potential resource for news pieces.

Radio

The mature market loves the radio, especially talk radio, which presents good, solid information. I have found radio producers to be fairly receptive to my suggestions to interview me on the air. Be prepared to suggest topics and to back up your suggestions with facts and current news events. The producers are always looking for topics that are timely, and of interest to their listening audience, and for someone credible to interview. Always go prepared with questions you want the host to ask you. Be just as prepared to provide solutions. If you look at an interview as an opportunity to sell product, the show's host or producer will probably never call you again. This is partly because the station sells time on the air to advertisers and is not willing to give it away to the show's guests to promote their product. Just like with the print or TV media the show's host will often put a spin on your story, often portraying the listener as a victim. Always listen to the show's host several times before appearing for an interview. You will be better prepared to interact with the interviewer's style and you will come off as knowledgeable as you need to be.

BE PROACTIVE IN THE MEDIA
Write Your Own Articles

If you have ideas for news articles, consider writing your own pieces. If you lack the expertise or time to write, go to a local college or university and ask around the journalism or English department. Students are often willing to write for a reasonable fee. Fees for editors can range from $15 to $50 per hour. If you lack the time to write, simply dictate your thoughts about a particular subject into a microcassette and have the journalist ghostwrite your article. Or, if you prefer to write the article yourself, have the journalist edit it for you.

Although I prefer to write my own articles, occasionally an editor can be very helpful. If you decide to retain one, I recommend that you select a mature adult who can grasp the concepts you are attempting to convey. Sometimes editors with limited life experiences have missed the point and changed the meaning of my copy.

Contact newspaper editors yourself to see if they will publish your articles, or use a public relations professional to market them for you.

In addition to appearing in publications, these articles can also be used in your newsletter or as a quality handout to demonstrate to other professionals and prospective clients and customers the depth of your knowledge and giving the reader the opportunity to get to know you and how you communicate. I have handed out thousands of copies of my articles to networking contacts, members of the media, and potential clients.

This strategy of distributing self-authored articles as a marketing tool has helped many financial service professionals establish themselves as experts. In the early years of his practice, New York elder law attorney and author of numerous articles, books, and papers, Peter Strauss handed out 5,000 copies of his article "Planning for Aging and Incapacity" whenever he gave lectures. That essay, which was written for the lay audience, became his "Bible." According to Peter, that article led to radio interviews and other speaking engagements. He became a regular guest on a radio talk show and is still a much-sought-after speaker both to public and professional audiences. As a result, his practice grew and he became known and respected nationally as an expert in elder law and estate planning.

Become a Newspaper Columnist

If you are skilled as a writer, try establishing yourself as a columnist. This will give you an opportunity to choose the topics to be addressed and the content. However, you are not totally safe from being misquoted even if you write your own articles. I write monthly articles that are distributed over a senior wire service to senior citizen newspapers throughout the country. One newspaper took the liberty of changing the title of one of my articles. The article was about how long term care insurance has changed and that even if you currently have insurance it might be prudent to rewrite your coverage from time to time. The title of the article was "Long Term Care Insurance Isn't What It Used To Be." The editor of the newspaper changed the title of the article to read "Long Term Care Insurance Isn't What You Think It Is." No doubt this title might have attracted more attention from the readership, but not in the way I had anticipated, since the new title did not reflect my intended message. I had failed to check with my intellectual property attorney before entering into the agreement with the publisher/distributor of the articles about my rights in the work.

Always place your copyright on any written piece so that if it is reproduced you must be cited as the author. This lets others know that you are entitled to compensation for licensing someone else the right to use your work. Be certain to check with your attorney about copyright laws to assure that you retain the rights to the work for your future use in other formats.

Host a TV Show

If you are real ambitious, put together your own weekly TV show. Inviting colleagues on the air to be interviewed can be an effective way for you to network with them as well as to be visible to your viewing audience. Offer a "giveaway" to viewers so you will have an opportunity to gather feedback from them. Be sure to have the show professionally produced so that the tapes can be marketed. Check with your attorney to be sure you own the necessary rights to the shows.

Host Your Own Radio Show

If you decide to have your own show, choose the station carefully. The best station could very well be an AM rather than an FM station. If you know more about marketing to the mature market than the station's advertising staff, you might want to look elsewhere. If the station's salespeople are not knowledgeable about their listeners, it would make me wonder how committed the station is to the mature market. If it is not committed, it might eventually be purchased by an owner who has no interest in continuing with the programming that appeals to your market. It would be better to select the right station from the start.

Having your own show is a lot of work, especially if you need to find your own sponsors, but it can be worth the effort. Chose the name of your show very carefully. In a nutshell, it tells people what the show is about. Plan carefully what you will be talking about on the air. If you have a cohost, be sure you agree about program format, content, who will do the talking and the research, who will secure the sponsors, and how to share other responsibilities. My current cohostess is a marketing executive with a prominent Medicare HMO. She also has impeccable professional and educational credentials. The name of our show is "Life Choices...Getting Straight to the Point about Your Issues." The only airtime the station currently has available for our show is 9:30 on Sunday mornings, which is not an ideal time. However, we produced a flyer promoting the show that has been distributed to thousands of the older members of our listening area. In addition, we had poster-size prints made of the flyer, which my cohostess has distributed to all the physicians in the Medicare HMO provider network to display in their offices. Between the exposure from the flyer and our promotional message, which is aired at least 10 times per week, we feel that the visibility we are receiving is worth our effort.

A call-in talk show is usually more effective for marketing your services and products. People love to call in and ask questions about their investment, legal, and other financial concerns. And I suspect that they often become serious prospects and clients of the talk show host. To enhance your effectiveness offer a free giveaway that the listeners can call in or write for such as "This Week's Hot Investment Tips" or "This Week's Retirement Planning Tips." This can enhance their loyalty to you and your show while promoting your product or service, and provide an opportunity for feedback to see if you are reaching your market.

I prefer to have a talk show that does not take calls from the listeners. My goal in being on the air is to educate the public about issues that have to do with aging, money, and managed health care. To control the content, my cohostess and I need to have total control of the airtime, which is not possible with a call-in show.

If you decide to have your own show, be clear about your goal. When marketing the show, in addition to promoting it with flyers, consider display advertising in the local senior citizen newspaper. Be sure to include your picture on all promotional material, unless it is cost-prohibitive. Be creative about how you market the show and the station. I am currently working with KAAM to put together a swing dance team of about four couples to perform around Dallas. I will coordinate and perform with the team, while the station will raise the money from sponsors for expenses. The team will perform at local big band dances and at other events where the mature audience is likely to be. As a member of the dance team, I will be positioning myself as a radio personality and a financial service professional who understands the market. There are other ways you can key into the interests of the older market to market yourself, incorporating your personal interests as well as your need to market your business or profession.

Advertising

A newspaper in your area that targets or appeals to the mature market is an ideal place to advertise. Consider creating a write-in column or a regular column, even if you have to pay for the space. This can create credibility if you are persistent and if your message follows the guidelines we will discuss in Chapter 6. If you do not have a "seniors" newspaper, advertise in the local community paper. The "small town" newspaper is less expensive and usually more effective than the daily "city" paper since it often has a longer shelf life, and your advertising will be more likely to stand out. Look into other advertising opportunities such as church bulletins and health club newsletters.

You will need to advertise consistently for at least 6 to 12 months in the same publication before evaluating the feasibility of continuing with that publication. Most advertisers will stop advertising if they receive no response within the first few months. While a younger audience might respond quickly to your advertising, the older reader will usually need to see or hear your advertisement for at least 6 to 12 months before he will call you. Many new prospects will come to my office holding a stack of my advertisements or newspaper columns. They volunteer that they have been reading the information for 6, 8, or 13 months in many cases. Often they will say that the deciding factor about whether or not to call me was a quote they saw in *Modern Maturity* or some other publication. Figure 3–1 is a sample of a question-and-answer column I have run in *SR Texas* (a quality, local monthly newspaper for the mature market). The column is paid advertising that results in prospects as well as visibility among other mature market professionals who send me referrals. Figure 3–2 is a sample of another style you might also use that is more transaction oriented. Your particular style will determine how you approach the sharing of information.

TV and Radio Advertising

TV and radio advertising can be very effective in this market, depending upon the advertisement itself and the ad placement. If the need for your service is urgent, you might experience an immediate reaction. Geriatric care manager Joyce Robbins in San Antonio built her business by advertising on both television and radio. She targets the mature audience for geriatric services on TV as well as personnel for her business on a radio station that targets the younger under-40 audience. While marketing for personnel she also gets the word out about her services. Both radio and the TV advertising have produced significant business. She has received as many as 50 responses in one day to her radio advertising, and numerous positive responses to her TV ads. We will take a look at a sample of Joyce's TV advertising in Chapter 6.

NETWORK

Networking might be the most effective for the mature market. Like all marketing, it is slow but it can have far-reaching and long-lasting results.

FIGURE 3–1

Tips from the Pro's

Finance

What's all the hoopla about the budget deficit and Social Security? The money I deposited into Social Security is in the Social Security Trust Fund and can't be used for anything but the payments I was guaranteed—right?

Not so. The money is being loaned out to the federal government to pay for other expenses. The Trust Fund currently holds about $400 billion in notes and enough cash to pay for approximately 13 months of benefits to current beneficiaries. Prudent planning includes keeping an eye on entitlements and how changing benefits could affect you. We need to rethink how we view "guarantees." The government can giveth and the government can taketh away. By the way, we are the government. **Joan M. Gruber, CFP, GRI, is a fee-only advisor. She works exclusively with the maturity market, advising clients in matters regarding their financial affairs. For additional information, contact Joan M. Gruber, 3010 LBJ Freeway, Ste. 1209, Dallas, TX 75234. Call (214) 888-6045.**

FIGURE 3–2

Tips from the Pro's

Finance

I recognize that I need to buy long-term care insurance, but I can't see putting out money for premiums before I'll need the coverage.

Statistically, your chances of needing care are much greater than are the chances of your house burning down. Nearly one out of two people over the age of 65 will require care. So buy coverage while you're young. Shifting this enormous risk of spending $36,000 to $100,000 annually to an insurance company with deeper pockets than yours and mine makes good sense from an investment standpoint. Call us for an appointment if you want independent advice about what to buy. **Joan M. Gruber, CFP, GRI, is a fee-only advisor. She works exclusively with the maturity market, advising clients in matters regarding their financial affairs. For additional information, contact Joan M. Gruber, 3010 LBJ Freeway, Ste. 1209, Dallas, TX 75234. Call (214) 888-6045.**

It can also lead you to the most lucrative clients. It is an art that can be acquired. The most transaction-oriented salesmen often find it boring and unproductive because it rarely produces clients and customers overnight. But it often leads to the most loyal clients who are ready to do business when they finally meet you. Networking often requires that you be in the right place at the right time and that you be able to spot another professional who is most likely to refer well-qualified business to you, or one who can introduce you to someone else who can. In the maturity market, it is especially important to network. This is because professional advisors of older clients are not likely to refer their clients to someone about whom they know little, one who is not known to their colleagues, or one who has not demonstrated that he can be trusted. We all work hard to obtain and retain good clients, so we are not likely to refer a client to someone who has not taken the time to let us get to know him. Please refer to Chapter 3 Appendix B for details about how to network effectively.

PROSPECT NETWORKING

Participate in activities where you are likely to come into contact with members of the mature generation. In his book *Marketing to the Affluent*[1], Tom Stanley talks about one very successful securities salesman named Harry who determined that telephone cold calling was not going to work for him since his target market, the affluent business owner in the apparel business, had too many people running interference for him blocking incoming calls. So Harry used his ingenuity and discovered that many of these business owners had breakfast early every morning in the low-rent part of town near their places of business. Harry, determined to capture their business, began to frequent the same diner at 6:00 A.M. for breakfast, became acquainted with his target prospects, and eventually captured their business. This is an excellent example of network prospecting. Get to know your prospective clients or customers. Walk in their shoes, go where they go, and find out what makes them tick. Not only will you become more visible to your target market, but you will get on their wavelength, improving your ability to relate to them when they do finally show an interest in your line of work.

If you recall the characteristics about the mature market discussed in Chapter 1, it will be easy to come up with places where you are likely to come into contact with those you seek to serve. Members of the mature market can be found in places that have something to do with:

- *Nature:* Sierra Club, garden clubs, Audobon Society.
- *Spirituality:* Church groups, temple, Jewish Community Centers, metaphysical study groups.

- *Community service:* Rotary Clubs, Kiwanis, Lions Clubs, women's auxiliary groups, nonprofit organizations (American Cancer Society, Public Television, etc.).
- *Physical activities:* Dance studios, health clubs, walking clubs.
- *The arts:* Art galleries, chamber and symphony groups, museums, theater, performing arts.
- *Family activities:* Church-related, entertainment-related; sports and physical activities; country clubs.
- *Educational facilities:* College and university adult education classes, museum lecture series.
- *Epicurean groups:* Cooking classes, wine-tasting groups.
- *Travel clubs:* Smithsonian tours and other travel groups, especially those that go to more exotic destinations or are related to community service (Habitat for Humanity).

With prospect networking, your goal is to get to know those who might be good prospects for your product or service. Gently and subtly let it be known what you do for a living after you have come to know them. Always have business cards handy and a pen to write with. When someone shows an interest in what you do, ask them to call you at the office for an appointment, or ask if you may call them later on that day to set an appointment. It usually is best to meet with them privately to discuss your products or services, deferring any discussion until then. Even if the prospect initiates the discussion, other potential prospects might be turned off for any of the following reasons: they think that you are imposing on the group; you could be viewed as one who cannot be trusted with personal information if you openly discuss private matters; or they might feel the need to leave the group or ostracize you if they think that you might pursue them next. It is better to offer to set a time to meet with the prospect outside the group.

Offer to present seminars and workshops to these groups, but only after you have earned their trust. Presentations that target multiple generations within one family can be very effective. Don't forget to invite other professionals with whom you are networking, even if you know they will not be able to attend.

DIRECT MAIL

This market is hooked on information. They do read their mail, and a well-designed direct mail piece will catch their attention. Discounts seem to be very effective, but be careful since you could end up giving away your service or product if the response is more than expected. Of course make certain that the piece is readable, so remember to follow the guidelines in Chapter 2. When designing your marketing mailer, apply what we will discuss in Chapter 6. You might need to write your own copy and work directly with an artist or photographer, since most advertising firms are not aware of how to design advertising pieces that are effective with the mature consumer.

In terms of how to mail out a piece, first-class mail is more effective than bulk mail, but not a must. I have never participated in a mass mailer, since the mailing lists often target by annual income, which can be useless for retirees. I am more interested in targeting the older person who has a higher net worth, especially with a disproportionaly lower income. That usually means he really needs my help with his investments. If you know exactly which neighborhoods are included in the list, and you personally know the demographics of those neighborhoods, a direct mail piece might be very effective. Be certain to include quality testimonials, a recent picture of yourself, and a quality message. Offer a "giveaway" or some sort of bonus or price reduction to anyone who calls you in response to your advertisement.

CAUSE MARKETING

It is my belief that the line between for-profits and nonprofits is beginning to blur and will continue to do so as the U.S. government continues to turn responsibility for themselves back to the people rather than looking to the government for assistance. This is already resulting in a softening on the part of nonprofits to enter into joint ventures with for-profits. This joint initiative is called "cause marketing." It can be very effective if it is sincere and well intentioned on the part of the for-profit. It can involve the marketing or development of a product or service, with a portion of the proceeds going to the nonprofit. Or, it can involve a time commitment for involvement in the efforts of the nonprofit. To be effective, the two groups or their missions must be related, and the for-profit needs to show commitment to the cause. One example would be Realtors working in groups with Habitat for Humanity, where a portion of their sales commissions would be set aside to pay their travel and other expenses when lending their manpower at the work sites. This intent would be noted on all marketing material. Another example would be for a stock brokerage firm to announce on all marketing materials that a portion of all sales commissions are used to fund a not-for-profit financial information clinic open to the qualifying public at announced times and places.

If you wish to develop a cause marketing campaign, you need to be aware of certain things:

- You will need the permission of the nonprofit to make the public, clients, and customers aware of your donative intent. For-profits cannot announce such an intent without complying with local and state laws. This is to protect the public from fraudulent fund-raising where the money is never given to the nonprofit.

- You will need to convince the nonprofit that your proposal is legitimate.

- You will probably be asked to enter into a written coventure agreement with the nonprofit.

- You might need to register your coventure agreement with various local and state governments whose job it is to monitor your activities.

I have been involved in such projects and am convinced that they will become more popular in the future. For instance, a portion of the profits from my first book are being donated to Ronald McDonald House Charities. I chose that nonprofit for several reasons: (1) I wanted to become involved and raise money for that group the first time I visited their local "house." It was a very moving experience. (2) The book is about families and money. Even though it focuses on older adults and their adult children, I wanted to involve the younger members of the family. (3) I wanted a charity that every reader could relate to. A portion of my profits from this book will be donated to the National Coalition for the Homeless, which I feel will have relevance for any reader of this book who is involved with personal finances. Perhaps more than any other professionals, we are acutely aware that for many, homelessness is only a paycheck away.

HIGHLY TARGETED SEMINARS

Seminars, like any other advertising or marketing, need to be positioned in a place or institution the mature person trusts. Ideal settings are churches, temples, museums, government buildings, civic centers, agency offices, schools and other academic settings, and banks. Cohost seminars with someone in a profession related to yours. If your only business is to sell product, consider retaining a professional in a related field to be a guest speaker. Of course, you will want to choose someone who complements your product. For instance, if you sell life insurance, an estate-planning attorney would be an excellent copresenter or guest speaker. If you have a product that you actively sell, consider cohosting a seminar with the product sponsor. Often the product's wholesaler is an excellent speaker and can give you valuable tips on how to put together a successful seminar. Be certain that the presentation is not too sales oriented. Be creative about your topics and copresenters. Don't forget to invite adult children as well as retirees. Remember that the audience wants to be entertained as well as informed. If you are new at speaking, work with a veteran copresenter. I urge you to first attend several presentations where he is a copresenter to see how he handles himself. You want someone who is willing and able to make you look good and to smooth over any errors you might make without demeaning you in front of your audience.

Gordon Caswell, president of the Baylor Health Care System Foundation, has been highly successful at reaching his market by inviting key people to a first-class luncheon or breakfast at one of several of Baylor's private dining rooms. During the meal for his small, hand-picked audience of 5 to 12 people, he delivers a concise, meaningful presentation. He targets professionals such as CPAs, attorneys, financial planners, life insurance agents, and stockbrokers. Other groups include potential donors and potential repeat donors, Baylor hospital volunteers, hospital administrative personnel, hospital and foundation directors, and just about anyone else who could be a donor or lead Gordon to a potential donor. According to Gordon, he has hosted such affairs for a total of over 900 guests, resulting in numerous gifts for the foundation. He also has orchestrated similar affairs at the homes of current donors who have invited other potential donors.

The planned-giving seminars are successful for a number of reasons: Gordon Caswell understands his market; he knows what they wish to hear about; and he knows how to speak effectively. He tells the Baylor story, in very human, caring terms, and then addresses the issue of gifts and how the client can benefit personally, especially during his lifetime. Like any presenter, he believes in what he is doing and is able to get his point across through effective storytelling. Most importantly, he understands that charitable giving is all about compassion, connectedness, beneficence, and lastly value in the form of financial benefits. His method is an excellent example of appealing to the client's heart first, then confirming the intent with the brain or intellect.

If you are inviting the public to a seminar or other assembly, you need to be aware of the Americans with Disabilities Act (ADA). It guarantees those with disabilities full access to and participation in American society. It affirms the rights and responsibilities of those with disabilities, and guarantees them several things, including equal opportunity regarding telecommunications and public accommodations. The law defines the *disabled* to include those with a physical or mental impairment that substantially limits one or more major life activities. This definition includes deafness and blindness. The act requires that the individual, not the facility, is to determine which aids are appropriate for him, such as hearing devices, visual aids, and wheelchair access. In other words, the facility has not met its responsibility unless it offers to make available aids that each individual disabled prospective attendee deems appropriate. However, the aids requested by the disabled person must be reasonable and readily achievable. Title III of the act prohibits fees to be charged to individuals with disabilities for the use of aids and services that make public facilities accessible to them. The burden of proof is upon the facility that it make every effort to accommodate each disabled patron. Check with your attorney to make certain that your event's public announcement complies with the law and how you would handle a request for aids and devices for the disabled.

COLD CALLING

If you are new to sales, cold calling is the fastest, and perhaps the only way, to get started, unless you have a ready clientele in a related area such an income tax preparation. Until you have established yourself enough to generate a steady stream of referrals and to pursue other types of marketing, cold calling will be the best way to market yourself. However, I have known many great salespeople who continued to cold call once they were well established simply because they loved it and they were experts at it. When cold calling, be sure to observe the new laws that went into effect in 1995 about what you can and cannot say over the telephone, and what you must disclose to the person you are calling.

Eric Baruch, General Agent for John Hancock Mutual Life Insurance Company, established the McLean, Virginia, office as Hancock's number one agency for long term care insurance sales by developing the cold calling skills of a young salesforce. Eric, now John Hancock's general agent in Milwaukee, is using the same methods to increase that agency's long-term care sales. According to Eric, his agents are having to educate their prospects in his new territory, since long term care insurance is not a familiar product to the Milwaukee community.

Here is the Baruch agency's cold call prospecting method:

1. Each agent places 80 dials per day using a well-rehearsed script. This results in 10 appointments, 3 closes, and 1 policy delivery per week. See Figure 3–3 for the Baruch Agency's telephone script.

2. Prospects who do not agree to an appointment are invited to a seminar resulting in sales that might otherwise have been lost. They are shown a presentation by satellite which includes Boston elder law attorney Harley Gordon. Sales as a result of the seminars account for 2 percent of the agency's sales.

Cold calling is a technique used by nearly every salesperson at one time or another, especially those new to their business. I agree with Eric Baruch, who cites several characteristics that a new, young salesman must have to be successful with the mature market. He needs to be (1) well educated, (2) well groomed, and (3) well bred. To that list I would add the following characteristics:

1. Humility.
2. Dignity.
3. Sincerity and integrity.
4. Impeccable manners.
5. Self-discipline.
6. Determination.
7. Impeccable telephone skills and diction.
8. Qualified prospects.
9. A quality product or service.
10. A quality, well-rehearsed script.
11. A thorough knowledge of his product or service.
12. A product with a favorable public image.

For those who possess these qualities, age is no barrier. In fact, often a bond is established between the client and the younger salesperson, or in Eric's words, the older person "adopts" the young salesman. This usually occurs if the older person can picture the younger person as if he were his own grandchild.

Because long term care insurance is a relatively new concept for most of the marketplace, it could take at least two personal interviews once you are able to get an appointment with the prospect to close a sale. Cold calling is hard work and frustrating at times, but I know from personal experience that it works.

FIGURE 3–3

Long Term Care Phone Language

Mr./Mrs. _____ please?

Mr./Mrs. _____ , this is _____ , calling, how are you today?
   Response: Will be one of the following: Who is this? What is this about? Fine.

Well Mr./Mrs. _____ , again this is _____ , calling. I'm calling
about a letter you received from me concerning the problem of **Long Term Care**.
Do you recall receiving it?
   Response: Yes or no or what was it about?
   It was about the problem of Long Term Care. Then continue...

Mr./Mrs. _____ , I represent John Hancock Financial Services.
I do most of my work with people your age in planning to meet the cost of
Long Term Care. The reason for my call, is that I'm going to be in your area
next week and I'd like to swing by, review the information with you, and give
you a free Medicare Guide. Are mornings or afternoons generally better for you?
   Response: I'm not interested.

Pause! I can appreciate how you feel Mr./ Mrs. _____ but you know
that's exactly why I called. Initially many of my clients felt the same but found
the time well spent, and as I said, the reason for my call is that I *am* going
to be in your area next week, and I'd just like an opportunity to swing by and
review the information with you. Generally, is early in the morning good for
you or is the afternoon better?
   Response: Well, afternoons are better, but...This is implied consent, if they
   don't say this then it isn't, and don't use implied consent close!

Implied consent: (after handling the objection) say,"and since you don't have
any objection is early in the week good for you or is later better?"

Objections
   Send it in the mail.

I could do that Mr./Mrs. _____ but as I said the reason for my call,
is that I am going to be in your area next week anyway, and I'd just like to
swing by and review the information, take a few minutes, and drop off a free
Medicare guide. Generally is early in the week good for you?

   I'm too busy.

I can appreciate that Mr./Mrs. _____ , that's why I called to let you
know that I'll be in your area next week. When is usually the best time to catch
you? Early or late in the week?

   I have a plan.

That's great. As I said, I'm going to be in your area next week and what I'd like
to do is compare your plan with ours and show you why Consumer Reports said
we were among the best. Is the morning good for you or do you prefer the
afternoon?

After obtaining the appointment.

Mr./Mrs. _____ , just so I can be better prepared, have you been in
the hospital in the last two years? Also, the average cost of Long Term Care in
the Milwaukee area is about $40,000 per year, could you afford two or three
years of care?

Thank you, I look forward to seeing you at (time), on (day) the (date).

As a young Realtor in my mid-20s, I knocked faithfully on at least 100 doors a day, in 100° weather, as well as in sleet and snow. In fact, my efforts probably made the greatest impression when I knocked on doors in the most severe weather. Homeowners were more likely to remember me, which they often did when they were ready to sell their homes. The benefits of cold calling far outweigh the frustrations, although at times you might question the wisdom behind this method.

EXUDE SINCERITY AND INTEGRITY

If you lack these two qualities probably nothing in this book will work for you. If you seek to work with the older generation for monetary reasons alone, it might be wise to concentrate on another target market since this market can sense insincerity, seemingly on a visceral level. If your goal is only to sell, no amount of marketing will make you a lasting success with this mature group. These people want someone they can trust. Forget about working with the mature market if you are not willing or able to put your customer's needs ahead of your own.

When I was a Realtor, my broker used to say that "the dollars we earn can only be the product of the service we provide." I attribute this quote to P. Wesley Foster, president of Long & Foster Realtors, Inc., in Washington, DC, although I suspect that many successful businessmen had made this their credo long before him. The mature consumer seeks out only those professionals who display the utmost integrity, sincerity, and respect. They are interested in purchasing products, but only if a quality service is rendered first. They do not wish to be sold to and most of them instinctively know whom they can trust.

PROJECT AN IMAGE OF EXPERTISE

The best way to project an image of expertise is to be an expert. At last there are courses a professional can take to learn more about the issues that pertain to the mature consumer. To learn about the financial issues of the aging, I recommend that you attend workshops and listen to tapes offered by The International Association for Financial Planning, the College for Financial Planning (a division of The National Endowment for Financial Education), The Institute of Certified Financial Planners, The American College, the National Academy of Elderlaw Attorneys, the National Association of Professional Geriatric Care Managers, the National Association of Planned Giving, the American Institute of Certified Public Accountants, and similar organizations. By attending you will have an opportunity to gather more detailed information, network with professionals to whom, and from whom, you can send and receive referrals, and usually come away with excellent handouts to which you can refer later. The professional who wishes to become an expert will find himself reading and networking constantly. The amount of material is endless.

There is so much to know, whether you are a registered representative in a bank, a stockbroker, an insurance agent, a financial planner, a geriatric care manager, a public policy developer or marketer, a development officer, an elder law attorney, a CPA, or a Realtor. It is particularly helpful to be knowledgeable in the areas contiguous to your own profession. It adds to your credibility when networking with other professionals and when marketing for prospects. For instance, an attorney or a CPA who attempts to give investment advice will probably lose credibility unless he is properly credentialed and is knowledgeable about the client's investments. A stockbroker who understands the basics of long-term care, Medicare, and Medicaid and the effect long-term costs are likely to have on an investment portfolio will appear as more of an expert than one who does not. I often hear of financial service professionals who tell clients that since they have a net worth of $1,000,000 or more,they will not need to purchase long term care insurance since their assets will be sufficient to cover the costs. Point-blank statements such as this damage your credibility and can sabotage your networking efforts.

To acquire expertise and to network with other professionals, I suggest that you become aware of various organizations that concentrate on the mature market. In addition to those mentioned above, you might wish to join the National Council on the Aging's (NCOA) National Institute of Financial Services and Issues of the Elderly constituent unit (NIFSE), the American Society on Aging's International Society for Retirement Planning (ISRP), and the American Association of Retired People (membership under age 50 is available). By reading their material and attending their conferences you will be surrounded by those who work with older Americans and come away with a great deal of useful information. You can also learn a great deal about your market by reading publications such as *Modern Maturity* and *New Choices* on a regular basis.

As a part of becoming an expert learn the basics about investment and insurance products even if you are not a salesperson. Likewise if you are a salesperson, become at least acquainted with the other professions and services that interact with your potential client. In one way or another, they will nearly all have something to do with his money.

From a marketing standpoint, you will have a tremendous amount of credibility. Coldwell Banker Realtors includes a very powerful statement in their advertising that goes to the very heart of what I am saying: "People will care about what you know when they know that you care about them." You will have an easier time impressing a potential client with your sincerity if you have taken the time to learn about what is of interest to him.

The Impact of Public Policy

Both product and nonproduct salesmen and professional advisors would be wise to know about public policy. The changes happening on a national level will affect every one of our clients. Any salesman or marketer who adds this dimension to his presentation will be seen not only as an expert but as one who really cares and whose broad viewpoint and perspective on the future can be relied upon. It also makes you a more interesting talk show guest and writer. I urge you to take the time to learn about the basic issues surrounding coming changes in Social Security, Medicare, Medicaid (including block grants), and income tax. These changes are not the usual adjustments but rather major structural changes in the entire system and the role of government in the lives of our clients. We can choose to be visionaries, leaders, and stewards of change in our society. We can be the experts the media seeks out because we understand the public's reaction to the proposals. If you are interested in acquiring credible information on these issues, read the material produced by the Cato Institute, the National Center for Policy Analsis, Concord Coalition, and other nonprofit research and educational groups.

OFFER PRODUCTS AND SERVICES THAT APPEAL

If you feel that you are marketing effectively and that you are knowledgeable and sincere, but you are disappointed with the results, it could be that you need to take another look at the products or services you are offering. Apply what we will discuss in Chapter 7 to the products and services you currently offer to see how yours stack up. Several salespeople with an abundance of integrity and all the other necessary features often ask me to send them referrals. When I point out to them the shortcomings of their products, they became defensive and try to sell me on their product, or worse yet, they attempt to demonstrate the inadequacies of their competitors' products.

Many salespeople who sell one product, particularly in the insurance business, are not as particular as they might be. Many claim that their product is the best but demonstrate little or no knowledge of their competitors' products, nor why theirs is the best. They are able to repeat often verbatim what they have been schooled to say by home office sales trainers, but they lack any depth of knowledge about what they are saying. This rote method of learning about product can be a death knell to any salesman in the maturity market.

Compare the top products available from the standpoint of the client or his financial advisor (disregard for the moment the commissions involved). You might find that there are far better products out there than the ones you are currently recommending. In many cases prospects know more about product than do the salesmen. This market reads and studies about products and services before they purchase. Representing that your product is the best when it is only mediocre will send them running for the door, and you will lose credibility. If your product is the top of the line, but the marketing pieces are not appropriate for the mature client, consider developing your own marketing pieces (marketing materials for investments will require your broker's and NASD approval) or look for another product to sell. In Chapter 6 we will discuss examples of quality advertising that incorporate the physiological and psychological characteristics of the mature consumer.

ASK FOR THE BUSINESS

The mature consumer does not want to be sold something, especially if selling means manipulation. But you do need to ask for the business. The best way is to be very clear about the products and services you are offering; where and how you can be reached; how you are compensated; and how you bill if you work for a fee. Much of this information can be included in your advertising, brochure, business card, fee schedule, and other marketing pieces. This is a tough market that demands value. The less sophisticated often assume that you are providing your services free of charge. This is particularly true of the client who has never worked outside the home, whose wealth is inherited, or who is not familiar with how a business or practice works. We will get into this more in Chapter 8 when we discuss some practice management tips.

MORE MARKETING IDEAS

1. Serve your local professional or financial services trade association as the public relations director. This will open doors to the

media if you are knowledgeable and have a natural inclination to communicate.

2. Write letters to the editor of newspapers, the local senior citizens newspaper, and magazine editors whenever you feel a need to comment about an article or editorial. This is a subtle way to demonstrate your expertise. It is also a great way to get the attention of reporters.

3. Communicate often with clients and prospects and let them know that you are always receptive to meeting prospective new clients. Some clients might feel more comfortable if you do this by way of written correspondence. Use humor in your correspondence. It can be very effective with this market. (When it comes to referrals, I have found men to be more likely to refer other people to me while older women are less likely, unless they were professionals or entrepreneurs themselves.)

4. If you sell insurance or other products, establish relationships with advisors who are willing to send you referrals in return for a share of the commissions or fees. Be sure to check with the appropriate regulatory bodies to be certain that you are totally in compliance. Be certain that you properly disclose any sharing of fees or commissions with your customers or clients where it is mandated by law, or if not mandated, where you feel it is necessary in the interest of proper disclosure and fair dealing with your clients.

5. Host Sunday Mother-Daughter Teas in a warm, comfortable setting with lots of ambiance such as a very private room in an old hotel. Include a discussion on a topic of intergenerational interest. Take a very soft approach. It might be best to have a woman for a guest speaker.

6. Host a Sunday Tea Dance featuring 40s big band music, or any event where your guests can be entertained by music, an art show, arts and crafts exhibits, travel films, or lectures. Always serve light refreshments. Solicit commercial sponsors to keep the admission fee very low; $5 to $10 per person is recommended. Be sure to include several door prizes such as books on financial topics, magazine subscriptions, works of your own authorship, and complimentary consultations with financial service professionals.

7. Speak at national conferences, especially those mentioned above where others who work with the aging attend. Public speaking is a great way to hone your communications skills while establishing you as an expert before other professionals who can send you business. Remember to send out press releases every time you speak at a conference.

8. Check with your professional membership organizations to see if they produce regular radio spots or newspaper articles that are available to their members for a small fee. Stay in touch with the media by keeping them supplied with these items on a regular basis. This is one way to avoid having to write your own pieces or hiring a writer. The Institute of Certified Financial Planners produces excellent pieces on timely topics for their members to send to the media.

9. Contact companies that contract elder services to corporations such as Work Family Directions and The Partnership Group and offer to be a workshop facilitator for their corporate clients.

10. Hire someone with expertise in your profession to join your staff as a professional (such as a financial planner, geriatric manager, etc.) whose responsibility is to market the entire firm. Do not expect increased revenues overnight. It takes time to see results from marketing efforts, and many times you might not be able to attribute increased business specifically to public relations or advertising efforts.

11. Put together a "Senior Expo" supported by sponsorship dollars and media exposure. The media is often willing to provide free advertising space in exchange for other benefits. Be sure to include a nonprofit organization as a cosponsor. It will boost your marketing efforts. "Senior Expo" popularity seems to vary widely. Always do some marketing research before committing major dollars and time.

12. Host impromptu discussions on unannounced topics of interest to depositors during peak traffic hours in the local bank lobby. Be sure to have plenty of refreshments such as coffee and donuts or food that cannot easily be eaten on the run. This will encourage them to stay and participate.

13. Contact your AARP regional office and offer to speak at the next Women's Financial Information Program. This program was developed by AARP and is cosponsored by a local nonprofit seniors organization. Women leaders in financial services are selected to speak at these workshops. AARP screens every speaker to be certain that the platform will not be used to promote product and that the speaker will not be solicitous or giving a sales presentation. The benefits to the speaker are numerous: these programs usually draw a large crowd; all the seminar logistics are taken care of by the hosting organizations; and the networking opportunities with the other speakers is worthwhile. Contact your local AARP office and request information about the Women's Financial Information Program.

14. Work with a local seniors nonprofit organization to develop an ongoing financial information clinic for your community. This is an ideal way to bring together for-profit and nonprofit organizations for a very worthwhile cause. The Financial Information Clinic for Women 55 + was established in Dallas by several financial service professionals in partnership with Senior Citizens of Greater Dallas (SCGD), a local non-profit organization partially funded by United Way. Once a month we offer a private 45-minute counseling session with a well-qualified financial service professional for any woman for a small fee ($10), which is donated to the SCGD. The program was originally underwritten by a New York Life Medicare HMO, but is now operating under a grant from Women in Finance. The program, which targets mature women who lack financial sophistication but not necessarily assets, has been immensely successful. We have counseled over 250 women since the program was founded in May 1994. We attribute much of our success to the exposure we receive through a very supportive local media. If you wish to develop such a program in your community, call Senior Citizens of Greater Dallas at 214-823-5700 for a copy of the manual the steering committee wrote on how to set up the program.

15. Develop a newsletter with topics of special interest to your aging customer, clients, networking contacts, prospects, and concerned adult children. If you lack the time or writing skills to write your own articles, I recommend that you hire a writer or editor to prepare your own publication. Several excellent newsletters are available that you can purchase and send to your clients. However, for maximum credibility and to increase the likelihood that it will be read, publish your own newsletter. You will have more credibility, and it will give you an opportunity to demonstrate your own expertise and communication skills. Always include a personal message and a picture of yourself. Be sure to put key members of the media on your mailing list.

16. Sponsor a support group for caregivers. Consider cosponsoring it with professionals in related areas, or with businesses that target the aging.

17. Sponsor a networking group made up of professionals and businesses that serve the aging community and their adult children. Steve Guerney, publisher of *Retirement Living,* has sponsored such a group very successfully for the last few years in the Washington, DC area, Baltimore, and Philadelphia. I also cosponsored such a group in Dallas in 1992 with *SR Texas,* the local newspaper for the aging community, which was very popular. I did not continue with it due to the immense investment of time it required. However, if you have sufficient help from a number of cosponsors, it can be a very worthwhile venture.

18. Organize a boat cruise up the Mississippi on the *Delta Queen* or the *Mississippi Queen* just for women: mothers, daughters, aunts, nieces, sisters, grandmothers, granddaughters, and so on. Make it a four-day cruise with women guest speakers and workshops that focus on financial self-care, health care, and relationships between women, as well as lighthearted activities such as line dancing. Speakers can be psychologists addressing money issues, financial planners, stockbrokers, geriatric care managers, insurance agents, attorneys, development officers, and anyone else who can address the issues of women and money. Work with a well-established travel agency that is willing to help you promote the cruise to its own customers as well as yours. Most travel agencies can produce attractive promotional pieces such as oversized postcards featuring a picture of the boat and details about the cruise and the speakers. (Leftover postcards make terrific inserts for your marketing kit.) Consider involving product sponsors to reduce the cost of the cruise for passengers, to provide product information, and to answer their questions about products. Consider sponsors such as mutual funds; life, disability, Medicare HMO, and long term care insurance; companies and firms offering financial planning; asset allocation and private money management firms; and services related to do-it-yourself financial planning. Ask a local dance studio to provide a dance instructor (preferably a male) to teach line dances and to dance with the ladies.

19. Develop a high-quality letter endorsing you and your services, to be sent out to the clients and contacts of a professional in a related field. Have the letter reproduced on that professional's letterhead and printed on a laser-jet printer, signed by that professional. Select an unusual, attractive 32-cent stamp. Always proofread each letter.

20. Enter into an agreement with a local newspaper to write a column about personal finances in return for free advertising, or advertising for a reduced fee. Include that publication as a sponsor in your public events

21. Cohost personal finance seminars with others who have access to highly targeted audiences. See Figure 3–4 for suggestions for hosts, subjects, and audience.

22. Produce audio- or videotapes that address personal finance issues and make them available as a giveaway (or sell if they are high quality) to the audience whenever you are a guest on a radio or TV show, a guest speaker or a speaker at your own seminars, or at any event such as a Senior Expo. Offer them as door prizes at any event your market will attend.

23. Give out an attractive calendar every year to business contacts and clients with your name, logo, and a short message about your services or products. Professionals prefer a desk calendar while others seem to prefer a wall calendar. Nearly everyone prefers the type of

FIGURE 3–4

Personal Finance Seminars

Hosts	Subject	Audience
Medicare HMO/ financial planner	Private money management	Physicians
Financial planner/ hospital system	Gift of practice	Physician specialists
Church/insurance agent or broker	Long term care	Congregants
Church/insurance agent/ financial planner/ geriatric care manager	Adult children and aging parents	Baby boomers
Elder Law attorney/ financial planner	Estate planning	Hospital or corporate wellness program members

calendar that has a separate block for each day that is large enough for personal notes.

24. Host a one-day buying spree at a children's clothing or toy store where the buyers are your clients who make a small donation and receive a 10 to 20 percent discount on all items. The donation is for the benefit of a children's foundation such as a children's hospital.

25. Sponsor a day at the zoo with a special lunch (such as Ronald McDonald Happy Meals) for clients and their grandchildren for a small fee, a portion of which is donated to a children's foundation, such as a hospital or Ronald McDonald House Charities. Transport all guests in a comfortable, air-conditioned van. Provide entertainment for all guests and refreshments while en route to the zoo.

26. Arrange to have a portrait photographer at an event grandparents and their grandchildren will attend. Offer a $50 gift certificate for a sitting and prints as a door prize. Be sure to have a large picture of yourself (ideally with a younger member of your family or an elderly relative) on an easel with a promotional message about your business or practice indicating that the photographer is available compliments of you or your firm. A good place to offer this is at a special event where people are all dressed up. An event at Christmastime is ideal. Be sure to be available to greet people and to hand out a quality marketing piece about you or your firm and your services.

27. Develop a Web site offering your services, written material, financial information, videos, and audiocassettes. Appeal to potential clients and be sure to solicit referrals from other professionals in other parts of the country.

28. Host outings to benefit charity sporting events. Attend basketball, hockey, and baseball games. Host charity golf tournaments. Invite men as well as women clients and prospects. Create outings where it is appropriate to invite the children of clients (or other younger family members) as well.

29. Compile the newspaper articles you have written over a period of time for publication in a book. Indicate your intent to donate a portion of the proceeds to a charity that appeals to your readership. Give the book out as a door prize. Hire a public relations professional to schedule book signings, speaking events, and interviews and book reviews in the media.

30. Establish a partnership between a group of experienced professionals from several disciplines (law, tax, financial planners, etc.) and a local health care system to develop a series of seminars about personal finances. The professionals develop the content of the material and the health care system pays for the production costs (slides, etc.), provides the seminar facilities, and promotes the seminars to their list of invitees. The professionals present the seminars. Be sure to have an intellectual property attorney draw up an agreement that addresses issues such as who owns the various rights to the seminar, to be signed by all parties before the work begins.

How to Work Effectively with the Media

Here are some guidelines that might help you be a more effective guest on a show or help when being interviewed by a reporter. They might also help you avoid talking yourself into a corner or being misquoted:

1. Always respond to the reporter as quickly as possible. Instruct your receptionist to discreetly interrupt meetings or whatever you are doing at the time the call comes in. Set a time with the reporter when you can get back to him to answer his questions and give him your undivided attention. He will be less likely to go on to the next person on his list, since he now knows that he will be interviewing you. Return his call from an in-flight phone, car phone, or wherever you happen to be when you receive the message that he has called. I once did an interview with a reporter for *Money* magazine while in flight since I knew that I would not be able to connect with her once I landed. She was very appreciative. By the way, this is one good reason to always have your receptionist politely determine the nature of any incoming call, since reporters often do not voluntarily identify themselves as such.

2. Never attempt to do an interview if you are the least bit distracted. Always be polite and give the reporter your undivided attention. A miscommunication could result in a misquotation.

3. Politely ask who else the reporter has interviewed for the article, but only if appropriate. This will give you a clue as to what information he might be lacking.

4. Never attempt to answer a question about a subject on which you are not well versed, or a hypothetical question.

5. Offer to refer the reporter to someone who is knowledgeable about a subject if you are not, especially if you have an indication that he has been given incorrect information by someone else.

6. Have recent professional photos available to send when requested.

7. Never make a statement or inference you do not want repeated. Everything you say to a reporter is fair game. *Everything.*

8. Don't be informal or take liberties with a reporter or interviewer, not even just before or just after the interview. This is a professional relationship. Everything you say is for the record.

9. When being interviewed on radio or TV, always be prepared with three to five statements you wish to make on the subject. If the host goes in a direction that would cast you or your topic in an unfavorable light, or if he is dwelling on an aspect of the issue that is not relevant, politely give an abbreviated answer and then go right into what you wish to say or move on to another subject. Often hosts will attempt to be controversial, ignoring information that would be more useful to the viewing or listening audience.

10. When being interviewed on the radio or TV, take a list of questions on the subject the interviewer can ask you on the air. Offer the list to the interviewer before the interview begins so that he has the option to use them.

11. Keep your answers general, but tell the reporter that you can go into detail if he requests.

12. Do not go off on tangents unprompted by the reporter. His time is valuable, and it is unwise and inconsiderate to break his train of thought while he is asking questions, even if it does feel like a friendly conversation.

13. Share statistics, facts, and figures to support your statements, and state your source.

14. Briefly point out angles the interviewer might not have thought of. He will let you know if he is interested.

15. Avoid jargon and technical terms and concepts unless you can explain them in laymen's terms. The more the interviewer or audience understands from your comments, the smarter they feel and the more they will like and trust you

16. Offer anecdotes that corroborate your statements but omit clients' names and other identifying information.

17. Have names and phone numbers available of clients who might be willing to be interviewed by a reporter, but only after securing the client's permission in writing.

18. Have short statements to make about the subject that have meaning out of context. These are attention grabbers that can be placed in the margin, set in a border box within the text, or under your picture attributable to you in the final copy.

19. Speak slowly and distinctly, giving the reporter an opportunity to digest what you are saying and to formulate new questions.

20. Drop a line to a reporter complimenting him when he produces a particularly interesting or informative piece, whether or not you were used as a resource for the article.

21. Before being interviewed on the radio or TV, listen to or view the show to become familiar with the interviewer's style.

22. Treat the reporter with the utmost respect, even if he is awkward at interviewing or is unfamiliar with the subject at hand. The reporter is your megaphone. Speaking through the media is an efficient and cost-effective way to promote financial services as well as factual information about financial products, without selling. View the media as your ally. It is in your best interest to cooperate and to help the reporter do his job since the public gives a great deal of credence to what it reads or hears in the media.

Media Relations No-No's [2]

1. Do not ask a reporter to let you review his story prior to publication.
2. Do not call a reporter to ask his source for a story.
3. Do not promise to provide an answer or information and not follow through. Always honor the reporter's deadlines.
4. Do not ask the reporter to send you a clipping or audio- or videotape when the story is published.
5. Do not threaten to pull advertising from a publication because it published a negative story.
6. Do not assume that because you advertise in a publication you will be interviewed or quoted.

How to Network Effectively with Professionals

Here are some simple steps to take if you wish to become a quality networker:

1. Identify other professionals from whom you would like to receive referrals and to whom you would like to send referrals.

2. Call the professional on the phone and request either a meeting in his office or a meeting over a breakfast (it's less expensive and more time-efficient), lunch, or dinner.

3. If he declines or delays a meeting, start sending him quality information about your product or service. This would be an excellent person to whom to send any articles you have written. Assume the posture of a problem solver, a provider of solutions both for him and for his clients. Focus on him and his clients, and not on yourself and your product.

4. At your first meeting, play show-and-tell. First ask what his practice or business is about, his fees, and services. Most importantly, ask him to describe his typical client and the type of referral he would like to receive from you. Always listen patiently and avoid the temptation to jump in and talk about your service or product. This is where most of us sabotage our own networking opportunities. By letting the other person go first, you can gather clues to what might interest him about your service or product rather than going off in a direction that might not be relevant. Also, by letting him go first, you might discover an angle you might not have thought of otherwise.

5. After you have carefully listened and are certain you have a clear picture of his business or practice, offer to share with him relevant information about you and your practice. Name-drop only if entirely appropriate, effective, and truthful. Of course, never, ever mention a client's name or a confidential identifiable situation. Let it be known if you are an officer or committee chair in your professional association or society. Be very clear about how you are compensated. Make it easy for him to send you referrals. Leave him with a few business cards, some appropriate reading material such as a brochure, newsletter, something you have written, and an audio- or videotape from a presentation you have made. Offer to meet with his client the first time in his office with him present, and a family member, especially if the client is advanced in age or impaired. Ask if he would be interested in receiving any information from you on a topic you know well. If you have a fee schedule, be certain to leave one with him.

6. Follow up with a warm, personal thank-you note.

7. Look for opportunities to send him referrals.

8. Thank him in writing or by phone if someone he has referred to you attempts to contact you. Do not wait until the referral becomes a client.

9. If someone he refers becomes a client, never refer that person to someone else for another service without calling the original referring person first. He might have someone else in mind to whom he wishes to refer his client, or that other person might be a competitor of his in some area. He will appreciate your thoughtfulness.

10. Stay in touch. Place him on your mailing list. Do not bombard him with product information, especially lots of company-produced pieces. Better to send short samples of how the product can be applied to a client situation. He will be better able to visualize who among his clients could benefit from your service or product.

CHAPTER 3 ENDNOTES

1. Thomas J. Stanley, *Marketing to the Affluent* (Homewood, IL: Dow Jones–Irwin, 1988), p. 73.
2. Harriet Hoffman and Noel Holmes, "How to Work with the Media," presented at a special meeting of the Dallas Fort Worth Society of the Institute of Certified Financial Planners (Dallas, Texas, April 1995).

CHAPTER 3 REFERENCES

Bartelstone, Rona, president, Rona Bartelstone Associates, Inc., interview with author, Ft. Lauderdale, Florida, January 11, 1996.

Baruch, Eric, general agent, John Hancock Mutual Life Insurance Company, interview by author, Milwaukee, Wisconsin, January 3, 1996.

Caswell, Gordon, president, Baylor Health Care System, interview by author, Dallas, Texas, January 8, 1996.

Foster, P. Wesley, president, Long & Foster Realtors, Inc., interview with author, Arlington, Virginia, January 11, 1996.

Gordon, Harley, partner, Gordon & Friedler, interview by author, Boston, Massachusetts, January 15, 1996.

Gurney, Steve, publisher, *Retirement Living*, interview with author, Arlington, Virginia, January 3, 1996.

Kniseley, Sandra, director of professional development, College for Financial Planning, interview by author, Denver, Colorado, January 11, 1996.

Lovick, John, general agent, John Hancock Mutual Life Insurance, interview by author, Dallas, Texas, January 3, 1996.

Nay, Tim, principal, Law Offices of Tim Nay, interview by author, Portland, Oregon, January 22, 1996.

Tanner, Michael D., director of the Social Security Project, Cato Institute, interview by author, Washington, DC, January 2, 1996.

Thayer, Leah, ed., *Selling to Seniors*, Silver Spring, Maryland: CD Publications. Interview by author, January 11, 1996.

4

CHAPTER

Successful Client Interaction

MARTHA: THE TRAVEL WRITER

I worked with Martha many years ago, but she remains one of my favorite clients to this day. To look at her you would think that she did not have two nickels to rub together. She drove a beat-up old car that gave her trouble from time to time. But that did not seem to bother her. Although she was always well groomed, her clothes were out of style and she always had a somewhat disheveled look. This woman was not a beauty by conventional standards. In fact she was rather plain, never wearing makeup and letting her long silver-streaked brown hair flow naturally down around her shoulders. Martha's beauty was in her peaceful demeanor and in her joyous outlook on life. Her husband had passed on when she was in her mid-50s, about 10 years before I met her.

Shortly after his death, she had decided to pursue a dream that had been in the back of her mind for many years, to become a travel writer. She would be gone for months at a time traveling throughout the Far East, writing about her experiences for travel magazines. She enjoyed learning the languages of the countries she traveled, and her adventuresome palate welcomed an opportunity to sample exotic cuisines. A lover of the arts and nature, she cherished the world and the people in it, and all the things they created. She would stroll into my office humming a bar from

---

Martha: The Travel Writer (continued)

Beethoven or Mozart. She loved to share stories about her travel adventures. It made no difference to her whether she stayed in first-class accommodations or a thatched hut on a riverbank in some faraway place. Although compassionate and empathetic, she had a clear sense of who she was and what she was about. She was very independent and knew how to make her way in the world. Martha saw beauty in everything and everyone she met, but was quick to put you in your place if you did not treat her with respect.

I worked with Martha while still in my early 30s. During a meeting with her I suddenly realized how much my older clients had learned from life and how much wisdom they had acquired. I knew how much I had learned about life through the experiences I had both enjoyed and endured in my first 30-some years. I could only imagine how much people like Martha must have known having lived twice as long as me. That's when I became aware of why I had so much respect for the older generations. They had endured and learned. Martha was a shining example of how life's experiences can be turned into wisdom.

EVERYBODY IS SELLING SOMETHING

This chapter could easily be called "how to sell to the maturity market." We are all selling something, whether it is a product, a service, or our alleged indispensability to our employer. Ultimately, our ability to sell depends upon our ability to communicate. If your livelihood depends on your communication skills, and it usually does, how you relate to other people becomes critical. Keep in mind that no one wants to be sold anything. Any member of the maturity market will tell you so.

Over the years salesmen have been bombarded with countless strategies and methods for selling. We have heard everything from "harmonizing the sale" to the "my dear old grandmother close" to "nonmanipulative selling." I have often wondered what our customers and clients would think if they could be privy to all these gyrations we go through just to get them to do what we think they ought to do.

Successful communication can be attributed to four things:

1. Attitude
2. Preparation
3. Environment
4. Skills

ATTITUDE

No matter who the client is, the desire to serve the highest good should be our goal. While it is important that clients have confidence in your expertise and experience, it is just as important for them to know they are your priority, not the product or service you are offering. We need to serve our client based on his needs, goals, aspirations, and value system, not ours. Most importantly, we need to treat every prospect and client with the utmost dignity and respect. Every individual has his own view of what he needs in order to be comfortable. It is not our job to redefine his needs according to our own value system but rather to discover his own personal definition of abundance, and to educate him, allowing him to make his own decisions and to facilitate the lifestyle he desires. Always serve with joy, and no matter what you do for a living, view it as your personal mission to help people realize *their* goals. Empathy is probably the most important skill for anyone to have who works with customers. Thankfully it can be acquired, but we need to leave judgment at the door.

Veteran elder law attorney Tim Nay, in Portland, Oregon, values his clients' satisfaction above all else. "I will do anything to make them happy." According to Tim, there are what he calls "gatekeepers." "A gatekeeper is anyone who can send you business. They are not going to send you business if they aren't happy. Unfortunately people will often forget the times they were happy with you, but will rarely forget the times they were unhappy. So we go out of our way to keep them happy. We really bend over backwards." Tim was a practicing psychotherapist before he became an attorney in 1984. His keen understanding of people is evident in how he runs his practice. He even brings in a psychologist to coach his staff on how to work effectively with clients. He is a good example of how important attitude is. Between January 1 and January 11, 1996, he saw 35 new clients. His average is 26 new clients per month, and the highest ever is 55 new clients in one month.

PREPARATION

Part of your preparation for client interaction is having expertise about his issues, which we already discussed in Chapter 3. What I am referring to here is preparation for the meeting or telephone conference with the client and his other professional advisers. I would rather cancel a client meeting than to go unprepared. Part of the preparation includes setting the agenda so that everyone knows what we are coming together to accomplish. Sometimes the client will call the meeting and he will set the agenda. That's fine. The important thing is that everyone needs to have a clear understanding of what is to be covered and the anticipated result.

If you have difficulty remembering what items to take to each meeting and what needs to be done to prepare, put together a checklist. Either you or your assistant can check off each item as it is gathered or prepared for the meeting. When I sold residential real estate, I used a "Listing Checklist" form to be certain that I had everything I needed when I went to an appointment, including all forms to be signed (filled out in advance). It included a list of items to review with the client, which I checked off during the meeting as the item was discussed. This form became a permanent part of the file to remind me later of what we had covered. Include on your checklist anything you will need during the meeting, including calculator, mints, tissues, memo tablet and pen (tablet and pen for the client also), *Morningstar Report*, client file, colored markers, sticky notes, marketing pieces, disclosure forms, laptop computer, fresh coffee, or whatever your profession requires. This list does not include your handheld telephone, unless the client is expecting a phone call.

The client might find it annoying if you must leave the room to gather things you forgot to bring into the conference room, or if you cannot continue with the meeting because you forgot to bring an item to their home or their advisor's office. While this information applies to a meeting with anyone and not just the mature market, it is especially important to be prepared for meetings with our older clients, since they have more difficulty with distractions and the focusing of attention. Meetings with this group need to be especially organized. In either case, your time is valuable and so is your client's, and this must be respected by both parties. Some polite social conversation is expected, especially at the start of any meeting. But a meeting that meanders with no identifiable purpose is fruitless and leaves the client with the impression that you are willing to give away your time, and your goal of providing a service or a product is not likely to come to fruition. It is also very confusing to the client.

ENVIRONMENT

A warm, private, friendly atmosphere is most conducive to conducting business. Always close the door before beginning a meeting and instruct someone to hold your calls. If a very important call does come in, politely excuse yourself and return as soon as possible. Avoid the temptation to tell the client who the caller was or what the call was about when you return. Any disclosure could be viewed as a breach of confidentiality or an indication of an inflated ego. Either way, you lose. The exception is an emergency that demands the abrupt termination of the meeting, such as a family emergency. Be sure to tell the client that he will not be billed for the time. This is important if you bill for your time, since clients need to know that they have your undivided attention.

SKILLS

We all have our own ways of communicating and ways of understanding what is being communicated. Communicating with our older clients can be particularly challenging since they have had several decades to develop their own ways of listening, viewing, and comprehending. I often marvel at the ways my colleagues who came from the educational profession are able to explain complex personal financial concepts to people. Whatever we are trying to sell, we need to realize that the terms and concepts we use are usually not part of our client's everyday conversation. Our challenge is to relate these ideas so that the client can make an informed decision. Then there are the clients who have done a lot of their own homework and can converse with us on some of these topics as well or better than some professionals.

Some of you might already be using some of these strategies. The important thing to remember is that all strategies do not work with everyone, so you will need to be mindful of how your client receives information and to use the strategy that works best both for him and you.

Story Selling

I have found that people do not really care about the features of a product, service, or a financial strategy. They care about how it relates to them personally. When they know how the product or strategy can work for them, then they might become more interested in the facts. One strategy that works with just about everyone is what I call "Story Selling."

Here's how Story Selling works. Older people especially tend to be able to create images in their minds better than most younger people. According to Joseph Chilton Pearce,[1] this is because they grew up at a time when storytelling around the dinner table and stories told on the radio were commonplace. Listeners were left to their own imagination to create an image or a visual picture of what they were hearing and from their own personal interpretation. Generations who grew up with television had the image created for them, so their ability to create mental pictures might not be as well developed. Although Story Selling might work best for the older generation, it might work for baby boomers if their exposure to television has been limited. Anyone who reads a great deal might also have a highly developed ability to create imagery.

I listen carefully to the client from the very first time I meet him, whether in person or on the telephone. I pick up clues about what is important in his life and how he receives information. Then I create a story about the product or service using the information he has shared with me. This personalizes the service or product so he can see, in his own terms, how it can fit into his own life. Let's look at one example.

Kathryn Smith, the Gardener.

Mrs. Smith calls you for an appointment, having been referred to you by her CPA. (Call her CPA or drop him a line immediately to let him know that she has called you, and to thank him for the referral.) She arranges to meet with you next Thursday afternoon when she learns that your office is not far from where her garden club is meeting that day. She arrives right on time. When you meet her in the reception area of your office, she is giving your receptionist tips on how to rejuvenate a drooping plant. During the meeting you discover that she is 77 years of age; she has three children and nine grandchildren (commit their names to memory) scattered around the country; she often travels by herself with travel groups to foreign countries; and she loves gardening. Her CPA has referred her to you because he is concerned about the rate of return she is receiving on her investments and the lack of diversification in her portfolio.

Ask her if the directions you gave to the office were helpful. Her answer will give you a clue about her physiological abilities. Mrs. Smith does not mention making a "dry run" as many older clients will do in order to be sure they can find your office easily on the day of their appointment. During the meeting ask questions about her gardening, travel, and her relationship with her children and grandchildren. Any one of these areas could provide information for a story selling "script." Since it seems as though her real passion is her flower gardens, spend some time getting to know more about this hobby. See how you can create a story about investment diversification around the theme of flowers. You also discover that she is a very busy lady, and although she is quite capable of learning how to select and manage her own investments, she makes it quite clear that she has no interest in this. And as long as she is comfortable financially, she sees no need to diversify in hopes of receiving a higher rate of return. However, she respects her CPA's opinion and makes an appointment to return to your office to discuss your recommendations. She also gives you permission to confer with her CPA so that she can benefit from your combined expertise. You also obtain her permission to invite him to your next meeting. You call the CPA to review your recommendations with him and to invite him to your next client meeting.

Let's say that you decide to recommend that she retain a private money manager to select and manage her investments. While Mrs. Smith might not have much interest in the financial aspects of your recommendation, her CPA most likely will. Review with him ahead of time information about historical performance (especially after taxes and inflation) and lifetime financial projections using first her current portfolio and then the projections based on your recommendations. Show him samples of the quarterly reports the portfolio manager will send her, and to him if he wishes. Mrs. Smith might have some interest in the lifetime projections, but only if they demonstrate that her current lifestyle might not be sustainable without making your recommended changes. But I suspect that she might respond better if you tell the story in her terms. By the way, I almost always address the client, regardless of her age, by her first name, unless I get an indication that it is not appropriate. Your discussion might go something like this:

Joan: Kathryn, I have carefully reviewed your current portfolio and prepared a short report that will show us how long you will be able to maintain your current lifestyle. What this shows us is that in about five years, you might not have enough income to support your hobbies, traveling, and the gifts you have planned to give to your grandchildren. Tom, your CPA, has reviewed my figures and finds my assumptions and the results to be accurate. Do you want me to review the details of this report with you before we continue?

Kathryn: No thank you, Joan. If you and Tom agree that these figures are correct, then I am certain they are. Tom probably knows more about my finances than I do. (She laughs.)

Joan: I am real glad that you called me when you did. You are lucky to have a CPA who has the wisdom to spot a potential problem, and who takes a personal interest in your financial security. It's not too late to do something about your situation to put you back on course. What I am recommending will increase the likelihood that you will be able to maintain your financial independence for many years to come. And, you will be able to afford to travel and to do all the things you love to do. Let me share with you the basic concepts, and then we can get into the details later.

I recommend that you retain a private money manager to personally select and manage your portfolio. It will be his job to make sure that your investments produce enough income for you to enjoy life. He will buy and sell investments based on your own personal needs, as well as changing market conditions. He will also work with Tom to minimize your income taxes. I will also stay involved. My job is to make sure he is doing his job, and to communicate with you, and with Tom if you wish, about how the investments are doing.

Kathryn: It sounds pretty complicated to me. If I have enough income now, why can't I wait until there is a problem and deal with it then?

Joan: Kathryn, that's a good question. Let me explain. I know how you love to garden. Remember sharing with me that your goal is to have a healthy garden where a plant or flower is always blooming, no matter what the season or what the weather is doing? (Wait for her to nod or respond.)

Well it's the same way with investments. I think of the investment portfolio as your own flower garden. Our goal is to always to have a healthy portfolio where at least one type of investment is always doing well. Sometimes some investments will do well, just like sometimes some flowers will be blooming. And at other times, some investments will do poorly, due to the market conditions, just like some flowers will not bloom during certain seasons of the year, or perhaps a particular flower has become unhealthy. As the flower expert, you are able to distinguish between the flowers that are not blooming because they are out of season from those that have become unhealthy and must be replaced. Well, so will your portfolio manager know the difference between the investments that are still healthy but are simply responding to out-of-favor market conditions from those that are not likely to ever perform well for one reason or another in the future.

You know how you need to keep your flower bed healthy by constantly pulling weeds, adding nourishment to the soil, checking the light exposure, and replanting? Well it's the same way with investments. This is what is not happening to your current portfolio. Your current portfolio is not getting watered and nourished. And your investment portfolio, just like your flower garden, will eventually die if it does not receive the proper care and feeding.

Be sure to maintain good eye contact with her while you are speaking so that she will hear everything you are saying. Turn to Tom in between sentences to include him. I recommend that you seat Kathryn directly across from you and Tom. It is important for her to communicate visually and verbally with him. Also, solicit her nod of approval as you are speaking to be sure you do not lose her in your analogy. She might either correct you or offer more information. If she's really in sync with your analogy, she might take over and tell the story for you.

If your analogy has been succinct and accurate without long complex sentences, she might begin to see how private money management is a solution to a problem she might have down the road if no action is taken. If she has processed what you have said, she will probably ask some questions, which might sound like objections. These might include:

1. I am not willing to give up control of my money to someone who might lose it.
2. Money management fees are too expensive.
3. How will I know if I am making or losing money if someone else is managing it?
4. I don't want someone I don't know making decisions about my money.

If she raises these issues, it usually means that your explanation made sense to her and now she is asking for the details. After you have told the story within her own context of understanding, respond to her questions with the facts. Remember, this is an independent lady who makes up her own mind. Maintaining dignity and independence is her priority, as it is with most older adults. Give her the space to ask questions and to make choices and decisions.

Kathryn has a clear idea about her goal (to maintain her lifestyle), and at least one professional whose opinion she trusts is joining you in this recommendation. At this point, you can review the details such as the expertise of the portfolio manager you are recommending, his track record (avoid any hype), and the quarterly reports she will receive (show her some samples). You can also reassure her that the portfolio manager is always available to you, Tom, and her, if an explanation of his investment activities is needed. Either you or Tom can explain the historical return for at least the last five years, after his fees, compared to the return on her current portfolio.

Even if Kathryn does not agree with you now that she ought to retain a private money manager, she might be receptive to the idea in the future. Sometimes delaying a decision is the client's way of maintaining control and of letting everyone know that she is still in charge. I have had clients resist such recommendations only to decide later to implement them. The members of the older generation are cautious; sometimes they are not necessarily resisting our recommendations, but are merely taking their time to digest what we have said and to become comfortable with a new idea you have presented. Many are simply taking the time to listen to their intuition and their wisdom before proceeding. I suggest that you give them some space and let them make up their own minds.

Ralph, the Tennis Player

Your stories will not always be as long and involved as the previous one. Let's take a look at another example of Story Selling. Ralph is divorced with grown children. He loves to hike, jog, ski, and play tennis. Ralph was introduced to me by a Realtor who listed his home several years ago. She was very concerned because all his money was invested in certificates of deposit and was planning to invest the proceeds from the sale of his home in certificates of deposit as well. This seemed very inappropriate to his astute Realtor, especially since Ralph was a young, active 58-year-old retiree at the time who could easily outlive his money. She insisted that he meet with me to discuss how he could invest the proceeds from the sale of his home and the certificates of deposit in a diversified investment portfolio. A nervous Ralph took a leap of faith implementing nearly all of my investment recommendations, and he took my advice and purchased long term care insurance.

We developed a wonderful relationship over the years and he continued to take my advice, except for one thing. I never could motivate him to implement my recommendation to meet with an attorney to design and implement an estate plan. Since he was a divorced parent with grown children living at a distance, this was of particular concern to me. He was very reserved about his feelings and rarely spoke about his children. But when he did, I sensed that these adult children were the most important thing in his life. During one of our meetings, he shared with me how much he loved to play tennis and that he had just won an important tennis match. So I took this as my cue to try one more time to motivate him to take action on his estate plan. The discussion went something like this:

Joan: Ralph, have you taken any action on your estate plan yet?

Ralph: No, I haven't. I'm OK. I'm as healthy as I have ever been. Nothing is going to happen to me. Besides, how can I deal with something that hasn't happened to me yet. I'll wait until I see what the future holds.

Joan: Ralph, when we address these issues from a legal and financial standpoint, we're really talking about your children. Taking personal responsibility and executing your estate-planning documents is a wonderful way to say "I love you" to your kids. It relieves them of the burden of taking care of your affairs, without specific direction from you, should you become incapacitated or when you pass on. Without the proper legal documents, properly executed by you, they would spend a considerable amount of *your* money and *their* time trying to convince a judge and a physician that they should honor your children's verbal requests about how your business affairs and health care decisions should be handled. And as for not knowing what the future holds, let's think of it this way: You know how when you are playing tennis you have a certain place where you stand on your side of the net so you can return the ball no matter where it lands? (Wait for him to nod in agreement.)

And you remember how you have demonstrated to me how you flex your knees and hold your racket so you can return the ball no matter how it bounces? (Use some gestures or stand up and demonstrate to make your point. At this point, Ralph was laughing hysterically because I looked so silly jumping around the conference room holding an invisible tennis racket. Wait for him to nod in agreement.) You have developed these strategies because you never know where the ball is going to land and you have to be ready for whatever comes your way? Right? (Check to be sure he is still in agreement.)

You just told me a few moments ago that you could not have won that match yesterday had you not used these strategies. Well, it's the same way with your estate planning. You never know what the future holds, and by executing these documents you will be prepared for whatever comes your way, both for your sake and for your children.

I finally got it, and so did Ralph. By looking at the situation from Ralph's point of view, explaining it in his own language, and interjecting some humor, I finally got my point across. My only regret is that it took me so long to think to use this approach. Up to that point I had been emphasizing all the benefits of the various documents when all I had to do was explain the solution to the problem I had identified in terms relevant to him personally. He called me two weeks later and said he was sending me copies of his executed estate-planning documents for my file.

By the way, I received a lovely note from Ralph the other day, out of the blue, expressing his gratitude for my "firm recommendations."

There are numerous themes around which you can develop a story to facilitate your client's understanding of your product or service, or your recommendations about action he needs to take. Some examples are golfing, fishing, cooking, baking, and card games, just to name a few. I suggest that you practice by writing out the sequence of your scenario first before trying this strategy out on a client. After a while it will be easy for you to develop a story spontaneously. I do not consider this to be a canned presentation since you are using your own words, it is interactive, and you will make adjustments as needed for each client. George Foelker, a psychotherapist who has a speciality practice with the mature market, shared with me that he too explains technical concepts to his patients in terms of their personal life experiences and interests. Dr. Foelker points out that we must constantly remind ourselves about our clients' educational level and their previous exposure to analytical concepts.

Avoid the temptation to create analogies or stories incorporating references to your parents, relatives, grandparents, or other personal experiences. This is about your client, not anyone in your personal life. Using examples from your own personal experience shifts the focus away from the client and his personal experience, which is the opposite of what needs to happen to maintain his interest and involvement. If you are young or inexperienced, all you will accomplish is to remind the client how old he is and how young and inexperienced you are. If you cannot avoid relating their situation to your own limited life's experiences, they will be wondering if you have enough "maturity on board" to handle a family crisis in a professional and empathetic manner. I point this out because I have often witnessed this reaction in younger salespeople, who will respond to a client's statement, comment, or objection with a reference to something in their own personal lives, such as: "Oh yeah, I have heard my mom say that," or "My friend's dad is in a nursing home too," or "My mom and dad just retired too." Such references come off as an inexperienced salesperson's desperate attempt to relate to a more mature person by calling to mind his own unseasoned frame of reference. This does not inspire trust.

When Story Selling, a simple reference to food to create an anology might be sufficient, since food is something everybody can relate to. For instance, it is very common for an inexperienced investor to want to put all his money in one star performer. "If it is currently the best performer, why not invest all my money in that one investment?" he might ask. Your response might be, "Tasty seasoning enhances the overall taste of a meal, but I don't think you would want to eat a whole plate of seasoning and nothing else, would you?" This can be done gently and even with humor.

Charts, Graphs, and Other Visuals

Story selling is not the only strategy you can use to help your client understand your explanations and recommendations. Charts and graphics appeal to those who are visually oriented. This is why the Ibbotson charts, produced and distributed by Ibbotson Associates, have been immensely popular with clients and customers. They tell the story about investments in a visual format. Unfortunately, they are produced on shiny paper and the colors are often difficult for the older eye to see. But evidently they are worth the effort, since my clients really take the time to study them during client meetings, squinting and straining their eyes to read them. They also have credibilty, since they represent information free of the perceived taint of a product sponsor's message.

Hand-drawn charts with colored markers on a white board or on a piece of large off-white paper are an effective way to explain financial concepts such as estate-planning strategies, financial-planning strategies, charitable giving, and your services, just to name a few applications.

Since geriatric care management is a relatively new profession, a chart might be an effective way to explain your services to a prospective client or during seminars where you are introducing your services. Show your prospect or audience how your services fit together with those of other professions and advisers.

Several clients have commented to me that they really like one estate-planning attorney to whom I often send referrals. They like both his low-key approach and the way he explains things to them. He often uses a white board with colored markers to tell the story about his vision for their personal estate plan design.

If you are not particularly artistic and feel uncomfortable drawing extemporaneously, develop some basic graphics on your computer, leaving room to personalize the visual when you are in front of the client. If you fill in some of the details during the meeting, the client will feel more involved in your explanation and the chart or graph will come off as more personalized, and less as a "canned presentation." Your approach will be more of an interactive discussion and less like a sales presentation.

Nasty Words

In the 1970s, veteran sales trainer Tom Hopkins developed for Realtors a list of words and phrases he called "nasty words." These words and phrases often have unpleasant connotations. There are different ways to express what we wish to say and different ways to phrase questions. Sometimes our choice of words and phrases can result in a breakdown in communication with our clients. We need to be mindful of how our understanding of words and phrases is often based on cultural, generational, educational, experiential, and developmental differences between people. It is in your best interest to tune in as soon as possible to the client's understanding. It is possible to be direct as well as pleasant in your choice of words. I have expanded Tom's concept of "nasty words" and applied it to financial services and the maturity market. Figure 4–1 presents some examples of different ways of sharing or requesting information.

FIGURE 4–1

Nasty Words

Don't Say...	Say...
1. How old are you?	1. What is your age? What is your date of birth?
2. How much money do you have (to a widow who did not work outside the home)?	2. What was your husband's profession?
3. When did your husband die?	3. When did your husband pass on or pass away? How long has your husband been departed? [2]
4. I recommend that you establish a trust.	4. I recommend that you write a special agreement. [3]
5. He had a stroke.	5. He experienced a stroke.
6. He is handicapped.	6. He is physically challenged.
7. We placed or moved her into a nursing home.	7. We settled her in a nursing home.
8. Did you have any trouble finding us?	8. Were my directions helpful?
9. You will run out of money.	9. You might not be able to maintain your current lifestyle. You might not have the resources to do all the things you love to do (*list them specifically*).
10. Nursing Home	10. Extended care facility [4]

CHAPTER 4 ENDNOTES

1. Joseph Chilton Pearce, *Evolution, Intelligence and the Future*, audio-tape of interview with Michael Thoms for New Dimensions Radio (San Francisco, 1991).
2. Tom Hopkins, interview by author, May 5, 1996.
3. Gordon Caswell, interview by author, January 8, 1996.
4. Tom Hopkins, interview by author, May 5, 1996.

CHAPTER 4 REFERENCES

Bagley, Martha. *The Americans with Disabilities Act: A Revolution of Opportunity.* Sound & Video, January 20, 1993.

Bartelstone, Rona, Rona Bartelstone Associates, Inc., interview with author, Ft. Lauderdale, Florida, January 11, 1996.

Caswell, Gordon, president, Baylor Health Care System, interview by author, Dallas, Texas, January 8, 1996.

Foelker, George, psychotherapist, Iatreia Institute, interview by author, Fort Worth, Texas, December 1, 1995.

Foster, P. Wesley, president, Long & Foster Real Estate Realtors Inc., interview by author, Arlington, Virginia, January 11, 1996.

Nay, Tim, principal, Law Offices of Tim Nay, interview by author, Portland, Oregon, January 22, 1996.

Robbins, Joyce, president, Geriatric Services, interview with author, San Antonio, Texas, January 8, 1996.

Slack, Judy, and Sharon Callosney, Permissions, Tom Hopkins, International, interview by author, Scottsdale, Arizona, March 25, 1996.

5
CHAPTER

Keys to Client Loyalty

JACK: THE CONSUMMATE GENTLEMAN

Jack and his wife Cathrine were referred to me by their attorney when Cathrine's illness had reached the final stages. Although she passed on last year, Jack has remained a client. He is a very handsome, virile man in his early 70s and, like most retired military, he stands erect and has a commanding presence, although his demeanor is surprisingly gentle. After Cathrine's passing and taking the time he needed to get resettled, he started making plans to travel. He especially enjoys the British Isles. His travel companions are usually his adult children and grandchildren. He is particularly fond of his grandson, who likewise enjoys traveling with him. Jack is a busy man. Like many of my clients, he can be difficult to reach by phone. When he's not traveling, you will find him involved with his hobby, photography, which he teaches at a local university just for fun. Although Jack is a very gentle man, he minces no words. He lets you know exactly what he wants. His straightforward approach makes him easy and fun to work with. And, he is very charming. Recently as he was leaving my office, I extended my hand to shake his. Instead, he bowed and kissed the back of my hand. What a lovely gesture. It was spontaneous and could only be pulled off by someone as genuine and spontaneous as Jack.

I have found it relatively easy to attract the mature market and to address their present needs. The greater challenge for me has always been providing ongoing service. Once they have rearranged their portfolio, purchased long term care insurance, and implemented estate planning recommendations, they need little else from me except for periodic minor repositioning of assets and a great deal of information. However, this market needs and appreciates special attention to their *perceived* needs. And it is in your best interest and theirs to stay in touch with them, since eventually someone passes on, experiences an illness or injury, inherits assets, sells his home, or desires to give assets to family or a charity. These events are all an occasion to do business. Unless you stay in touch, the client might not think to call you when these events occur. Of course, we cannot overlook the issue of how you will be compensated for providing ongoing services. We will explore this issue in Chapter 8, which addresses practice management.

Let's assume for the moment that you are being adequately compensated for providing ongoing service and focus on what you can do to create a willingness on your client's part to continue to work with you. The delivery of services and products that inspire loyalty in the maturity market often apply to all markets, except that the need is intensified in this market. This group usually depends upon the performance of their investment portfolio for income, unlike those still in the workforce. For them, Social Security, pensions, annuities, and investments have taken the place of the employer.

If you were to lose your job tomorrow and were without income, you might begin to understand how a retiree must feel when his investments are not producing income. Cash in hand is all that matters to the average retiree. Preserving principal and entitlement benefits is the same to him as preserving your job is to you. Both are sources of income.

Until I understood this, I really could not appreciate why the little things we can do to ease their minds are so important. If you manage the personal affairs of a family member, you probably have a sense of what I am talking about. For them, this is it. There will be no pay raises, no bonuses, no fringe benefits, and perhaps no inheritance. If they are not in excellent health, or if their job skills are obsolete, there is little they can do to increase their income. You can perhaps begin to understand why so many older people play state lotteries. By the way, I include lottery tickets on my client's monthly cash flow statements since they do represent a real expense. It also lets them know that I am in touch with their reality. Whether or not they play the lottery, they find my reference to it amusing, if not insightful.

I have worked with mature clients for many years, and have made mistakes along the way. I wish to share a few of my mistakes with you as well as the things I have done that have worked. Let's take a look at how you can keep these hard-won customers loyal to you.

HOW TO KEEP YOUR CLIENTS' LOYALTY

Be Empathetic

I am placing empathy at the top of the list because it is so important. Webster defines *empathy* as "the intellectual identification of oneself with another." I would revise this definition to read: "the combined heartfelt and intellectual identification with another." Empathy does need to be balanced with the practical aspects of doing business, but compassion and empathy will go a long way toward furthering your success and underlies everything else on our list. Staying in touch with the other person's reality is not easy. It often requires that we place our own reality on hold to hear what the other person is saying, feeling, and experiencing.

Let me share with you an example of when I misread a situation, probably because my own reality got in the way. I was meeting with an adult child and his dad who was in his late 70s. The son was a CPA who had requested a meeting to discuss his mother's long-term care. His mother had had a stroke nearly three years before and at that time had been expected to live less than two months. The family settled her in one of the finest and most expensive nursing homes in the area. Her husband had visited her faithfully every afternoon for three years even though she could not communicate with him. Three years later at the time of our meeting, Dad was nearly out of money and he and his son wanted to know what resources might be available to pay for her care. The physicians were amazed that she was still alive due to the enormity of her physical challenges, and there was no indication that death was near. I incorrectly assumed that the husband could relate in a detached way to his wife's condition and her ability to survive despite all of her physical challenges. I made a comment to the effect that "I always marvel at people in such circumstances who choose to remain alive." While some clients could relate to the situation in an unemotional, detached way, this man was still involved emotionally. Because he seemed so calm and peaceful, I failed to recognize what he was really feeling, resulting in my inappropriate comment. My detached, intellectual approach was entirely inappropriate. I had forgotten to engage my heart. The sad thing is that I really could have helped this family and, due to my carelessness, the opportunity was lost for them and for me. I have always regretted my blunder.

Being empathetic means understanding the client's fear of losing his independence. This becomes especially important when the adult child is making the introduction to you. And it is quite possible that the older adult will lose, or is already losing, some of his independence. At any rate, he needs reassurance that your job is to facilitate his independence and dignity.

Be Sincere

A sincere desire to help people find solutions is an important quality for anyone who works with people. It has not only endeared clients to me, but I am convinced that it is the biggest reason that I have never been sued, nor has any client ever mentioned the possibility. Most litigation against financial planners is initiated by disgruntled adult children, and I am a likely candidate to be sued someday because I work intensely with the mature market.

In the early 1980s, nearly every financial planner and stockbroker was selling limited partnerships. Even some of the best conceived partnerships offered by the most respected general partners did not work out. I made every effort to sell only the most conservative partnerships and only to well-qualified (suitable) investors. While it was distressful for me when these programs did not work out financially, I was heartened to hear from several clients that they recognized that I did not sell them these investments out of self-interest, that they had made an informed decision, and that they knew I had sincerely thought they were quality investments and entirely appropriate for them. It seems that people search for someone to work with whom they can trust because in the end they need to know that you have their best interest at heart.

Understand the Issues

We touched on the need for you to be an expert on the issues that affect the mature market in the section on working with the media and as an important component in attracting prospective clients. But there is a very practical reason for including it here. You really need to be well versed on their issues so that the client does not feel the need to educate you every time he needs your advice or when a decision needs to be made. For instance, you need to know the difference between Medicare and Medicaid; health care issues and the basics about Medicare HMOs and Medical Savings Accounts; and estate planning for the elderly and the incapacitated, just to name a few. You do not need to be an expert in these areas if they do not fall within your specialty. However, if you know where to refer them for further information, this will go a long way toward maintaining their loyalty.

I receive countless calls from the over-65 group wanting information about an issue affecting their finances. They often work with other financial services professionals, especially product salespeople, who seem to lack an interest in or understanding of the client's issues. Sometimes they also share that the other advisors do not explain things to them to their liking. This could be because the salesperson lacks understanding or interest in the older person's point of view, understanding of the physiological and psychological changes that the customer is experiencing, or time. It could be that the broker is under pressure to sell products and does not have the time to give his clients the attention they demand unless they are purchasing product. If you demonstrate at least a willingness to keep up with the customer's issues as he ages, he will be inclined to remain with you.

Demonstrate Value

People tend to forget the benefits they derive from a relationship with a financial professional. The client needs to be reminded in a practical way, and often very subtly, the benefits he derives from working with you. This is especially true if you charge a fee for your service. Every time they write a check they will ask themselves if your service is worth the fee. If they are paying you to manage their money, hopefully they can see the value of the account increasing by more than the fee you are charging. But the result of most advice is often less visible, since it frequently helps to keep them from losing money, rather than helping them to make money. I readily admit that I sometimes forget to point out to my clients the benefits they are receiving compared to the fee they are paying me. This is a big mistake.

One way to remind clients of your value is to include stories in your newsletter about people in situations similar to theirs who have benefited from your sound advice. Of course these stories need to be either fictional or very well disguised. Confidentiality needs to be observed. Another strategy is to show them with charts, graphs, or some other visual how much money the strategy you are recommending is saving them. Compare this savings to your fee. Your goal is to make the intangible tangible. Show them again after they have implemented the strategy the benefits of your advice.

Be Responsive

Respond quickly to requests for service, even if the activity is not important to you. Your priority should be what is important to the client. Older clients are often disgruntled by lost statements, misspelled names or incorrect addresses on account registrations, incorrect Social Security numbers on statements, and fluctuations in market values. Take immediate action to let them know that you are aware of the situation and that you are doing something to correct it, or explain to them what is going on. When explaining market conditions to them, use nontechnical terms. Anything else will sound like nonsense. It is not a good idea to use a string of technical concepts to head them off from asking more questions about a market condition even you do not understand. It will seem as though you are trying to put them off, which might be your motive. Such a strategy is insincere, insensitive, and foolish for anyone trying to create client loyalty. Commit to provide the information they seek and then deliver on that promise. If there is no answer to their question, tell them.

Be Proactive

If you have an investor who is not yet comfortable with a repositioned portfolio that favors growth, and the market takes a tumble, or if you are expecting a correction, call him first. Let him know what you think is coming, or what has just happened. Never feel compelled to try to "fix" the situation by moving money around unless that really is the best strategy. Mature clients can live with unknowns. Your attentiveness and ambiguity lets him know that you understand his concerns and that they matter to you, even if you cannot do anything about the situation. I survived the stock market crash of October 1987 with my clientele intact. I had many retirees invested in the market at the time, and in anticipation of a correction I had sent them a letter a week earlier urging them to call me to discuss reallocating to protect from the anticipated downslide. Some called, some did not. After the crash, I called all of them to let them know what our next move was, if only to do nothing. Most of them were nonchalant about the recent drop in asset values. Just knowing that I was right there with them reduced their fears.

Over time, many of them, including Ralph the tennis player I referred to earlier, assured me that they were now comfortable with the ups and downs of the market. Many have told me that I need not call them every time the market takes a tumble. "Don't worry, Joan, it will be up again." "This is just the way the market works." "Without these drops in value there might be little opportunity for portfolio growth in the long run." "We need to view these drops as an opportunity over the long haul." "You don't need to call me every time the market goes down." They really had committed to memory what I told them and then played it back for me.

Be Interactive

Ask your clients directly what services they need. Solicit their viewpoint about the pricing of your services. Just like they want to be involved in their health care decisions, they also appreciate the opportunity to voice their opinion about how you can serve them. Ask their opinion about your brochures and other written materials. Can they read them? Do they like the colors? Would they like to hear from you more often? I think of my practice as more of a partnership, or a club. I solicit and welcome my clients' opinions. These people enrich my life, and speaking with them, for the most part, is a pleasure whether or not I agree with them. They are the reason I am in business, and they are the reason I will stay in business.

I see client meetings as an opportunity to exchange information. I solicit their opinions and feedback often. This is not used as a closing technique but as an opportunity to gain insight into how I can serve them better. It also lets me know if we understand each other, if I am hearing what they are saying, and if they are comprehending my thoughts and recommendations.

Communicate Often

If time permitted, I would spend the entire day on the telephone chatting with my clients. They seem to enjoy our conversations and so do I. The only problem is that it is not economically feasible. So I send them notes. I often include a short one-sentence note on their invoices, or I drop them a line in the mail. The handwritten note is more time-efficient than a telephone call, although I realize that it is not interactive. But it lets them know that I am thinking of them. Holiday greetings sent in December or early January are a must, although I feel most comfortable sending a nonreligious message expressing my wish for joy and peace. Many of my clients are not Gentiles so I feel a need to send a greeting that is appropriate for everyone. If you have developed a relationship with the client's adult child, it is thoughtful to send him a short greeting now and then to let him know that your relationship with him and his parents is important to you.

It seems as though every business sends out a newsletter, and clients seem to expect it from anyone with whom they do business. Clients seem to enjoy receiving my newsletter, which addresses the issues important to them. It is expensive and time-consuming, but it disciplines me to keep in touch with them. I recommend that you send out a quarterly newsletter. It can be as simple as the front and reverse of an 8 1/2 by 11 page with a few short paragraphs about important, timely topics. If your business addresses several different markets like mine does, enclose an extra, separate page with the basic newsletter to the other markets with whom you work. For instance, in addition to working with individuals, I also consult with corporations and other groups about how to work with the mature market. My message for that group is inappropriate for my individual clients, so it is included on a separate page sent with the main newsletter. If your company sends out a newsletter to your customers or clients, including a special note from you would be a nice touch if that's possible.

When sending out forms to be executed and other brief communications to clients, I prefer to enclose a handwritten note rather than a formal typed letter. I have a one-half page memo with all the information that appears on my formal letterhead on the masthead. The memo page is two part so that a copy can be placed in the file as a permanent record of what I have said to the client.

Some of my clients are very computer literate. I am looking into the possibility of communicating with them on-line. While doing so might be more of a novelty at this time, I envision that as my clients continue to age, I will be working more with their adult children, who will most likely welcome the convenience of this method of communicating. This could be a tremendous time-saver for the adult child who lives in another time zone, making the placement of telephone calls during business hours inconvenient if not impossible.

As time goes on it will be important to be able to communicate with clients and prospects in a variety of media such as video and audio. Although many of my clients are very technology literate, the majority of the current older market is not as enamored of the various communication media. However, this will change as the baby boomers age. More about this in Chapter 10.

Observe Confidentiality

I would never intimate that someone is a client or a prospect unless I have that person's explicit permission to do so, let alone divulge any information to anyone about the client's or prospect's personal affairs. Older women in particular are very secretive about their personal finances. In fact, they rarely send me referrals. Many seem to think that their friends have more assets than they do. They are so insistent that others not know what they have that they are not even willing to take a chance by referring a friend to me for fear that their friend might find out from me how much they have or do not have. I suspect that this is a holdover from the days when a woman's worth was measured by the wealth of the man she married. It took me a long time to figure this out. It became apparent when many older women would say to me, "My friend Mrs. Smith really needs your help. I might give her your card. She has quite a bit more money than I do. Her husband was a surgeon." Older men on the other hand have always been very generous in sending me referrals. If I am working with an older husband and wife, it is common for the husband to send me referrals, but not the wife.

I have at least one client who is a member of the media or who is married to a columnist or a reporter. If you find yourself in that situation, it would be a very good idea to have the client sign a reverse confidentiality agreement. This might protect you from having your relationship with that client exposed if an unfortunate disagreement should arise. You surely would not want your business dealings printed in the city newspaper or broadcast on the evening news.

Recognize That Loyalty Is the Client's Option

No matter what we do to engender client loyalty, it is their option. Expecting them to give us all their business might be unrealistic given their need for independence. Demanding their loyalty or that they take all of your recommendations is demeaning and insulting to the client who wants to be treated with dignity and respect. This means honoring his viewpoint and allowing him to make his own decision, even if the decision defies logic from your point of view.

I was asked by a reporter a few years ago how many clients I have. He was surprised to hear that the size of my active clientele is by most standards fairly moderate. However, in addition to active clients, over the years I have worked with a substantial group of people who consider me to be their financial planner even though I might not have had any contact with them for over a year. They have told me that they do not see a need for me to remain in constant contact with them, but they just need to know where to find me should the need arise.

Offer Flexible Fees and Services

Because this group is so diverse, remain flexible in the services and fees you offer. Explain the options to the client or prospect. He will appreciate having the opportunity to make his own decisions. When recommending products, I have found it beneficial to offer two options, or on occasion three. More than three product options will usually create unnecessary complications. Offering the client options is another way to allow him to maintain his independence. If you are compensated by a fee, offer both a set price for a package of services and an hourly rate as well. Be certain to put your agreement in writing, or if this is not appropriate for your profession, give him a fee schedule that states very explicitly how and when he will be billed. He will be more comfortable if he knows all this information before engaging your services. I generally do not charge for the time I spend with a prospective new client in telling him about my services and fees.

Work with the Team

Let the prospective client know from the very start that you are very comfortable with—in fact, that you prefer to communicate with his other professional advisors when it is in his best interest. Tell him that you will seek his permission before contacting his other advisors, except for an initial introduction by letter or telephone. This is to assure him that you are not going to run up his bill with his other advisors without his permission. I have found that people are generally very pleased that you are willing to get involved. If the client has worked with the other professional for a period of time, he welcomes another opinion about your abilities and expertise. The very fact that you have volunteered to reveal yourself to the other trusted professionals indicates that you have nothing to hide and that you can be trusted. Introducing yourself to the client's other professional advisors presents an excellent networking opportunity, since you already have the endorsement of their client.

You can be an invaluable resource to the client and his family just by knowing where to refer him for other services and products. I maintain an up-to-date database of geriatric care managers, elder law attorneys, insurance agents and brokers, and other professionals throughout the country with whom I have developed relationships or whose expertise I know. In addition, I am a member of several organizations that give me an opportunity to access information about other professionals throughout the country to whom I can refer the client. Sometimes knowing where to refer the client is the most valuable service you can offer him.

Be Honest

Let the client know right from the start that you are not an expert in all areas but that you make it your business as a service to your clients to know someone who is. In my case, I do not work with younger people unless we are addressing the issues of the older parent or relative. In that event, I usually advocate for the older person, and the younger person is his agent. I often refer younger people to other financial planners. I also let prospective clients know that I do not prepare income tax returns, draft legal documents, or sell insurance, real estate, or securities. However, as a part of my services, I can introduce them to other professionals and salespeople when they need their services. I volunteer in the very first meeting that in some cases I might receive a referral fee if they purchase a product from someone to whom I refer them. This includes the sharing of fees paid by private money managers.

When speaking about products and services, it is important to be brutally honest about what these products and services can and cannot do. You can gain credibility by making clients aware of the shortcomings of products as well as their strong points. Besides, when better products become available, they will be more likely to take your recommendation to purchase the new product if you were honest from the beginning about the product you originally recommended.

It is also important to be honest with the client about his own situation. Try to be matter of fact, supporting your assertions with the facts. Be gentle when explaining the reality of the challenges he is facing, and be prepared to offer solutions. Many retirees have no idea how long their money will last, nor whether or not they will face substantial expenses due to future "unexpected" health care costs. I am often the messenger of the sad news that they will be out of capital before their natural life span is up at their current rate of spending. I back this up with a year-by-year projection of expenses and income, taking inflation, taxes, and other variables into account. My job is to develop a strategy to extend the life of their investment portfolio. While they might not be receptive at first to your unswerving honesty, they will respect and trust you, knowing that they can always count on you for straight answers.

One of the most difficult things to do when working with clients is to admit when you have made a mistake. If you know that an investment is going sour, that you simply misread the market, that an insurance company is getting into financial trouble, or that you made any recommendation that is turning out to be a poor choice, admit it to the client and be prepared to offer solutions. Do not make excuses or blame someone else. Clients are more likely to remain loyal to an advisor or a salesman who is willing to admit to his misjudgments as soon as possible and take personal responsibility as soon as the error is discovered so that the client has the opportunity to make decisions. The only benefit in delaying is that it buys you time to cover your tracks. This strategy can only get you into deeper trouble.

Avoid Hyperbole

Exaggeration and overstatement of the facts will cost you your credibility. Resist the urge to make promises and statements about products, services, and your capabilities in order to make the sale. I have been told time and time again that what the mature clients want is a "low-key" approach when they are being offered a service or product. This might take a great deal of patience on your part, but your detached, realistic approach to presenting products and services will create a bond between you and the customer.

I remember an older couple in their 70s, call them Mr. and Mrs. Feinstein, who were referred to me by their son, a life insurance agent. Their son was concerned about the lack of diversification in their investment portfolio, so I recommended that they rearrange it to include a very conservative balanced mutual fund and a U.S. government bond mutual fund. Up to that point, every dime they owned had been invested in certificates of deposit. They agreed to implement my recommendations and were pleased with the results, although it required a great deal of hand-holding on my part. Mr. Feinstein was afraid of losing money. He asked me what seemed like hundreds of times if his money was guaranteed as it had been at the bank. Surprisingly he was most concerned about the government bond fund, not the balanced fund. Every time we spoke, he would ask me if the bond fund was guaranteed and I would respond that while the income from the bonds was guaranteed, the value of the bonds was not guaranteed and the value of the fund would fluctuate. We went through this so many times it became a joke.

He totally understood the risks he was taking, but he found it humorous to raise the issue just to hear me repeat my explanation, since he knew I would not bend the story just to please him. It actually took me quite a while to catch on to his humor. It became our private joke.

Invite Family Members to Your Meetings

When making the first appointment with a prospective client, I ask him to feel free to invite a trusted family member to join us. Once again, during the first meeting I tell him that I would welcome an opportunity to meet whoever would be assisting him in the event he were unavailable or unable to carry out his own affairs. I share with the client that I do not want to meet his family members for the first time during a crisis, should he become ill or pass on. I need for him to know first that I am a person who can step in and work with his family members to be sure that his best interests are observed during his absence or incapacitation. Secondly, he needs to know that I am comfortable working with his family during a crisis and that I have the empathy as well as the levelheadedness to guide and advise them about action to be taken, and to help them make important and timely decisions.

Provide a Comfortable Meeting Environment

We will discuss special features of your office design in Chapter 8 under practice management. But for now you need to know that no matter how much the client likes and trusts you, if he has to meet with you in an environment that in his opinion is unsafe, uncomfortable, or inconvenient, he might not wish to continue the relationship. Clients are sometimes embarrassed or uncomfortable about telling you why they do not wish to continue a relationship with you. They might see their disease as their own shortcoming such as their declining ability to see documents clearly in your office due to poor lighting, or their inability to hear you due to poor acoustics. Maybe your office is noisy or not private. Others might not be able to identify the reason for their discomfort. They only know that meetings in your office are not pleasant, despite the fact that they might genuinely like you and trust you.

Getting Intimate

If you are very present when communicating with clients, you will pick up on their deepest fears and their greatest joys if they trust you enough to share these with you. When I think about the personal advisors I have had the most rewarding and enjoyable relationships with over the years, they all have allowed themselves to be vulnerable enough to allow me to share my fears and joys. They always validated my feelings before offering solutions. How we view money is tied to these joys and fears. When we work with people and their money, we are getting very close to their very core. It requires patience on our part and a willingness to accept them as they are. Whether we think they are right or wrong is not the point. If we want them to feel comfortable working with us and to remain loyal, we will need to accept them right where they are.

Author Olivia Mellan has developed a method by which financial service professionals can identify how clients view money, resulting in a stronger rapport with the clients. Says Mellan, "I've noticed that the advisors with the most successful client relationships do more than just give good financial advice. They understand how particular clients are motivated to act around money, and they build their recommendations around this understanding. The resulting plan is usually readily accepted by the client because it reflects his inner needs and values as well as the stated financial goals."[1]

Getting Physical

I have saved this thought until last because it usually inspires very positive or very negative reactions when I bring it up in seminars for financial service professionals. It is just a suggestion and is not right for everybody. I find that when people open up and share their intimate feelings and thoughts with someone, a certain closeness often develops. It sometimes results in a willingness, perhaps a need, on their part for physical contact more intimate than a handshake. At first, as a new financial planner, I was not sure how to handle this. I thought that my colleagues would think that a pat on the arm or shoulder or a hug was inappropriate for the client-professional relationship. But over the years I have come to accept it. If the client wants to hug or wants to be hugged at the beginning, end, or during a particularly challenging meeting, I just let it happen. Older women in particular seem to want to hug or to be hugged. Some clients have a very charming way of expressing this feeling of affirmation or closeness, such as "Jack, the Consummate Gentleman."

You can decide for yourself what is comfortable for you. This is often a cultural thing, so try to be aware of the various acceptable salutations and greetings of your clientele. Many years ago I held a particular fondness for an older Japanese client. When greeting her, I would extend my hand to shake hers and then lay my left hand on top of her right hand so that I was shaking her one hand with two of mine. One of the partners of the first financial planning firm I worked with cautioned me that this could be offensive to someone from the Japanese culture who was more accustomed to bowing instead of shaking hands. Evidently the overcrowded conditions in Japan resulted in a particular need to avoid entering one another's space. Being aware of such protocol is important. As for me, I will continue to allow the client to let me know what is comfortable for him. I will continue to accept whatever gesture of endearment comes naturally for the client, as long as it does not violate my own personal boundaries.

CHAPTER 5 ENDNOTES

1. Olivia Mellan, "Beyond Reason," *Fee Advisor Magazine*, November/December 1995, p. 62.

6

Marketing Messages that Work

RUTH: THE HOMEMAKER TURNED INVESTMENT GURU

I am reminded of Ruth, a gentle, but feisty woman in her mid-70s, who had always relied upon her husband to care for her. Her husband had recently passed on after battling cancer for five years when we met. She had heard me speak somewhere and decided to work with me. By now she knew the ins and outs of their finances and had become very independent, having taken on all the jobs her husband used to oversee. She had learned how to cut the grass, negotiate with the auto repairman, and actively manage her financial affairs. She had educated herself about personal finances and felt very comfortable making important financial decisions. No longer did she sit back and wait for someone else to take action on her behalf. Ruth, who by her own admission had not known how to balance a checkbook until her husband fell ill, was now totally comfortable charging ahead and implementing her own financial decisions. She could have turned to their accountant or a family member to tell her what to do. But she chose to take this opportunity to learn about their finances.

Having educated herself over the previous five years, she was concerned about her portfolio, which was comprised entirely of debt issues (bonds and money market funds) only. "This is much too conservative,"

Ruth: The Homemaker Turned Investment Guru (continued)

she shared with me during our first appointment. I recommended a portfolio of mutual funds with moderate growth. But according to her, this was still too conservative, so I redesigned my original portfolio recommendations to include several very aggressive funds. She was delighted and later shared that she found the volatility exhilarating. I have found this to be the case with many older women. Given the opportunity, they revel in the newly discovered aggressive, masculine side of themselves. Ruth is an excellent example of the mature woman whose personality is integrated so that she is comfortable expressing characteristics commonly attributed, at least in her generation, to the man. Ruth's aggression, as is the case with many older ladies, is couched in a gentle, peaceful demeanor.

WHY YOUR COMPANY'S MARKETING MESSAGE SHOULD MATTER TO YOU

How your company or any product or service you recommend presents itself can have a profound, sometimes unconscious, effect on your client's attitude toward both the product and you. Your client is responding to this image, one that is often developed through advertising, although favorable or unfavorable media coverage can also have an effect. A logo, product spokesperson, the name of the company, and its slogan or byline all add to image development. And that image can affect your ability to attract potential clients and their willingness to do business with you or to purchase a particular product.

The Purpose of Advertising

In addition to creating an image, advertising can have other purposes. Here are a few:

1. To educate the consumer.
2. To remind the consumer about the product or service.
3. To distinguish the product by comparing it with accepted benchmarks, competitors' products, or by demonstrating its performance.

Without a clear purpose, it would be difficult to create an effective message, decide upon the ideal medium, or determine its timing and placement. For instance, if you want to advertise your geriatric care management service, you might first need to tell the consumer what a geriatric care manager is, since it is a relatively new profession. At one time, the purpose of advertising financial planning was simply to let the consumer know what the service was. Once the public is educated, then a frequent reminder about the product or service, or a comparison between competing products or services, is feasible.

Eric Baruch, General Agent for John Hancock Mutual Life Insurance Company, says that when his agents are cold calling to develop long term care insurance prospects in the Milwaukee area, they must first educate their prospects, since this product is not well known there. He says that quite often the prospect will say "Lawn care? No we don't need any. We already have a lawn service." (Perhaps part of the problem is the prospect's declining ability to hear.) Or, just as with prospects in previously unschooled markets, they will say, "No I don't need any insurance. Medicare pays for that." Any advertising of long term care insurance in that area will need to be educational, at least until the market becomes more knowledgeable. Advertising can be very effective in educating the target market. But the ads must speak directly to the consumer, and they must be well placed.

A product image can also be impacted by its packaging. The best product might never be bought if the packaging is undesirable or offensive. The same goes for point-of-sale brochures and other marketing pieces. Although we will look at some examples of these marketing pieces, most of our discussion will be about advertising, since it reaches a broader audience. Although little current advertising is appropriate for the mature audiences, I have decided to focus on a few samples that incorporate what we have previously discussed about the psychological and physiological aspects of aging.

The Message Is Critical

Most advertising is created by young personnel in advertising agencies who lack an understanding of and an interest in the older consumer. Nor are they encouraged to create advertising that speaks to the older markets. Customer Marketing Consultant Dick Lee wrote a report, "Ageism in Advertising," based on research done in 1994 by his firm, High Yield Marketing, in St. Paul.[1] According to Lee, agency personnel are encouraged to create advertising that appeals to their own age group (30–39), despite all the data demonstrating the immense resources held by the more mature consumer. Thumb through any magazine and you will begin to notice that many ads are not only designed with the younger consumer in mind, with countless type styles and sizes and noncontrasting colors, but the message itself does not speak to the more mature individual. Even TV advertising is geared toward a younger audience although, from a demographic standpoint, the more mature audience would be the more likely target since it holds the majority of resources.

Packaging of products, brochures, prospectuses, annual reports, and other client communications needs to reflect the changing needs and capabilities of the aging consumer. I recall a broker-dealer conference several years ago where a wholesaler for an investment product and a young man from his company's advertising department were to make a joint presentation of a new product. It had many features that would appeal to the mature client, and the product sponsor was very reputable and well known. The advertising representative was very proud of the packaging he had designed. It included a shiny white folder with the name of the product across the front in no less than six different colors and in as many shades. I lost count of the number of type styles and sizes—at least ten, and they were all going in a different direction across the folder. Fortunately, the design of the new product better reflected the company's understanding of its prospective customers' needs than did the packaging. Packaging is more important than many product and service developers might expect. I have watched mature clients approach a package, attempt to read it, and then put it down when they perceived that it was not worth the effort.

Consumer Needs and Values Should Inspire Advertising

We spent some time discussing the values of the mature person in a previous chapter and how they differ from those in preceeding life stages. Here is a quick review of important things that should be addressed in advertising to the maturity market:

1. Family, especially multiple generations.
2. Multiple cultures and races.
3. Spirituality.
4. Comfort rather than luxury.
5. Nature.
6. Social connectedness and relationships.
7. The arts.
8. Solitude.

9. Altruism.
10. Peace and contentment.
11. Humor.
12. Timelessness.
13. Dignity.
14. Independence.

I have selected a few samples that exemplify quality print and visual advertising. However, even in these samples the text could sometimes be more readable or the colors more discernible to the aging eye. But the messages in the ads are so appropriate to the reader or viewer and so powerful that I have chosen them since their strong points easily overcome any shortcomings they might have. In previous chapters we discussed the physiology and psychology of aging in great detail. Let's look at a few examples of quality advertising that exemplify an understanding of the mature target market.

UNUM

UNUM's advertisement for its long term care insurance product has been very effective in educating its readers (Figure 6–1). I admit that when I first saw the ad, I was both impressed and concerned that if improperly placed, it could actually repel the older consumer. In speaking with Charlie Hurdman, Director of Corporate Advertising for UNUM, I learned that this ad was created primarily for group benefits personnel. Its purpose is to educate the reader about long term care, and the potential risks for employers and employees if they find themselves having to care for an aging parent. These risks could cost the employer money in terms of reduced employee effectiveness on the job, unscheduled time off, and personal phone calls at company time and expense. UNUM, of course, hopes to sell their product as a group benefit, but they are first educating their consumer, the policy makers in group benefits.

While this ad, created by the Goodby, Silverstein & Partners advertising agency, might have been inappropriate for publications that target the older consumer, it has been very effective in educating corporate decision makers through placement in industry trade publications and a variety of consumer publications. The text refers to UNUM's prominent position as a leader in the disability insurance market. In a subtle way, the ad educates the reader by comparing UNUM's better-known and better-understood disability coverage with the newer long term care product.

FIGURE 6–1

*C*ongratulations.
YOU'VE JUST BECOME
THE PROUD
PARENTS
of a beautiful
78 YEAR OLD
MAN.

When I speak before groups of financial service professionals or groups of adult children, I show this ad and solicit their comments. Overwhelmingly, the adult children love it and see it as almost visionary, while those who work with the aging, such as geriatric care managers,

F I G U R E   6–1 (Continued)

You grow up looking to your parents as your providers and protectors, then one day, sometimes quite suddenly, the shoe's on the other foot. As you yourself grow older, how can you be assured that you won't be forced to depend on your own children for your care and security?

We're Unum, *the disability insurance leader, and we have some thoughts on the subject. For instance, we pioneered the idea of making long term care coverage a natural extension of short and long term disability insurance. To protect a lifetime of savings even after retirement,*

and allow people to remain independent into their later years. And our long term care policies offer a number of innovations that can help people live more comfortably, by doing things like compensating family members or friends to take care of their loved ones at home.

It's simple. Because we're continually looking toward the future, we can help you be prepared when it gets here. For more information about the Unum *family of companies, contact your broker. Here's to a long life.*

UNUM.
We see farther.

Unum Japan
Tokyo, Japan

Commercial Life Insurance Company
Piscataway, NJ (All states except NY)

First Unum Life Insurance Company [New York State Only]
120 White Plains Rd. Tarrytown, NY 10591

voice concern that it could be demeaning to the older person. But according to Hurdman, "UNUM's advertising is designed to communicate to all its audiences in the same human, caring voice. Long term care is something that most people don't think about and advertising can help raise awareness levels. These ads have some shock value, but they deal with the issue in a very dignified manner. The message is as much about the kind of company UNUM is, and its forward-looking approach to meeting customers' needs, as it is about a specific product. By presenting long term care in terms that our target can readily understand and relate to, UNUM is providing a very real value in the marketplace." Since the ad is positioned for the younger benefits personnel, it is very appropriate, and an excellent example of quality advertising of a product for the mature market.

AARP's Scudder Stevens Funds

Comparative advertising, in which a product is compared to a well-known and accepted benchmark or to a competing product, is the purpose of many mutual fund ads. Once the market is aware of what a mutual fund is, advertisers can focus on the fund's performance. One good example of an advertisement that targets the mature market has appeared in AARP's magazine, *Modern Maturity* (Figure 6–2). The ad features AARP's IRA and AARP Growth and Income Fund, managed by Scudder. It states the rates of return for the fund over three different time periods. Although this type of ad is common, I selected this one as an example of quality advertising because of its design. It is uncluttered and uses contrasting colors. The ad appears with purple and black copy on white stock. But most importantly, the type style and size are very readable and the content and design of the text is uncomplicated. And, there is no fine print. This is no surprise, since AARP has developed very strict guidelines advertisers must follow for advertising to be accepted in its magazine.

Shearson Lehman Brothers

Although the TV ad in Figure 6–3 has not aired for a few years, many will remember it. The spot was created before Shearson Lehman Brothers was acquired by Smith Barney in 1993. It remains one of the better examples of visual advertising that depicts altruism in the mature client, demonstrating in a very tasteful way how older people often follow a calling. Often money is no object. The older gentleman in the ad, a Shearson client, is meeting with his stockbroker to tell him about his important decision to retire in order to take advantage of an "offer" to work with "some kids." His voice is soft and his body language conveys a feeling of intimacy with his investment advisor, the Shearson broker with whom he is confiding a special secret. It also conveys his desire to be discreet about his decision, which appears to come straight from

FIGURE 6-2

Three Reasons To Transfer Your IRA To The No-Fee AARP IRA.

**AARP Growth and Income Fund
Historical Total Returns*
Period Ending 9/30/95**

14.55%

Ten year average
annualized total return.

17.12%

Five year average
annualized total return.

20.43%

One year total return.

Call for the most up-to-date
performance.

Your IRA may not be working as hard as it can. That's why you should consider transferring your IRA to the No-Fee AARP IRA and investing those dollars in the AARP Growth and Income Fund. Here are three good reasons why:

1 **High Returns and Lower Risk.** The AARP Growth and Income Fund is a conservatively managed AARP Stock Mutual Fund designed to offer you competitive returns, long-term capital growth and regular income. In addition, the Fund seeks to keep its share values more stable than other growth and income funds. (You should be prepared to invest your IRA for three to five years or more, giving you time to help ride out market and share-price fluctuations.)

2 **The only IRA designed for AARP members.** The No-Fee AARP IRA was created by the AARP Investment Program from Scudder to help meet the needs of AARP members. And you can be confident that AARP is actively involved in overseeing every aspect of the Program's services.

3 **No fees.** Many IRAs charge you fees to open or maintain your account. With the No-Fee AARP IRA, *all your money works directly for you.* What's more, when you transfer your IRA to the No-Fee AARP IRA, we'll even take care of all the paperwork.

AARP Investment Program
from SCUDDER
A family of mutual funds designed for AARP members.

*Past performance is no guarantee of future results. Investment return and principal value fluctuate so that, when redeemed, shares may be worth more or less than their original cost. Contact Scudder Investor Services Inc., distributor for a Prospectus which contains more complete information about expenses, the roles of Scudder, Stevens & Clark, Inc. and AARP, and the fees they may receive. Please read it carefully before you invest or send money. Scudder Investor Services Inc., Two International Place, Boston, MA ©1996.

Call 1-800-322-2282 ext. 8521
for a free Investment Kit or return the attached card.

the heart. The broker's quiet acceptance assures the viewer that he is genuinely interested in his client's needs and objectives. He listens closely, does not react except to take notes, giving gentle reassurance that he understands what the client desires and that he is dedicated to making the client's dream come true.

FIGURE 6-3

Where do you want to be next year?

You know, I don't plan to be a partner in this firm forever.

In fact, I've been doing something on the side that could be very rewarding.

I have an offer to work full-time with some kids.

It pays $11,000 a year.

How can we restructure my portfolio so I can tell them "yes"?

You can get there from here.

Shearson Lehman Brothers.

Who Is Your Audience, the Adult Child or the Older Consumer? A Tough Call

Determining your audience is not so simple as it sounds, especially in the maturity market. Often your audience will not be the actual user of the product. For instance, if you are selling beds in a nursing home, your audience will probably be the medical community that makes referrals, or adult children who usually decide where a parent should settle. But this is not always the case.

Geriatric Services

Geriatric care manager Joyce Robbins has been immensely successful in developing her practice through TV advertising. Joyce not only advertises on television, which is unusual for a care manager, but she often targets the patient himself, another unusual approach, as well as the adult child and the medical provider. Her ad agency, Altgelt and Korge, developed the three 30-second spots in Figure 6–4, which include testimonials from families of deceased clients. As the interviewee is speaking, piano music is playing softly in the background.

The ads air during the week at 8:00 A.M. on shows such as "Good Morning, San Antonio" and "Good Morning, America" to target the adult child, and during the day on "The Price is Right" to target the older adult and his medical providers. Joyce chose these time slots because that is when physicians are making their rounds in the hospitals. Her message reaches both the consumer who is currently in the hospital and will soon need a care manager's assistance in selecting a nursing home, and the referral source, the hospital medical providers. To reach the affluent market and the patient, she airs these ads on Sundays as a sponsor of "Face the Nation" and "The David Brinkley Show." According to Joyce, she invests $3,000 per month (recently increased to $5,000) in TV advertising. These testimonial ads, in addition to another ad she runs, result in 40 to 50 inquiries and 15 to 20 new clients (she calls them customers) per week.

The Westwood

The ad in Figure 6–5 might appear at first to defy everything we know about the mature consumer. An ad that speaks about comfort rather than luxury, and comaraderie rather than 24-hour medical staffing, would more likely appeal to the older consumer. But this ad was designed and well positioned in publications to appeal to the younger, upscale adult child who, unlike the older parent, responds well to messages about safety, luxury, security, food, and being catered to. This ad is a good example of "external cueing," as David Wolfe calls it, where the reader is told what to perceive, leaving little to his imagination. This kind of ad is more likely to appeal to the younger market. And it did. The ad was so successful that it immediately resulted in bookings six months in advance and a waiting list. Because of the extraordinary success of the "Queen Mother" ad, the owners of The Westwood, an assisted-living facility in the Washington, DC, area, commissioned the creation of a "Queen

FIGURE 6-4

Joyce's Script

"Daddy lost 90–95% of his eyesight. He could no longer cook, which was his love, cooking. And he just needed full-time care." (Live-Ins) (Home Nursing) (Physical Therapy) (Home Health Aides) (Transportation). "We liked the one-on-one care. Geriatric Services took a real burden off of our shoulders." (Voice over with Geriatric Services screen: "Geriatric Services 822–9494".)

Chas's Script

"Geriatric Services gave me real peace of mind because I knew someone who was professional was there with them at all times. Twenty-four hours a day they had the best of care." (Live-Ins) (Home Nursing) (Physical Therapy) (Home Health Aides) (Transportation) "I would recommend Geriatric Services to a friend because they are dependable. They are professional and they are always willing to help." (Voice over with Geriatric Services screen: "Geriatric Services 822–9494".)

Lucille's Script

"Geriatric Services, when he had the need of it, they worked as hard as they could to get him the right mattress, or the right doughnut or whatever it was he needed." (Live-Ins) (Home Nursing) (Physical Therapy) (Home Health Aides). "Well the most important thing to me about Geriatric Services was the fact that I trusted them." (Voice over with Geriatric Services screen: "Geriatric Services: Always Willing. Always there.")

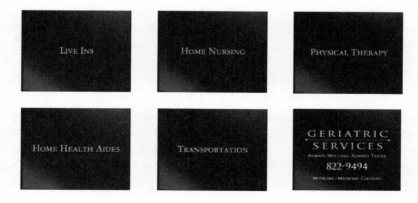

FIGURE 6-5

"While I vacationed in England, Mom was being treated like the Queen Mother in Bethesda."

residence in Montgomery County.

Where else can you entrust her to a 24-hour on-site licensed nursing staff. Cater to her special dietary needs three times a day in an elegant dining room or in the privacy of her suite. Provide her a chauffeured limousine to go places. And give her a jolly good time with plenty of social activities.

After all, Mom deserves a break too. And much more.

Once she tells you about her Westwood stay, you may wonder who had the better vacation.

Plan your next trip with peace of mind. For details about our **Royal Fortnite Package**, write or call us today at 301-657-9111.

*I*ntroducing The Westwood's 'Royal Fortnite Package' ...for Moms (and Dads) who need a little extra care. The next time you're away on vacation or business — for 2 weeks or 2 months — there's no need to worry about your parent's safety and well-being.

For a real royal treatment, check

your mom into a luxury suite with private bath and daily housekeeping for a short stay at The Westwood, the premier Assisted Living

Name_____

Address_____

City_____

State_____ Zip_____

Phone_____

Mail to : The Westwood, River & Ridgefield Roads, Bethesda, Maryland 20816

The Westwood

More Than Assisted Living. Much More.

 No Entrance Fee. Affiliated with Fernwood House and Bethesda Rehabilition and Nursing Centers.

Mother" brochure. According to Kathy Faber, then director of Communications and Quality Assurance at The Westwood, this was by far the most successful one it had ever run, although many of its previous ads were also media award recipients. The ad was created by the Entry USA agency, a mature market agency located in Arlington, Virginia.

John Nuveen

John Nuveen, investment sponsor of tax-free mutual funds and unit investment trusts, by its own admission targets the mature consumer. Nuveen's Human Bond Campaign, created by Hal Riney & Partners, leaves the reader with no doubt that the company understands its mature customer.

The ad in Figure 6–6 is one sample of the print ads from the Human Bond Campaign. Time seems to stand still as the viewer eavesdrops on a mature couple engaged in a quiet, intimate moment. The beauty of this ad is that it allows the viewer to project his own scenario onto the picture, creating a script drawn from his own personal experience. For instance, he can fantasize about whether the couple is a father and daughter, close professional colleagues (perhaps two professors), husband and wife, an older gentleman and a cherished daughter-in-law, or any of several other possibilities. An ad which engages the consumer, allowing him to create his own story and to determine his own needs is more likely to create a favorable impression with the mature person. This ad would appeal to the older consumer who does not need, nor does he wish to be told about anything in a didactic way, especially how to use a product or whether he needs it.

The ad in Figure 6–7 is also from Nuveen's Human Bond Campaign. It features two Asian ladies, a grandmother and granddaughter, sitting on a porch enjoying a special moment together. The photograph could have been taken in the spring or fall, a wonderful parallel to the stage of life of the subjects. The ad demonstrates the bond which often exists between the older and younger generations, where age has no meaning. The photographer has successfully captured the caring and softness in their facial expressions and the closeness which they share. This connection, which the older person feels, mirrors the connection she feels with life, humanity, and nature, colored with pride in the younger person's accomplishments. Just ask any older person and she will willingly share pictures and stories about his grandchildren and other younger people in her life at the slightest suggestion. In fact, my clients often send me pictures of their grandchildren, which I am pleased to display in my office. This ad demonstrates the financial advisor's awareness of the mature person's devotion to family, and an appreciation of her value system.

If you have ever worked with mature, older ladies, you know that they often possess a certain serenity, joy, kindness, compassion, and wonder about life. The ad in Figure 6–8 captures those qualities so well. Warmth, affection, and companionship often develop between siblings, despite their past when they might not have been so compatible. The viewer is left to speculate about what they are looking upon. Are they expecting a visitor? Are they watching children at play? Grandchildren perhaps? The viewer is given the space to tell the story from his point of view, assigning his own meaning to the ad. This ad which targeted the financial service professional not only portrays the beauty and dignity of the older lady. The ads in Figures 6–7 and 6–8 cast the investment advisor in a favorable light as caring and compassionate about his clients, and one who understands what is important to them. Yes, investment performance is important, but just as important to many mature clients, is the relationship which they have with their investment advisor.

The pictures in these ads were taken by Chicago photographer Dennis Manarchy whose artistic eye recognized and captured the timelessness and beauty of his subjects. The ad copy enhances the photographs, allowing the reader to fill in the blanks. These ads are a wonderful example of how advertisers can appeal to the viewer's right brain, the feeling intuitive side, and perhaps more importantly, appealing to the heart first, before trying to sell something. These three ads are a part of a larger campaign which included print and T.V. advertising. Some ads targeted the investor, while other print ads targeted the investment advisor. Manarchy used older photographic techniques to create the soft tones which are so appropriate for evoking a feeling of nostalgia, peace, and the mellow gentleness which often characterizes those in the later years.

According to Peggy Gudenas, Advertising Director at John Nuveen, these ads are no longer in use. It is my contention that they would be well-received if they were to be reintroduced. Other investment sponsors are now attempting to create advertising which appeals to the mature consumer, some with mediocre results. This is usually the case when the product's advertising decision makers or the ad agency personnel do not understand the mature market. Perhaps the ads were slightly ahead of their time. I vote that Nuveen reintroduce this campaign.

Kemper Funds

Kemper Funds has developed the "Nest Egg" campaign, which segments and addresses several retirement markets including:

1. Those At or Near Retirement.
2. Retirees.

FIGURE 6-6

He

can go hours at

a time

without saying a

word. And yet,

she still

knows exactly what

he's thinking.

It's something you

have to experience to

truly understand.

If you have,

no explanation is

necessary.

If you haven't,

no explanation is

possible.

The human bond

Reprinted with permission of John Nuveen & Co. Incorporated

For more complete information on Nuveen Tax-Free Mutual Funds and Unit Trusts, including charges and expenses, send for a prospectus. Read it carefully before you invest or send money.

For the best advice on Nuveen investments, call your investment advisor. Or 1-800-379-6413. Income may be subject to state and local taxes. Capital gains, if any, will be subject to capital gains taxes. ©John Nuveen & Co. Incorporated 1993.

FIGURE 6–7

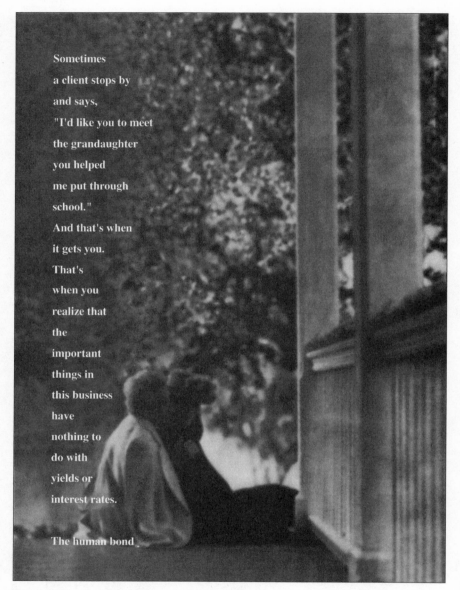

Sometimes
a client stops by
and says,
"I'd like you to meet
the grandaughter
you helped
me put through
school."
And that's when
it gets you.
That's
when you
realize that
the
important
things in
this business
have
nothing to
do with
yields or
interest rates.

The human bond

Reprinted with permission of John Nuveen & Co. Incorporated

Taken from our ongoing conversations with members of the Nuveen Advisory Council across the country.

It's through the efforts of investment advisers like you, that our tax-free investments have been able to play a role in people's dreams for nearly one hundred years. And you're the reason we still believe our strongest bond is human.

NUVEEN

To learn how investment advisers have used Nuveen tax-free investments to build their client's trust, call 1-800-626-2216.

FIGURE 6–8

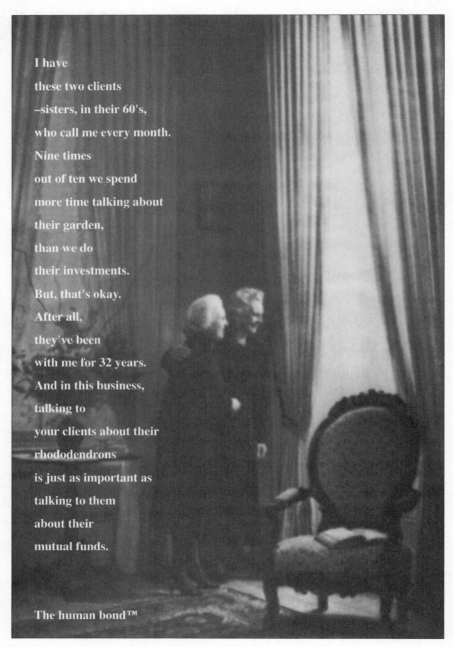

I have
these two clients
–sisters, in their 60's,
who call me every month.
Nine times
out of ten we spend
more time talking about
their garden,
than we do
their investments.
But, that's okay.
After all,
they've been
with me for 32 years.
And in this business,
talking to
your clients about their
rhododendrons
is just as important as
talking to them
about their
mutual funds.

The human bond™

Reprinted with permission of John Nuveen & Co. Incorporated

Taken from our ongoing conversations with members of the Nuveen Advisory Council across the country.

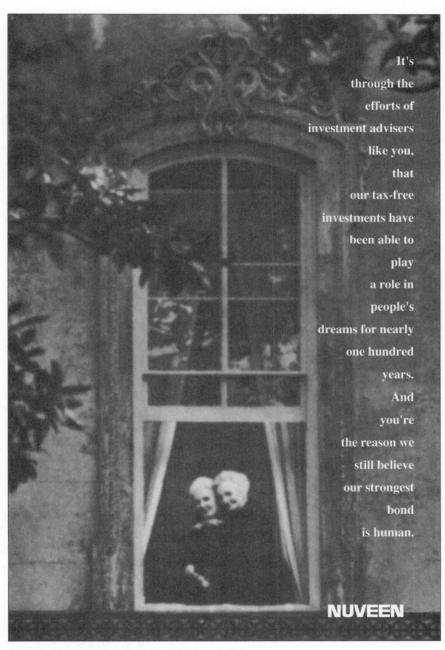

It's
through the
efforts of
investment advisers
like you,
that
our tax-free
investments have
been able to
play
a role in
people's
dreams for nearly
one hundred
years.
And
you're
the reason we
still believe
our strongest
bond
is human.

NUVEEN

Reprinted with permission of John Nuveen & Co. Incorporated

To learn how investment advisers have used Nuveen tax-free investments to build their client's trust, call 1-800-626-2216.

The campaign includes print advertising, as well as separate brochures, retirement kits, and seminar material (including seminar invitations, ad slicks, slides, and scripts) for each of those markets.

According to Lisa Huot, Vice President of Zurich-Kemper Investments, Inc., parent company of Kemper Funds, the Pre-Retiree campaign addresses those who are nearing retirement while the Retiree campaign addresses the needs of those who wish to preserve and grow their retirement nest egg. Kemper very cleverly sought advice from The National Council on the Aging, a nonprofit, which offered its assistance regarding the appropriateness of the text, artwork, and message. The text is very readable, and the symbol, an egg, has connotations for the older market as well as for those planning for retirement. In this example the reader is given some latitude to create the message for himself based on his own value system, level of sophistication, gender, educational background, and culture.

The ad in Figure 6–9, from Kemper's Nest Egg campaign, targets Retirees. The point-of-sale brochure in Figure 6–10 is from the At or Near Retirement campaign. The point-of-sale brochure in Figure 6–11 is from the Retiree campaign. Each piece appropriately addresses issues of interest to those who are either planning for retirement or are currently retired. The mature market experiences many phases, or life stages, simultaneously while planning for and living through the retirement years. It is refreshing to observe a product developer that recognizes that all "retirees" or members of the "mature market" are not alike, and that they will face a multitude of issues as they pass through the various phases of life in their later years.

All of Kemper's marketing pieces demonstrate an exceptional understanding of the retiree's and pre-retiree's needs and concerns. What is especially impressive is that the text of these pieces address not only investment issues but long term care and other noninvestment issues. They imply that the investment advisor recommending Kemper Funds has broad knowledge about the issues of retiring and retired people. This message appeals to the maturing individual who wants to feel that his investment professional is there to provide both quality investment advice and sound information in related, noninvestment areas. (Kemper plans to roll out another module targeting the late-stage baby boomer in the spring of 1997.)

Texas Tomorrow Fund
The ad in Figure 6–12 was created for TV by a group of five advertising firms, headed up by Bonner, Inc., to promote the new prepaid col-

FIGURE   6-9

We understand the importance of your nest egg. You worked hard for it. You nurtured it. But sitting on it won't make it last. Your financial advisor can help you make the right decisions. At Kemper, our philosophy is that diligence and a disciplined plan will help you meet your retirement goals. For 40 years our Family of Funds have focused on a long-term investment approach that helps build and preserve tomorrows today.

Talk to your financial advisor. And, for ideas about making smart retirement investing choices, get our "Investing Your Nest Egg" brochure. It's free. Just call 1-800-KFS-5555, extension 400.

Kemper mutual funds

We're Building Tomorrows Today™

Before you invest or send money, carefully read the Kemper Fund brochure and prospectus containing more complete information, including management fees and expenses. ©1995 Kemper Financial Services, Inc.   233940

RET-74

lege education fund sponsored by the state of Texas. The spot was created primarily for the 21- to 45-year-old age group, although it appeals to the mature market as well. The appeal of this ad is its humorous

FIGURE 6-10

Reprinted with permission of Zurich-Kemper Investments, Inc.

approach to a subject that often causes parents and grandparents sleepless nights. And, its intergenerational approach appeals to the older market. The ad has been extremely effective and its success easy to monitor, since viewers must call the Texas comptroller's office for further information. Calls are carefully monitored, providing support for the claim of the immense effectiveness of the ad. According to the lead advertising agency's spokesperson, Kathy Bonner, the comptroller's office received 37,000 telephone calls, 3,325 from grandparents, between January 1 and February 13, 1996.

Tributes to Aging

The ad in Figure 6–13 is one of several created by Phoenix Systems, Inc., in Sioux Falls, South Dakota. The agency licenses advertisers to use the

FIGURE 6-11

Reprinted with permission of Zurich-Kemper Investments, Inc.

ads in their respective markets, inserting the name of their company, hospital, or firm. Each ad in the series includes the picture of a famous American who initiated a great accomplishment in his later years. The ads demonstrate that the older person is to be admired for his imagination, wisdom, compassion, patience, and other virtues. This type of ad is effective for enhancing the advertiser's image and maintaining visibility in the marketplace. Compared to the type of ad meant to educate the reader, this ad is simple and merely lets the reader know that the advertiser appreciates and understands the older consumer. For some readers, the ad might evoke memories. It offers others the space to project themselves into the story, much like we project ourselves onto our heroes, giving us, if only for a moment, the thrill of being a hero in our own right.

AARP

I include the ad in Figure 6–14, even though it does not address financial services directly, because it is a good example of quality

FIGURE 6–12

It's never too soon to start thinking

about your child's education.

That's why we've created the Texas Tomorrow Fund.

For only a little every month the state of Texas will help you

lock in the cost of tomorrow's tuition at today's prices because if tuition keeps rising,

four years at a public college could cost an additional $24,000.

Call now for a free brochure.

Tomorrow's tuition at today's prices.

advertising that typically appears in AARP's *Modern Maturity* magazine. It portrays the mature person in a very positive way as vibrant, active, and involved with life, more in keeping with the reader's self-image. The purpose of this ad is to stimulate interest in membership in AARP. Since the baby boomers began to cross the threshold of midlife on January 1, 1996, and since age 50 is the eligible age for membership, AARP is now aggressively pursuing this enormous potential new market. To attract this "younger" mid-lifer, AARP is doing all it can to demonstrate the image of older Americans as active and healthy.

FIGURE 6 –13

Age.
It sets the imagination free.

They said it could not be done. To move millions of tons of stone, even with adequate manpower and finances would take a lifetime.

Gutzon Borglum did not have a lifetime. But he did have what he said was the most precious thing on earth . . . imagination.

And with it he began his colossal tribute to democracy at the age of 62.

Age. It sets the imagination free.

Gutzon Borglum
Sculptor, Mt. Rushmore

FIGURE 6–14

For many people, age 50 is the ideal time to embark on new adventures. Or even a new business venture.

And if you've ever thought about putting your life's experience to work in new and different ways, AARP is ready to help.

We offer free publications that can help you manage — or even change — your career. Job-hunting seminars through our AARP Works program. Even mutual funds to help you invest for the future. You don't have to be retired to join. And it only costs $8 to join.

To take advantage of these and many other benefits, call today and join AARP.

After all, there's no time like the present.

1-800-227-7167

AGE 50 IS NOT
A TURNING POINT.
IT'S A STARTING POINT.

PARTNERS FOR THE NEXT
PART OF YOUR LIFE.

CHAPTER 6 ENDNOTES

1. Richard Lee, "Ageism in Advertising," *High Yield Marketing* (St. Paul, Minnesota, 1994).

CHAPTER 6 REFERENCES

Altgelt, Ernie, Altgelt and Korge, interview by author, San Antonio, Texas, February 19, 1996.

Ambrosius, Richard, president, Phoenix Systems, Inc., interview by author, Sioux Falls, South Dakota, February 13, 1996.

Asro, Sharon, principal, Market Entry USA, interview by author, Arlington, Virginia, January 5, 1996.

Bonner, Kathy, president, Bonner, Inc., interview by author, Austin, Texas, February 13, 1996.

Collins, Wendell, director public relations, Merrill Lynch, interview by author, Princeton, New Jersey, February 13, 1996.

Faber, Kathleen, (former) director of communications and quality assurance, The Westwood, interview by author, Bethesda, Maryland, January 5, 1996.

Gudenas, Peggy, director of advertising, John Nuveen Mutual Funds, interview by author, Chicago, Illinois, January 11, 1996.

Gurney, Steve, publisher, "Guide to Retirement Living, " interview by author, Arlington, Virginia, January 3, 1996.

Halper, Melinda, director, Membership, AARP, interview by author, Washington, DC, February 14, 1996.

Huot, Lisa, vice president, Zurich-Kemper Investments, Inc., interview by author, Chicago, Illinois, April 9, 1996.

Hurdman, Charlie, director, corporate advertising, UNUM, interview by author, Portland, Maine, March 5, 1996.

Igler, Karen, assistant vice president, Scudder Stevens & Clark, New York, February 28, 1996.

Janeike, Kris, senior regional vice president of Financial Advisers Division, Kemper Distributors, Inc., interview by author, Cleveland, Ohio, February 27, 1996.

Morgan, Diane, first vice president, National Advertising, Smith Barney, Inc., interview by author, New York, New York, March 13, 1996.

Nielson, John, principal, The Sandcastle Group, interview by author, Minneapolis, Minnesota, February 20, 1996.

Robbins, Joyce, president, Geriatric Services, interview by author, San Antonio, Texas, Janury 11, 1996.

Silvers, Cary, Advertising Research, AARP, interview by author, New York, New York, January 11, 1996.

Wolfe, David B., principal, Wolfe Resources Group, interview by author, Reston, Virginia, January 13, 1996.

7

CHAPTER

Successful Product and Service Design

SUZANNE: THE YOUTHFUL SAGE

Suzanne, a very attractive and articulate woman, is one of my youngest clients. Although in her early 50s, she exhibits most of the qualities usually found in those much older chronologically. She has an insatiable curiosity for nearly everything. She came to me at the recommendation of her CPA a few years ago, who felt it was in her best interest to learn about investments and retirement planning. Suzanne could dispel anyone's misinformed opinion that women cannot learn about investments and proper financial self-care. Her opening statement the first time we spoke on the telephone was, "I can't afford to be afraid anymore." She had previously invested the proceeds from the sale of her home in certificates of deposit and was coming to understand that unless she invested some money in growth-type investments, she would not have a secure retirement. My work with her has been mostly educational, and the pleasure has been all mine. She loves to learn about new things. Last fall she enrolled in college courses and is now pursuing a degree in business management. This is in addition to working full-time and fulfilling family commitments.

Suzanne is very close to her family, 4 sisters, a brother, and her mother. Two of her immediate family have cancer. Her sister, Michele, has the least promising prognosis. Suzanne and Michele are particularly close, so

---

Suzanne: The Youthful Sage (continued)

Suzanne travels to the West Coast to visit with her every chance she gets. I recall a conversation we had after she returned from one of their visits. "Why is it always the best ones who leave us so young. Michele is such a good person," she told me. I responded, "Maybe we could think of Michele as an angel in a body, that she will never really leave us, but will be with us always even though we won't be able to see her." When Suzanne started to cry even harder than she had been, I wondered if maybe I had said the wrong thing. She quickly assured me that hearing that made her feel better. In a subsequent conversation she shared, "when the family feels down, they reassure themselves that Michele is, after all, an angel in a body."

I asked Suzanne recently how she feels about death. This is what she told me. "It's not the end. We're on earth for a short period of time. I know that when my time comes we will all be together again because it's in the Plan. For now, it's my faith that keeps me going. Michele has given me a great gift in her strength and courage. She never complains, although she does tell me about her pain. She has taught me how to deal with it. Sister Maureen, my best friend, tells me just to listen, and to acknowledge Michele's pain, and to let her cry. It is hard for me, but I have to be strong and let her cry because she can't cry with many people. I do whatever I can to make her more comfortable. But I always let her cry."

Suzanne is a good example of many of the characteristics of the mature individual such as detached compassion, caring, and a thirst for knowledge and information. She demonstrates that the mature market cannot necessarily be defined by chronological age.

This is an exciting time to be working with people and their money. As our clients live longer and healthier lives, product and service designers will need to continue to develop new and innovative ways to address their needs and desires. If you select products or services for your clients, you will need to keep in mind their needs and values before making recommendations. If your products and services are not designed for the changing needs and values of the mature consumer, you will have a challenge both in engaging and in keeping them as clients.

DESIGN CONSIDERATIONS

The important thing to remember when designing or selecting products and services for the mature consumer is that they covet their dignity and independence above all else. Everything else seems to revolve around this reality. Here are the major features the mature consumer desires in financial products and services:

1. Flexibility in design.
2. Choices in pricing.
3. Value.
4. Convenience.
5. Performance.
6. Enhancement of vitality image.

All products and services will not appeal to all clients because of differences in socioeconomic status, educational level, gender, ethnic background, physiological capabilities, level of psychological development, and the client's value system, just to name a few. However, the items mentioned above are critical aspects to consider in the design of products and services for maximum appeal to the mature market. As we go along, I will mention several products and services that I think reflect the needs and desires of the mature consumer. However, this does not necessarily mean that the products' package design or advertising also reflects an understanding of the mature consumer. In addition, I offer these products and services by way of example. I do not mean to imply anything else about them, such as the financial strength of the company (unless specifically indicated) or feasibility of the design. Nor should my comments about these products and services be taken as an endorsement of those cited or as a nonendorsement of those not mentioned. Also, I realize that some of the insurance products we will discuss are not available in all states, and that perhaps newer, even better examples of mature market–friendly products and services have recently entered the marketplace.

Flexibility

Fluctuating Needs

Some products and services allow the client to tailor the product or service to suit his own needs, even after he has purchased it. For instance, needs often fluctuate in the long term care area. The client's ability to use benefits based on his needs at the time of a claim appeals to his need to express his independence and his need to make decisions about self-care. In addition, whether or not the client is likely to need these benefits is unimportant. What *is* important is ***his perception*** that he might require different levels of care, or that he might require care more than once in his lifetime.

Product Examples

- **John Hancock's** long term care products are a good example of flexible design. The Alternate Plan of Care option allows the policy insured to dip into his unused nursing home benefits to pay for in-home care once the in-home care benefits are exhausted, if he prefers to remain at home rather than to move into a nursing home. Hancock's Flex Care option (single pool) allows him to use his benefits either in a nursing home or at home depending upon his need. This gives him the flexibility to receive the needed care. With Flex Care all benefits can be used to pay for whatever type of care is needed. Hancock also offers the Shared Care option which allows spouses to use each others long term care benefits if they exhaust their own.

- **CNA's** Preferred Advantage 100 long term care product includes three ways for the insured to trigger Home and Community-based benefits: (1) Inability to perform two or more activities of daily living; or (2) Cognitive impairment; or (3) "Medical Necessity." These three benefit triggers provide an opportunity for broad coverage.

- **Fortis's** long term care product provides for a restoration of benefits after a nursing home stay, or in-home care, where the original benefits are restored after the insured has been off claim for a stated period of time. Should he need care again, benefits would be available to him, provided all claim requirements are met. Fortis's Long Term Security policies allow the elimination period for in-home care and nursing home care to count toward each other.

Multiple Objectives

Flexibility can also allow the client to address multiple needs with one product. This idea of one product serving many needs will become very important to the baby boomer as he searches for ways to stretch his dollar. The following securities and insurance products allow the client to address multiple needs with one product.

Insurance and Securities   Some products offer the investor an opportunity to invest for growth while protecting from the downside risks associated with participation in the stock market. These product designers recognize that while investors desire to participate in growth aspects of the market, they also feel a need to protect from the risks of loss of capital.

Product Examples

- **Keyport's Key Index Fixed Annuity. (Insurance)**
- **IDS Stock Market Certificate. (Security)**

Insurance

Product Examples

■ **UNUM Insurance Company of America's Lifelong Disability Protection** product is an outstanding example of a product with multiple objectives. During his working years, the insured is protected from the risks associated with disability. This protection extends beyond his usual retirement age of 65, up to age 70 if he is working at least 30 hours per week. He does not need to be working a full 40 hours to be eligible for disability protection.

When he does retire, he can transform his disability coverage to Unum's Long Term Care contract with a 20 percent discount off of the current long term care rates. The product designer is demonstrating here the company's awareness that people are not necessarily retiring at age 65, and that many are reducing their work hours gradually rather than retiring all at once. In addition, when people do retire, their disability needs do not necessarily end: They still need to protect their assets. The product is available to both individuals and to employer groups and is popular in both the group and individual markets.

Despite all the quality information available about the need for long term care insurance, many people will still resist purchasing it. While they might acknowledge that some day they could need coverage, they cannot justify spending money on a policy they might never need. Consequently, many are attracted to long term care insurance products that include investment features or return of premium benefits.

■ **Golden Rule's Asset Care Insurance** offers a long term care product that works like a single premium fixed annuity with a death benefit. In reality, the product is a single premium life insurance contract with an accelerated benefit for long term care. According to James Eddington, Advanced Sales Specialist, there will be changes in benefit triggers in late 1996 in response to the new NAIC regulations.

■ **John Alden's Independent Life Plan** is a long term care product that includes a return of premium feature. This feature attracts the attention of the older consumer who wishes to protect against the financial risk of long term care and is willing to "invest" more in premiums to assure a return of any premium dollar not paid out in benefits.

Flexibility in Management Style

Some variable annuities offer the investor the opportunity to invest his money in one product where he can chose from among several different portfolio managers within one annuity, allowing him to take advantage of several different investment management styles within one investment vehicle. This opportunity for investment choices appeals to the mature consumer.

Product Examples
- **Nationwide's The Best of America.**
- **Pacific Mutual's Pacific One.**
- **American Skandia's Advisors Portfolio.**

Choices in Pricing

Services

Clients respond favorably to choices in pricing as long as the choices are not so numerous or complex as to be confusing. If you are compensated by a fee, it is wise to offer the client a choice about how to pay for your services. Some would prefer to pay an hourly fee, while others prefer a fixed fee or a percentage of net worth or account value. I have observed that most mature clients would rather have a fixed fee for work to be done rather than an hourly rate. They respond well to a fixed fee for a "package" of services such as estate plans, care assessments, and financial plans. But perhaps even those who do not sell products might need to develop a variety of services and pricing schedules to respond to the various desires of the mature market.

Securities

In the product area, many pricing choices are available, especially in mutual funds. But now the client can choose to pay front-end, back-end, or annual commissions or fees. The various payment options range literally from "A" to "Z" shares.

The latest product development with an array of pricing strategies in securities is occurring in the private management of low-load or no-load mutual fund portfolios, and wrap accounts that provide management or advisory services for portfolios of individual securities or mutual funds. Firms that were formerly commission-driven now offer private management or advisory services for individual securities, or load, no-load, or low-load mutual fund portfolios that give the client choices about the services and prices. What is particularly exciting is that the money managers will accept moderate-sized portfolios for a reasonable management fee. Here are a few examples of companies offering innovative pricing of securities transactions and ongoing money management or advisory services for a fee:

Product Examples
- **American Express Financial Advisors** (including IDS Wealth Management Services and American Express Strategic Portfolio Service).

- **Brinker Capital's Destinations,** a third-party provider that manages portfolios of no-load mutual funds.

- **Most stock brokerage firms**.

Admittedly, these developments in ongoing money management are due in part to the salesman's need to receive annual compensation for ongoing services. The industry had at first responded to this dilemma by charging what is known as trails, or 12b-1 fees, in addition to upfront commissions, but there was little or no perceived value by the client, and the compensation to the reps for ongoing service was often inadequate. (This is especially true if clients are no longer making substantial deposits to their account.) However, clients seem to be willing to have their accounts debited automatically to pay the larger ongoing management fee, as long as they are receiving active discretionary money management with quality periodic performance reporting and account monitoring by the investment adviser.

Insurance

Even the insurance industry is creating innovative pricing choices. For instance, while most insurance companies have offered graduated premiums and discounted premiums for lump sum and accelerated premium payments for quite some time, no-load and low-load life insurance and variable annuities are now more readily available. Fee For Service, the only low-load distributor of multiple products, was purchased last year by GE Capital, which plans to become the major distributor of low-load insurance to fee-only advisors. The high-income mature client will probably be attracted to paying a fee rather than a commission for an insurance product, especially since the fee might be tax deductible while the commission is not. Also, no-load annuities are gaining in popularity.

A few companies, including Pacific Mutual have now joined Vanguard, Janus, USAA, T. Rowe Price, American Skandia, and a few others in offering a no-load annuity. American Skandia, which has long experimented with creative pricing features, now offers a variable annuity that gives investors a 3 percent credit on all new money when it is invested in the product.

Companies Offering No-Load or Low-Load Insurance Products

- **Ameritas**
- **Fee For Service**
- **Vanguard**
- **Janus**
- **American Skandia**
- **Pacific Mutual**
- **T. Rowe Price**
- **USAA**

Value

Discerning mature clients will seek out what they perceive to be the best service or product for the most reasonable price. This does not necessarily mean that they seek out the **lowest** price. This prudent shopper is looking for the best ratio of value versus cost. If he has done any research, he will favor products that have received the higher ratings for financial solvency and claims paying ability (insurance) or higher performance ratings (mutual funds and variable annuities) from the various rating services such as Standard and Poor, Moody's, Duff and Phelps or Weiss, and A.M. Best (insurance); or *Morningstar Reports*, Lipper Analytical Service, and *Value Line Mutual Fund Survey* (mutual funds and variable annuities).

Securities

Many mature clients do their homework and are attracted to products and services that offer real value. They do a great deal of comparison shopping before purchasing, whether the product is a certificate of deposit, a mutual fund, a long term care policy, or the services of an attorney. Many search out the mutual funds with the lowest annual expenses, no sales charges, the most consistent performance, and no-frills marketing. These clients are often drawn to mutual funds such as the Vanguard Funds. They are especially attracted to Vanguard if owning a portfolio of bonds appeals to them, which is usually the case. The conservative management style of the Vanguard Funds and of American Funds, if the load is not a deterrent, appeals to mature clients who are not impressed with flamboyant advertising campaigns but want a history of solid, consistent performance with low expenses. Sales hype and grandiose statements about product performance will often turn off the mature client. He is interested in the consistency of performance and quality service.

Product Examples
- **Vanguard Funds**
- **American Funds**

Insurance

The economic realities of longevity have led many long term care insurance carriers to eliminate the indemnity contract, which means that the vast majority of policies currently being written offer to pay a benefit up to a stated amount, such as "**up to** $3,000 per month" or "**up to** $100 per day." Once the client understands the indemnity concept where a stated benefit is paid if policy requirements are met, he recognizes its potential value and is often willing to pay more for this type of contract. At this writing, the UNUM individual policy continues to be an indemnity contract. AMEX also currently offers an indemnity contract in many states.

Product Examples
- **UNUM**
- **AMEX**

False Economy   The mature person simply will not buy some financial products and services, even if they are worth the price, simply because he is not willing to spend the money. He will avoid such a purchase even knowing that he will likely someday need it. Long term care insurance is one good example. Often the mature person's socioeconomic status will have no bearing on his spending posture. He will shop wisely for what he perceives he needs, carefully weighing value and cost. But when it comes to items he *perceives* he can do without, often out of denial, he will avoid the purchase altogether. Then there will be other times when he will invest or spend money on discretionary items with little regard for "value." This phenomenon does not occur often in financial services.

Convenience

The mature client will pursue products and services that are convenient to access and easy to use, avoiding those which are inconvenient or uncomfortable. These include client engagement contracts with small print, ill-conceived product packaging with illegible verbal messages and shiny covers, unintelligible billing practices or invoices, complicated products and services and strategies, and other indications of disregard of the psychological and physiological aspects of the maturing client.

I have found that clients are willing to pay for a product or service if they perceive value. This includes paying a commission for a product, even when they could have had a no-load, if the salesperson adds value and if doing business with the salesperson is convenient. One good example is the client who places high value on the salesperson who willingly takes the time to explain financial issues to his satisfaction, enhancing his comfort level.

Many mature clients get fully immersed in on-line financial services and other computer functions, especially if use of the computer results in convenience, and perceived value. If he thinks that using computer services and programs will save him money in advisory or planning fees, or if it will make his record keeping manageable, he will become immersed in financial services technology. Three examples of services that feature convenience with perceived value are:

- On-line computer services for account and transaction information, money management, budgeting, and tax preparation.
- CD-ROM product and educational information.
- Automated telephone information access.

Long Term Care Insurance
Some product sponsors are putting forth a great deal of effort to market their product and to make it easy for the consumer to make a purchase. This is especially important if the product is relatively new, such as long term care insurance. Many people are interested in learning more about it, but information about premiums and benefits is not readily available. Two companies, AMEX and John Hancock, are doing an outstanding job of making their products visible in the marketplace through highly targeted lead-generating mailouts, extensive telephone cold call marketing, and seminars. We discussed the John Hancock agents' telephone cold call marketing efforts in Chapter 3. AMEX, now known as General Electric Capital Assurance Company, also makes it easy for likely prospects to learn more about their product. LTC, Inc., which joint ventures the marketing of the AMEX product with AMEX, sends out 600,000 to 950,000 introductory letters weekly to prospects age 62 to 83. The company has 13.5 million prospects in its database. These prospects are distributed to 870 agents in 49 regions throughout the country. Since advertising of long term care insurance on a corporate level is almost nonexistent, most mature consumers find out about specific product details from cold calls and direct mail, although

they often become aware of the need for long term care insurance and the generalities about the products available through the media. I have observed that once the mature client determines that he is interested in long term care insurance, the agent or broker who calls on him and makes specific information available about the product is likely to make a sale, especially if he can demonstrate that his is a quality product.

Product Examples
- **John Hancock Mutual Life Insurance Company.**
- **AMEX (now General Electric Capital Assurance Company)**

Performance

Mature clients demand performance and good service. Period. They will not tolerate poor service and mediocre performance, especially in their investments and investment advisors. Most are well aware of investment performance, even if they do not understand the strategy behind it. Many investment companies are *perceived* by the mature investing public to have an outstanding performance history based on media image. Here are a few examples:

Product Examples
- **Fidelity Investment's mutual funds including the Fidelity Advisor Funds.**
- **AARP's Scudder Funds.**

Insurance

Many older clients will recognize value in a product by its association with another known and trusted product. One example is long term care insurance from AMEX, which is now known as General Electric Capital Assurance Company (GE Capital Life Assurance Company of New York in New York State). AMEX, formerly owned by the American Express company, may have a decided advantage over many of its competitors simply because of the name recognition of its parent company. However, AMEX, which offers a competitively priced, quality product, is one of a few insurers that markets aggressively to the individual market. The result is over 300,000 in-force policies and over 25 percent penetration rate in the individual market (12/95). Sophisticated clients recognize that because of the large number of in-force policies, AMEX has a demonstrated history of underwriting and claims adjustment, a wider pool over which to spread risk, and the ability to minimize the risk of unstable premium rates. According to a recent study of in-force long term care policies by the Society of Actuaries (1995), the smaller the number of claims for a company, the longer and costlier the claim. The results of this study tend to support the idea that the more policies a company has in force, the more resources it has to contain claims costs and premiums.[1]

Enhancement of Vitality Image

The mature client sees himself as vital and active, even though he might be slowing down or experiencing some challenges in his ability to participate in certain activities. The older client does not view himself as "sick" but rather as an important part of society. He will be attracted to products that emphasize this self-image. A type of long term care insurance that appeals to the mature client, once he understands it and if it is not cost-prohibitive, is the disability model contract, which is quite different from the medical model contract. A disability model reflects the client's view that the need for long term care is more likely a result of the normal aging process, or a dysfunction, and not necessarily a medical condition or sickness. At this writing, UNUM's contract is an example of a policy based on the disability model.

Product Example
- **UNUM**

EXCITING PRODUCT AND SERVICE DEVELOPMENTS FROM THE TRENDSETTERS

The days of having a product or service, then searching the horizon for some "body" to sell it to, are history. The message from the marketplace seems that be that the consumer will dictate how you are to do business with him. He seems to be saying: "Give me the freedom and all the information I request, and I will make my own financial decisions. I'll call you when I need you"; or "Relate to me and give me lots of attention and service, or I'll find someone who will." In addition to the products and services noted above, other products and services are appealing to the mature market. The following are some product and service providers that are particularly exciting, although the list is far from exhaustive.

Banking

I wonder if banks and banking services will at all resemble what they have historically been as we enter the new millennium. They have become social centers for the community and major "distribution" centers for all kinds of financial products. Not only have they added mutual funds, stock brokerage services, and insurance to their product list, but many now include on-line computer services as well. And they all want to capture the same dollars currently held by mature consumers because they have the majority of investible assets and are perceived to be more stable customers.

KeyCorp (formerly Society Bank) in Cleveland, Ohio, has been particularly successful in attracting the older consumer. At first the bank offered free checking and special rates on certificates of deposit to those with deposits above $10,000. This strategy generated significant new deposits. Although their certificates now are frequently 25 basis points below the market, their customers remain loyal, presumably because bank personnel are so active and visible in the community, and because of the relationship they have developed with their clients. For instance, the bank has been a major sponsor of the Kroger-Seniors Expo held every July. This event attracts tens of thousands of people from all over Ohio.

The bank carefully cultivates its image to provide information and to educate and serve its clients. Many of their key investment representitives are Certified Financial Planners. They, along with trust officers, go out into the community and give seminars at senior citizen centers, church groups, and other public gatherings in addition to presenting seminars at the bank, always taking a soft-sell approach. The bank's personnel have observed that what works in one market might not work in another. For example, although the seminars are effective in smaller markets, direct mail seems to be more effective in larger markets. In Columbus, for example, a "Society Club" meets on a regular basis to play cards. This works for that particular bank, since it already has a meeting room that lends itself to this type of activity. In the Indiana market, the bank sponsors successful big band dances.

Regardless of the activity, developing a relationship with bank customers seems to be the key in creating customer loyalty. Getting to know what is important to the people you seek to serve is one of the best ways to create and grow relationships. Society Bank reps are trained to recognize the issues that are important to the customer, even though they have seemingly little or nothing to do with products such as Medicare, Medicaid, long term care, and reverse mortgages. I had the opportunity to meet reps from several banks in the Southwest a few years ago at an investment conference. I was impressed by the reps from Society Bank (now KeyCorp). They spoke respectfully about their older customers, and in a genuinely caring way, unlike other bank reps I met. Their communication skills were more reserved, more low-key. And, unlike the others, they were committed to recommending only the most appropriate products to their clients. Society Bank's reps were not only well trained on how to work effectively with the mature market, they were the least likely to create liabilities by selling unsuitable products and making unrealistic or false claims about them. Fortunately, most banks are now training their reps to better relate to the mature market.

One of the best ways to become an expert in this, or in any other market, is through market segmentation. This strategy can change the bank from a product distribution center to a customer financial service center. Recently KeyCorp has identified several market segments, including the Mature Market Segment. Bank personnel are being trained in the various market segments, based on their capabilities and desire to work with a particular segment, matching the profile of the personnel with the segment.

KeyCorp intends to stay in contact with its clients' needs through its Advisory Group, which is a representative group of bank clients. The Group meets with one or more representatives of the bank to discuss their needs, feedback on current programs, advertising, and other image-building activities and services. It functions much like a focus group. Today's mature client needs to know that his opinion matters to the businesses he patronizes. The Advisory Group program lets the client know that he counts by exploring the development of programs and services, and improvement of systems suggested during the Advisory Group discussions. One of the services KeyCorp plans to implement by 1996 year-end is on-line services. This is in response to requests from the Advisory Group.

Comprehensive Marketing Initiatives

If you are affiliated in some way with a large financial services concern, you might have experienced a disjointed approach in marketing efforts. For instance, it is not uncommon for one department to develop a marketing campaign (usually with an outside agency) of print and visual advertising; another to develop products; another to do the package design; another to conduct research or to hire an outside market research firm; another to develop training materials for the salesforce; another to train the sales managers; and another to track sales results. As I interviewed numerous personnel in large financial service corporations, it seemed counterproductive to me for these companies to spend millions on the various steps to bring a product to the marketplace without a coordinated plan.

According to Michael Rybarski, Senior Vice President and Director of Age Wave Communications Corporation's Target Marketing Division, that company works with corporations that want to target maturing baby boomers and older adults. Age Wave does all the research, develops programs, designs customer communications, measures results, tracks sales, and designs and delivers integrated training. Age Wave identifies key issues, then creates, delivers, executes, and monitors a strategy of target marketing around the various life stages of maturing adults. This coordinated, integrated approach could save a financial service company millions of dollars in wasted efforts, generate more dollars as a result of delivering a product more suited to the target market, and attract that market through effective marketing, advertising, and training of personnel.

Market Segmentation

Such a simple concept—why didn't we think of it sooner? It includes such concepts as "niche marketing" and Dr. Thomas Stanley's concept of becoming an expert in your chosen market. Evidently when I made the decision several years ago to work exclusively with the Mature Market and committed to learn everything I could about their financial issues, I was creating what is called a market segment for myself. This approach to marketing and relating to the client should appeal to the mature person because it promotes relationships between the client and the professional. It appeals to his need to feel connected to others.

American Express Financial Advisors has created market segmentation within the ranks of its 8,000 financial planners. Segments include the Mature Market, Pre-Retiree, Achiever, and Small Business. Marketing brochures, advertising, financial plans, and products and services are designed specifically for each market. But the best feature of this strategy is the special training designed for the planner who specializes in each of these segments.

This strategy has worked for me, and my clients appreciate the fact that I make it my business to know about any issue even remotely connected to their finances. This includes the typical financial planning, health care, and public policy issues. One of the benefits for me is the confidence and satisfaction I derive from knowing just about everything I need to know about clients who are in the segment in which I specialize. Because you really are knowledgeable, you can help them and make a difference in their lives. And it makes it acceptable not to be an expert in all the other areas. I very unabashedly tell my clients that I am not an expert in other areas, although I might have a general knowledge due to my tenure in the profession.

Market segmentation also shifts your focus from "I have a product, now who can I sell it to" to "I have a lot of knowledge and understanding of a particular type of client, how much can I help him?" The focus has now shifted from the product to the client. The only real challenge is anticipating when your clients are moving into another segment so you can prepare for it ahead of time. For instance, surely the small business owner will eventually retire. He will expect you to remain loyal to him throughout his retirement years. But if you find the issues of the retired boring, your alternative might be to share him with or refer him to a colleague who specializes in the mature market segment.

Financial Planning

Financial planning is nothing new. In fact, the concept was created in the early 1970s. The American Express Financial Advisors financial planners might argue, and rightfully so, that their company, originally called IDS (Investors Diversified Services), created the concept back in 1894, although financial planning then was more product driven than it is today. So although the concept is not new, what is new and exciting is the recognition of financial planning, as a product or service in its own right, and that it is an important part of the client–financial advisor relationship by stock brokerage firms and insurance companies. The financial planning giant, American Express Financial Advisors is spending millions of dollars to let the public know that they need to retirement planning, both pre-retirement and post-retirement (my word) planning. It has also invested millions of dollars to develop more timely financial planning software, new insurance and investment products, and to train its salespeople to work effectively with the pre- and post-retirement markets.

Merrill Lynch

Merrill Lynch has long been a leader in spotting trends, and the aging of America is no exception. The 1995 Merrill Lynch Baby Boom Retirement Index was calculated by Dr. B. Douglas Bernheim of Stanford University. Like its two predecessor studies, it demonstrates the enormity of the baby boomers' unpreparedness for retirement. The typical baby boomer does not save nearly enough and will be forced to accept a significantly lower standard of living during retirement, or to delay retirement indefinitely if his or her investment habits remain unchanged. Merrill Lynch is responding by educating its clients, especially the boomers, about changing public policy, the need for financial planning, and how they must begin to save and invest now in order to be able to sustain themselves throughout the later years. Admittedly Merrill Lynch has a tremendous challenge of its own. Many of its clients are members of the mature market whose entitlements are costing Merrill's younger clients a considerable portion of their paychecks. This trend will continue to worsen if public policy does not address the fiscal imbalance in entitlement programs. Merrill is trying to use the important information uncovered by the Bernheim studies to educate its clients as well as policy makers. According to Karen Mair, assistant vice president, Merrill Lynch Strategic Planning, the firm is educating its younger clients one by one, face to face, financial planner to client, reinforced by reading material and brochures created for baby boomer clients about the need to do financial planning.

Prudential Securities

Prudential Securities currently has one of the most aggressive campaigns to encourage people to prepare for retirement, and they have the services to support their clients' needs. These services include on-site financial planning, on-line Internet account access, and basic financial planning. With the new Prudential Securities' Personal Financial Architect software, the firm's Financial Advisors can develop more detailed financial plans for clients. Additionally, Prudential Securities has a new informational pamphlet entitled *Families & Money,* which deals with the "emotional" wealth transfer issues of aging parents and adult children. Consultations are provided in the Prudential Securities office or at the client's home free of charge.

As a part of the bottom-up approach, selected Prudential Securities Financial Advisors are trained to understand the client based on his or her "Life Phase," which has to do with the client's stage such as widowhood, divorcehood, and special issues for women. The Financial Advisors go through a rigorous home-study program to qualify for a live one-day training workshop where such issues as longevity and longer lifespans and implications and the effects of inflation are explored. The Financial Advisors are trained on the unique needs created by Life Phase events. According to Steven M. Samuels, First Vice President, Director of Marketing Communications and Initiatives, "This approach is really working for several financial advisors because it's what the client really wants. Meeting client expectations requires ongoing service." Special brochures and newsletters, and client-interactive seminars are also provided which address these issues in a realistic way as well as client interactive seminars. Prudential Securities, through all of these services, is showing the client how to address any issue that could seriously impact his or her ability to prepare financially for retirement.

Reverse Mortgages

This is one of the most exciting and necessary products on the market. The U.S. Department of Housing and Urban Development (HUD) conceived of the first insured reverse mortgage loan in the late 1980s where the lender is insured against loss by The Federal Housing Administration (FHA), a HUD agency. Although reverse mortgages had been available for several years, they did not gain in popularity until FHA began to insure them.[2] Both FHA-insured and uninsured reverse mortgages are now readily available. Currently, all but two states in the country, Texas and South Dakota, permit such loans. A reverse mortgage is a loan to an owner occupant of a home, who retains title to the property, secured by the equity in the home. The borrower can receive payments in a number of ways. For instance, he can choose to receive a check periodically, usually monthly for a stated period of time, or as long as the homeowner occupies the home; or he could set up a line of credit that makes cash available when he needs it. The periodic payment amount is fixed, and the amount he receives depends on how long he stays in the home. The homeowner makes no payment on the loan. As the payments are made by the lender to him, the equity decreases, and the loan balance increases. Should the loan amount exceed the value of the home, FHA, which guarantees the loan, would step in and pay the lender the difference between the value of the home and the loan balance, up to a stated amount.

One feature of the reverse mortgage that appeals to the older adult is that he can never owe more than the value of the home, and the lender can only look to the value of the home for repayment, not to any other assets. Without this type of loan, many homeowners would need to sell their residence just to unlock the equity to pay their bills. This type of program responds to the need for many older people who either refuse to move out of their homes but who need more income to enable them to remain in the home, who cannot afford to live anywhere else, or who need the additional income for in-home or long-term nursing care, assisted living for home repairs, or for other expenses. It appeals to the older person's need to remain independent and to maintain a connection with his long-established lifestyle. I believe that the reverse mortgage, perhaps with some design variations, will become popular with baby boomers who might need to tap their home equity to support their lifestyle during their retirement years.

Transamerica HomeFirst, Inc., a wholly owned subsidiary of Transamerica Corp., is a private lender that offers proprietary self-insured reverse mortgages that are not insured by FHA. The company began offering its HouseMoney plans, which are now available in 14 states, in June 1993. According to Linda Hubbard, vice president of marketing and public affairs for Transamerica HomeFirst, "The plans are designed for people over 65 with homes valued at $75,000 or more."

Realtors' Mature Market Services

Realtors are often among the first to know when an older person needs to sell or rent his home, which is often his largest single asset. He could be selling or renting for any number of reasons: to move to a smaller home; to invest the equity for income; to go into an assisted living facility or a nursing home; to live with an adult child or a new spouse; or he has passed away and the executor wishes to sell. When an older person is selling or renting, he very often faces issues that require other professional services. Some residential real estate companies have awakened to the notion that many of their clients are older individuals who would benefit from the assistance of other financial services and professionals, but who do not know how to access those services.

Headquartered in Fairfax, Virginia, Long & Foster Realtors, Inc. is one of the nation's largest independently owned residential real estate companies. The company has a special program that trains willing Realtors how to assist their aging home buyers and sellers. The firm has developed a one-day training workshop to create awareness for Realtors about how to facilitate the independence of the older person. The training includes information about reverse mortgages, retirement housing options, and other professionals and services to whom homeowners can be referred. Experts on aging such as elder law attorneys and geriatric care managers, address the group as a part of their training. Upon completion of the training, the participant receives the Retirement Living Specialist Certification and is authorized to use that title on his business cards and in his advertising. While the Realtors do not charge a fee for the services they provide their clients, they are permitted to accept referral fees from other Realtors when referring clients and customers to other housing concerns such as retirement communities. The agents who are actively networking have been very successful in generating referral business. This program is a very creative way to provide a much needed service and to generate business in return for both the Realtors and for related professionals in aging.

Charitable Giving

Altruism is one characteristic mature individuals demonstrate by their willingness to give time and money to their favorite charities. Although the highest dollar amount of contributions per household peaks in the 45- to 54-year-old age group, the highest percentage of household earnings given to charities actually occurs in those age 65 and older.[3] While charitable giving is common among the mature generations, their choice of charitable beneficiaries differs markedly. Older individuals tend to support churches, religious organizations, and mainstream charities that focus on disease research, while the younger donors, particularly the baby boomers, are more likely to contribute to nonprofits that support political and social agendas.

Fidelity Charitable Services

Fidelity Investments has created a way to do well by doing good. To establish an account with the Charitable Gift Fund, a nonprofit public charity, ((501(c) 3)), a donor (individual or corporate) can contribute intangible personal property such as appreciated stocks, bonds, and mutual funds that the Charitable Gift Fund sells, reinvesting the proceeds in a pool of Fidelity funds that Fidelity manages for benefit of the Fund. The charitable assets grow tax-free in the Fund until the donor grants them to his favorite charity, either now or in the future. The donor does not need to select an ultimate charitable beneficiary when making the gift to the Fund. He can make the selection at a future date with the flexibility to change that selection at any time. Or, if he chooses, he can name an individual to take over his Fund account upon his death, including the naming of the charitable beneficiary.

The donor receives an income tax deduction when he makes a contribution to the Charitable Gift Fund. In addition, he is removing the asset from his estate for estate tax purposes. At this time Fidelity Investments offers several gift options. These include an outright gift, which is called the Charitable Gift Fund. There are also two planned gift options that include a pooled income fund and a charitable remainder or charitable lead trust. The pooled income fund and the charitable remainder trust pay the donor an income stream.

This product, although not widely advertised, has been extremely successful. It is an excellent example of a product whose design appeals to the mature consumer for several reasons: it appeals to his altruistic tendency; it is convenient; it offers value, since the donor need not retain an attorney to draw up the legal documents for the Charitable Gift Fund;

and the donor has the option to chose which Fidelity fund pools to invest in. The type of gift, the timing of when the fund is to give the gift to the charitable beneficiary, and where the gift sales proceeds are to be invested offer the donor even more flexibility.

The popularity of this product is demonstrated by the number of requests for more information and the amount of money given to the Charitable Gift Fund. Each advertisement in *The Wall Street Journal* has generated nearly 85 calls resulting in approximately 10 new donors. As of December 31, 1995, $450 million is under management and more than one-half of the donors in 1995 made additional gifts to their accounts. Since the Fund's inception in 1992, it has granted over $175 million on behalf of donors to more than 14,000 charities across the country and abroad. The average age of donors is 65, and 75 percent give appreciated assets.

On-line Services

Accelerated technology is opening up new vistas for products and services, the potential of which we have hardly even begun to imagine. To date 19 banks offer on-line services, with 15 more about to enter the market. Typical on-line banking includes account information, account-to-account transfers, account balancing, on-line bill paying with expense category recording, and 1040 income tax form data entry. You might wonder why I am talking about technology, since older people are not interested in computers and other high-tech equipment. This is just one of several misconceptions about mature individuals. According to one recent survey done by *Modern Maturity* magazine of its readership[4], 85 percent of those surveyed own a computer and 4 percent plan to purchase one in the near future. Of those who have a computer, 75 percent use it every day and 71 percent use it for personal budgets and spreadsheets. SeniorNet, a nonprofit that educates seniors about how to use computers, estimates that 9 percent of households headed by someone between ages 60 and 69 have computers.[5]

According to Kristin Julbert, Director for Compass PC, the new on-line banking service for Compass Bank, thousands of customers have signed up for the service since mid-October 1995, many more than expected. The third highest group to sign up is the 50 to 59 age group (the 30 to 39 and 40 to 49 age groups are the first and second highest). This was a surprise, according to Ms. Julbert, since the bank anticipated that the highest usage would occur in the 20 to 29 age group. Most of them claim to have responded to the on-line service offer as a result of the bank's Internet sites rather than as a result of mailouts. These are future retirees who will be surfing well into their retirement years.

I can testify from personal experience that many of my over-65 clients spend hours a day at their computers. They come to our appointments prepared with balance sheets, monthly expense sheets, and detailed investment tables. They have already printed out *Morningstar Reports* on their mutual funds. They expect me to do my analysis and offer recommendations based on the work they have already done. What appeals to the mature market about on-line services is the convenience and perceived value.

Product Examples
- **Compass Bank**
- **NationsBank**
- **Guardian Life Insurance Company**
- **American Skandia Life Assurance Corporation**
- **Fidelity Investments**
- **The Vanguard Group**

Financial Education

The Vanguard Group

While most financial services companies view on-line services as marketing opportunities, The Vanguard Group is implementing on-line services as an alternative way to educate consumers about financial issues, including retirement planning. Vanguard, in conjunction with the University of Pennsylvania, is currently testing a computer connection, with both visual and audio communication, to assist employees with their retirement planning. Employees are given an assignment, such as data gathering, which they must complete before their financial counseling session. They then "meet" on-line with their investment counselor in a one-on-one counseling session where the necessary calculations are done and displayed on both computers to demonstrate the employee's retirement scenario at his current rate of saving and investment allocation. He is then shown how much and where he must save and invest to meet his goals. He and the counselor can go through several scenarios in a session. The employee's financial future is calculated right there before his very eyes, and best of all, the employee is an active part of the process. All of this is accomplished through personal computers and a highly sophisticated telephone with visual and audio communications capabilities. Employees are given the computer application so they can work on their own retirement plan at home. Vanguard is currently evaluating the results of this pilot in meeting the needs of its 403(b) plan administration clients.

In addition to the above pilot program, Vanguard has an on-line educational program through America Online where the user completes reading assignments, then comes to "class" once a week to discuss personal finances with the "professor," a Vanguard investment professional. Transcripts from the class are made available to the students.

The Vanguard Fund Group also offers account information on-line to its individual and corporate employee shareholders. They can also obtain share prices by 7 PM based on the 4 PM market closing prices. Both shareholders and nonshareholders can E-mail Vanguard for information about the funds. They can expect a reply within two days. The innovative on-line educational initiatives being pioneered by Vanguard are responsive to the needs of the mature person, including value, choice, convenience, and vitality image enhancement.

Distribution

Many changes are taking place in how financial products and services are made available to the consumer. The "middleman," such as the wholesaler or the financial service professional, is being bypassed in many cases. The consumer can work directly with the product sponsor or service provider in obtaining information and in executing purchases and sales. For now, investment centers and on-line services are addressing the need for efficient distribution of products and services. Once sophisticated telecommunications are available for an affordable price to the consumer, and once all compliance issues are worked out, it will be just a matter of time before these services and products are available in the home. Before long the consumer will be able to turn on his TV or computer screen and meet face-to-face with the investment or insurance counselor who can provide him with the information he wants and implement sales, all without the client leaving his home. A few companies poised to develop these kinds of services include:

Product Examples
- **Fidelity Investments**
- **Charles Schwab & Company**
- **The Vanguard Group**

CHAPTER 7 ENDNOTES

1. InterCompany Subcommittee: Gary Corliss, Linda Ball, Mark Newton, Gregory Van Slyke, Long Term Care Experience Committee, Society of Actuaries Intercompany Study 1984–1991 Experience (Avon CT, January 1995), p. 37.

2. Ken Scholen, *Retirement Income on the House* (Marshall, Minnesota: NCHEC Press, 1992), pp. 197–98.

3. INDEPENDENT SECTOR SC, Washington, DC, 1994, as quoted in "The Official Guide to the Generations," Susan Mitchell, New Strategist Publications, Inc., 1995.

4. Al Cole, "Feedback-Computers: Readers Report Love-Hate Relationship," *Modern Maturity* (March/April 1996), pp. 14–16.

5. *Selling to Seniors* (Washington, DC, April 1996), No. 9604, p. 11.

CHAPTER 7 REFERENCES

Arena, Rob, product manager, American Skandia Life Assurance Corp., interview by author, Shelton, Connecticut, February 15, 1996.

Bagley, Martha, specialist to older adults at the Helen Keller National Center for Deaf/Blind Youth, interview by author. Dallas, Texas, February 8, 1996.

Bagley, Martha, "The Americans with Disabilities Act: A Revolution of Opportunity," *Sound & Video Contractor* (January 20, 1993), p. 10.

Beaman, Noreen, senior financial officer, Brinker Capital, interview by author, Radnor, Pennsylvania, April 10, 1996.

Beckwith, Mary, program director, Key Corp. Prime Advantage Program, KeyBank Corp., interview by author, Cleveland, Ohio, January 9, 1996.

Belling, Bronwyn, director, Reverse Mortgages, AARP, interview by author, Washington, DC, February 19, 1996.

Boeder, John, vice president and general manager, Segment Marketing, American Express Financial Advisors, interview by author, Minneapolis, Minnesota, January 18, 1996.

Boho, Cynthia, research and development specialist, Fortis Long Term Care, (underwritten by Time Insurance Company) interview by author, Milwaukee, Wisconsin, April 17, 1996.

Collins, Wendell, director public relations, Merrill Lynch, interview by author, Princeton, New Jersey, February 13, 1996.

Cortelli, John, senior vice president, Deposits Products Management, interview by author, Cleveland, Ohio, April 9, 1996.

Cox, Kathy, director, educational programs for women, Prudential Securities, interview by author, New York, New York, February 15, 1996.

Dahlberg, Larry, national leads manager, LTC, Inc. (for AMEX joint venture partner), interview by author, Seattle, Washington, April 10, 1996.

Eddington, Jim, advanced sales specialist, Golden Rule, interview by author, Indianapolis, Indiana, February 15, 1996.

Galvin, Janet, director, Curriculum Planning and Evaluation, Merrill Lynch, interview by author, New York, New York, January 11, 1996.

Garf, Jennifer, marketing manager, Fidelity Charitable Gift Fund, interview by author, Boston, Massachusetts, February 15, 1996.

Gaunt, Jan, advanced planner group, senior financial advisor, American Express Financial Advisors, interview by author, Dallas, Texas, February 19, 1996.

Glickman, Jim, president, LifeCare Assurance Company (reinsurer for John Alden Long-Term Care policies), interview by author, Miami, Florida, March 4, 1996.

Gularson, Suzanne, director, Retirement Living Program, Long & Foster, Realtors, Inc., interview by author, Fairfax, Virginia, January 11, 1996.

Halloran, Jane, policy planning, Merrill Lynch, interview by author, New York, New York, January 11, 1996.

Haywood, John, principal, Electronic Services Group, The Vanguard Group, interview by author, Valley Forge, Pennsylvania, February 22, 1996.

Hubbard, Linda, vice president, Marketing & Public Affairs, Transamerica Home-First, Inc., interview by author, San Francisco, California, February 13, 1996.

Julbert, Kristin, coordinator for electronic banking, Compass Bank, interview by author, Birmingham, Alabama, February 19, 1996.

Kreiger, Edith, director, Marketing Research, The Vanguard Group, interview by author, Valley Forge, Pennsylvania, February 15, 1996.

Kennedy, Pamela, The Principal Financial Services, interview by author, Des Moines, Iowa, February 11, 1996.

Larson, Dave, vice president, Product Strategy, LTC, Inc. (AMEX joint venture partner client), interview by author, Seattle, Washington, April 9, 1996.

Lloyd-Reese, Susan, director, Product Development Individual Disability, UNUM, interview by author, Portland, Maine, February 23, 1996.

Magee, Nancy, second vice president, Long-Term Care Markets/Product Development, UNUM, interview by author, Portland, Maine, February 23, 1996.

Mair, Karen, assistant vice president, Merrill Lynch Strategic Planning, interview by author, Princeton, New Jersey, February 21, 1996.

Mauer, Judith, director, Public Relations Fee For Service, interview by author, Tampa, Florida, April 8, 1996.

Meahl, Steve, senior vice president, Long Term Care, UNUM, interview by author, Portland, Maine, February 23, 1996.

Murray, Peggy, director of Micro Risk, UNUM, interview by author, Portland, Maine, February 23, 1996.

Nickels, Jean, assistant vice president, manager, Mature Market, KeyBank, interview by author, Cleveland, Ohio, April 11, 1996.

Norton, Mike, director, Public Relations, UNUM, interview by author, Portland, Maine, February 19, 1996.

Pols, Inger, director, Market/Product Development, UNUM, interview by author, Portland, Maine, February 23, 1996.

Rybarski, Michael, senior vice president and director of Age Wave Target Marketing Division, Age Wave Communications Corporation, Inc., interview by author, Emoryville, California, April 18, 1996.

Samuels, Steven, first vice president, director of Marketing Communications and Initiatives, Prudential Securities, interview by author, New York, New York, February 26, 1996.

Thompson, Todd, director, Marketing and Product Management, KeyBank, interview by author, Cleveland, Ohio, January 9, 1996.

Wakefield, Doug, Gold Team Financial Advisor, American Express Financial Advisors, interview by author, Dallas, Texas, January 26, 1996.

Wolferson, Linda, director, Marketing, Brinker Capital, interview by author, Radnor, Pennsylvania, April 9, 1996.

Worth, Richard G., interview by author, Dallas, Texas, April 26, 1996.

8
C H A P T E R

Some Practice Management Tips

M A T U R E   P R O F I L E

MIKE: THE JOYFUL ONE

Mike was one of those people you meet once in a lifetime but never forget because he touched everyone he met. He actually had very little when it came to material things, but if you were to ask him, he would have told you he was a wealthy man. He was not lying. It's just that he measured wealth by how many people he loved and how much he felt loved. And by those standards he truly was wealthy. Family was his greatest treasure, but that family extended well beyond those related by blood. He always looked forward to the holidays when his grandchildren came home from college. Well into his 80s, he would stay up half the night playing cards with his grandchildren and their friends, and he often beat them. The college kids loved him. When it came to having fun, they all knew that age had no boundaries. On Saturdays he would invite friends and family into his wine cellar where he would share a loaf of Italian bread, a hunk of cheese, and a glass of wine. He told the same jokes every Saturday, but they always seemed like new to his guests, who had heard them hundreds of times. The laughter, good company, and abundant food were cause enough for celebration.

Mike: The Joyful One (continued)

Mike was a cultured man. He spoke seven languages and was well versed in opera and works of art. An epicurean and a gourmet cook, he could create a meal fit for royalty out of what ever he could find in his garden. Mike's eggplant Parmesan and homemade pastas were legendary. Of course, his meals were accompanied by his homemade wine. Even if it was not properly aged, everybody drank it and enjoyed. He grew his own vegetables and seemed to have a knack for exactly what was needed to create the biggest tomatoes, the plumpest eggplant, and the sweetest green beans. But his real gift was his roses. He created the healthiest roses of the most vibrant colors. And every spring he would pick the first one to bloom and present it proudly to his wife, Concetta. It was an annual occasion for celebration.

Mike survived Concetta by nearly 30 years. He told his family many times, "There's $500 in my wallet. Don't mourn for me when I'm gone. Just take the money and have a party to celebrate for me because I will be having my own celebration." And that's exactly what they did. There was lots of laughter, tears of joy, and tears of sadness when Mike, loved by so many, passed on to his own celebration. He was a fine example of how people experience joy and peace in the later years.

OFFICE

Office Location

If you are establishing a practice or business that will require that the client or customer come to you, you will need to give a great deal of thought to where to locate your office. It is important to keep in mind the physiological changes we experience as we age, which we discussed in Chapter 2. Even though some of you might never have clients who come to your office to see you, keep in mind that you might have aging employees (anyone over age 40) to whom the entire following discussion might be addressed. Disregarding these basic concepts could result in a costly accident, leaving your employees with lost time on the job, not to mention increased group insurance premiums.

Traffic Patterns

Give some thought as to how the client will actually drive to your office. For instance, avoid locations where he must do a U-turn to enter your parking lot or negotiate extensive construction if coming from a particular direction. Any location where he must navigate busy traffic circles, cross oncoming traffic without a green arrow, or enter a busy highway and immediately cross several lanes of traffic to take your exit would be a poor choice. Most of my clients do not seem to have major challenges with negotiating busy traffic until they reach their mid to late 60s. At that point I begin to notice they have some difficulty. For this reason, I recommend that you not even consider office space that requires that the client drive onto a major highway.

My office overlooks an eight-lane highway with service roads, but it backs up to, and it is accessible from a slower-paced three-lane roadway. My older clients over age 65 will, almost without exception, use the slower-paced road. In fact, when making their first appointment, they invariably ask if they can reach my office without going onto the freeway. They make it clear that traveling the freeway is not an option for them. Most of them will even do a "dry run" as they call it to be certain they can find it the day of our appointment. Even if you meet with people in their homes but plan to hold seminars at your office, the location of your office building could be critical to the success of your events.

Travel Time

The hour of the day when you meet with clients, and whether or not they are still in the workforce, will have some effect on travel time and the best location for your office. Generally, if you are working with the already retired or the soon-to-be retired, your best choice for an office location might be in a suburban area closer to your clients' residences rather than busy downtown commercial areas. Even residential areas near shopping and low-rise office buildings might be ideal. I find that people resist coming to my office if the drive exceeds 20 to 30 minutes from their homes. This will probably vary with the geographical area.

Directions

If the office building you are considering requires tricky maneuvers to get to it, giving directions to someone over the telephone might be even more difficult. If you cannot give simple directions over the telephone, you might wish to consider another location. By the way, I suggest that you always keep a very legible map at the receptionist's desk. The receptionist should be able to give clear, concise directions to any caller regardless of where he is coming from. It would be especially nice if he could clearly describe landmarks near your office, know for instance exactly how many traffic lights you are from a particular roadway or traffic light. In fact, it would be a nice gesture to include typed directions with a letter of confirmation of your first appointment with a new client. A map might be of little use since the prospect might not be able to read it.

Exterior Parking and Access

Underground parking is ideal if it is very well lit. Covered ground parking is acceptable, as is exposed outdoor parking, as long as the client does not need to walk very far to your front door. Lighting both outside and inside your building is important. Your mature clients who are still working might be coming to your office at night, making exterior outdoor lighting crucial if they are to find you and avoid a mishap. The interior of the building as well needs to be well lit. There should be no dark hallways. Signage needs to be large, very visible, well-lit, and made of nonglare material. Shiny brass, glass, or Plexiglas nameplates, office building directories, and office or building numbers are very attractive but not very practical. Keep shrubbery clipped to reveal outdoor signage, which needs to be easily visible from the roadway. Avoid buildings that require the client to climb more than two or three steps to reach the front door or your own office door. Also avoid large office building complexes where the client must walk a long distance through parking garages, change elevators, or cross busy streets to reach your office.

Shared Office Space

If you choose to office with other professionals who are not involved with your practice or business, you will need to observe all of these guidelines, taking everything into consideration we have discussed so far in addition to the atmosphere that pervades the suite or office. If the others in your office space do not work with the mature market, they might not understand or appreciate your need to observe some of these guidelines and you could end up fighting a losing battle to create a mature client–friendly atmosphere. Sharing office space with someone else has many advantages such as the cost savings. But these advantages could pale by comparison with the frustration and lost business.

I once shared office space with an attorney. The building was a charming home built in the 1930s and located on a lovely tree-lined street in a prestigious Washington, DC, suburb. At first glance, it appeared to be perfect, both to me and to my clients. But in hindsight, it was less than ideal, except for the ambiance and nostalgia it evoked. The parking lot was a stone-covered driveway rather than a covered garage. It was noisy and exposed to the elements, and there were no marked parking lanes. Cars were always parked two or three deep. It was not uncommon for the attorney to interrupt my client meetings by sticking his head in my office door unannounced to ask my client to move his car so his client could get out of the parking lot. The exterior signage was large and well lit. The only problem is that my name was not on the sign until I had been there for over a year. Until clients were familiar with my building location, they often had difficulty locating me. This posed a problem, since we were located on a one-way street leading right into a congested business district. Some would get lost in the maze of new construction sites if they inadvertently passed my office.

The interior of the building was attractive, with shiny hardwood floors covered with oriental rugs with fringe borders. It was not uncommon for women to get their heels caught in the fringe or for someone to slide on the loose carpet. My office was very bright, since nearly half the wall space was paned windows, but it was drafty in the winter, and not very private since we were on the first floor adjacent to the parking lot. We could see and hear every passerby and hear every car in the busy, noisy parking lot. The situation was improved, and so were the acoustics, when I put up heavy drapes. Another deterrent to our privacy were the doors to my office, which adjoined the foyer. They were double doors that did not close tightly. They opened slightly every time someone came into the building because of the draft.

One of the worst features of this arrangement was the rest room facilities, which were on the second floor. The client had to climb two flights of stairs separated by a landing where the second set of steps took a sharp right turn. The stairway was beautiful to look at with its heavy wooden banister, but it was hazardous. The bathroom, like most of the original old bathrooms, was charming but not very private. Sound bounced off the ceramic floor and walls. It was surrounded by the attorney's offices, and the door lock was nothing more than a loose latch. It was not uncommon for an occupant to be intruded upon by a knock on the door to see if it was in use, or worse, for someone to attempt to open the door without knocking first. Then there were the times when the old plumbing failed and the toilet would either not flush at all, or would overflow. Fortunately, this never happened while a client was using it. We did have a backup facility for such emergencies, which was nothing more than an old commode set in the center of the cement floor in the damp, old cellar below my office. The point of all this detail? Think at least twice before selecting office space.

Office Design

When designing office space you can do many things to improve the client's comfort level and express your awareness of his values, lifestyle, and issues. Once again, keep in mind the physiological aspects of aging we discussed in Chapter 2.

Lobbies

If you are considering a move to a building with a common lobby area, or if you will be designing the lobby area, here are some practical tips to consider. The flooring needs to be glare-free and nonslip. Now that you know something about the visual and hearing changes we experience as we age, you can observe how impractical most lobby areas are, especially those in large, high-rise buildings. They are filled with large, expansive, shiny wall and floor surfaces with few or no coverings to cushion sound. Echoes are common because of the high ceilings. The directories are nearly impossible for the aging eye to see, as are brass numbers indicating which elevator to take and the numbers inside the elevators. Fortunately, manufacturers now offer both attractive and practical materials and designs for an aging society.

When selecting floor coverings remember to avoid large swirling designs in favor of smaller, simple patterns. Honed-finish marble is acceptable. Another suggestion is a softer floor covering made of quartz granules with a friction anti-slip surface such as a nonslip marblelike vinyl.

In order to cut down on the glare from glass, use gray tints or Mylar film on windows and doors. You can avoid unnecessary accidents by placing corporate logos on glass wall and door surfaces so people don't collide with glass they might not be able to see. Cover directories with antiglare Plexiglas. The directory should include larger black letters on a white background, or vice versa.

Lobby floors can be very slippery, especially when wet. On rainy days, put down nonslip mats in bright, attractive colors, that contrast with the permanent flooring.

Colors

The important thing to remember about your color scheme is to select contrasting colors, which are sharp and distinctive, putting together light and dark colors. Avoid muddy hues in favor of vibrant colors such as red and bold, vivid orange and yellow. Brilliant, bold colors are not only easily seen but they add vitality to the room. Avoid putting blues and greens together, for instance, unless you select blues and greens of varying density with a great deal of contrast. Some of the most unlikely colors for an office might be the best. Geriatric care manager Rona Bartlestone's office is pink, which, she claims, is very popular with her clients. I have found that older clients, both men and women, seem to like pink, especially bright pink.

I once had an office decorated in charcoal gray and mauve with country French furniture. Both men and women found the colors warm and attractive. I recommend that you step out of the box when it comes to color selection. Be unconventional. If you are uncertain about what to choose, bring in a geriatric care manager or other professional who understands the aging eye to help you select colors that might be pleasing and visible to your aging clientele.

Fabric and Carpet Patterns

The selection of fabrics is very important, especially the carpet. Any design should be moderate in size and simple. Avoid involved floral or geometric patterns. They can create the illusion of a floor elevation when there is none, and camouflage an elevation where one does exist. Hotels often have large, busy designs in their carpets, which can result in a fall, twisted ankle, or an embarrassing stumble. If you have steps in your office space, contrasting colored borders around the carpet, on the steps, or on the risers help to alert the client to a change in floor elevation. The step portion of stairs should be rubber, preferably in a bright, contrasting color to the riser, which also needs to be a bold color. Wood floors are lovely and can elicit a welcome feeling of nostalgia, but highly waxed, slippery floors, especially with a glare, are inviting someone to slip or misjudge a step. Oriental rugs, or any rug, over a hardwood floor are especially hazardous even if they are nailed down. A client could get a toe caught on the edge of the rug. Fringed or shag rugs are not recommended since a woman, especially, could get a heel caught in the fringe or loops. At the very least, careless design could result in an embarrassing stumble, an injury, or worse yet an outright liability.

Recently, a geriatric care manager recounted an incident to me that demonstrates the difficulty older people have with some carpet designs. He watched an older lady attempt to walk across a large room that had a white carpet with large black circles. As she walked, she carefully and deliberately walked around the black circles. If she could not avoid them because of furniture and other obstructions, she would either lift her legs much higher than necessary as though she were climbing stairsteps or she would place her foot heavily on the black circle as though she were descending a flight of steps. She appeared to be very frightened or confused by all these imaginary elevation changes. She could easily have stumbled or fallen, resulting in embarrassment, at the very least, and possibly an injury.

Acoustics

Since many of our clients will experience difficulty in hearing as they age, we can improve the quality of client meetings and telephone conversations by making certain that the rooms in the office have wall coverings, floor coverings, and ceilings that absorb sound. The acoustics in the rooms should cushion the sound so that your client can easily hear you, and to assure that your conversation will not be heard from another room, to assure privacy. Exceptionally high ceilings can produce an echo, as can hardwood floors and "flat " or "hard" wall coverings. Better acoustics can result from wall coverings made from heavier fabrics with ample yardage and an acoustical lining. Carpeted floors as opposed to slate, ceramic tile, or other hard tile floors, would also reduce the effect of sound bouncing around the room. There are different acoustical ratings for wall panels. A designer can help you select the best one. During construction of your space, work with an architect or designer to be certain there is ample acoustical batting between the wall board, and one who can help you select the best acoustical ceiling, placed at the right height. The position of the furniture can also improve the client's ability to hear. For instance, seating should be arranged at a 90° angle in the reception area. Avoid seating that faces the same direction. All of these points are very important to remember when designing private offices, but they become more of an issue when designing conference rooms or other larger rooms were you are likely to host events such as seminars.

Despite your efforts to improve the quality of sound in your office space, you might not be able to overcome some challenges. Consider acquiring some personal communication devices you can keep on hand in your office to aid those with hearing impairments. For instance, the battery-powered Williams Sound PockeTalker is a small device, about the size of a cigarette pack. It has an ear bud that fits into the user's ear (much like the earpiece on a small portable radio that joggers use). A microphone picks up the speaker's voice and it is amplified in the user's ear. Another device is the Audioport made by Sennheiser. It is a small amplifier, suspended under the user's chin by two tubes, which are attached to earbuds in the user's ears. These two items retail for about $160 to $180.[1]

If you will be giving seminars in your office space, or if you speak to groups of mature audiences outside of your office, you might consider purchasing a radio frequency listening system manufactured by Comtek or Phonic Ear. The speaker wears a lapel microphone and a transmitter that broadcasts to listeners within 300 feet who are wearing a receiver. If the acoustics in the room are poor, the sound transmitted directly to the listener will be free of any echo.

Lighting

In most cases, bright lighting is essential for the aging eye to be able to see printed material on the page, presentation materials on a board, or even your face. The most effective lighting in addition to overhead lighting is "task" lighting, which focuses directly onto the printed page. If you are hosting a seminar that lends itself to classroom-style seating, make individual lights available for each attendee. Avoid lighting that causes glare in mirrors or shiny walls or flooring. For instance, when designing any room where you are likely to make presentations using a projector screen, white board, or easel, work with a lighting consultant to be certain that the lighting and its placement will not create a glare on you or on your audio-visual aids. Lighting in hallways needs to be especially bright. As a matter of convenience and safety, make certain that lighting in restrooms is especially bright so as not to produce shadows. In conference rooms, consider installing lighting above the table, in the same or similar shape as the table, which can be remotely controlled to move up, down, or around the table. This will give you considerable flexibility to focus lighting as close to the client's writing or viewing surface, with the light positioned as directly above his space as possible. Movable lighting such as I am describing is much more flexible and can be customized for each client's particular lighting needs, compared to ceiling or track lighting mounted at the ceiling. Both are usually too high and too far away from the client's viewing area to be useful, and it often creates shadows.

Floor Plan and Floor Elevations

I spoke of floor elevations earlier, but it is so important that it bears repeating. It would be unwise to select an office with interior steps such as "sunken" reception areas, steps going to lofts, and the like. When designing or selecting your space, privacy, simplicity, and a safe environment should be your priorities. Changing elevations represent hazards to the mature client. If you are currently in a space with elevation variations, install bright-colored handrails and risers to help identify these obstacles.

Furnishings

The important thing to remember when selecting seating furniture for your reception area, private offices, and conference room is that the cushions should be firm and should not sit too low so that the visitor's hips are lower than his knees. Nor should the seat be too deep. The chair back should be tall enough to support the visitor's entire back, if not the neck as well. Armrests are also recommended. A chair that meets this description would create a feeling of safety and comfort. Keep plenty of firm, medium-sized pillows on the couch or in the chairs. They can be used behind the visitor's back for extra support. Lumbar rolls should be readily available for those with back challenges. An ottoman that can be used as a footstool to elevate the knee above the hip to relieve back pressure would be a nice touch, but keep it out of the traffic pattern of the room to avoid having someone trip over it. When not in use, it could be placed under a table. In selecting fabrics, smooth surfaces are recommended because it is easier to slide in and out of a chair with a smooth covering than a rough one. Wingback leather chairs are especially practical for this reason, and they lend an air of safety and security, bringing back memories of older offices of professionals and institutions that inspired trust, such as banks and attorney's offices.

Accessories

Up until now we have focused on office design and furnishings from the standpoint of function, utility, safety, and comfort. When I speak of accessories, I am referring to wall hangings, tabletop artwork, magazines, and other decorative pieces. This is the area where you can really demonstrate an appreciation for your clientele and create an atmosphere that says, "I understand you" or "I appreciate your experience. "Choose a theme first. You might want to tastefully frame *Look* magazine covers from the 1940s or pictures of scenes from well-known movies of that era featuring Fred Astaire, Ginger Rogers, and other celebrities, or pictures of sports heroes. People really do notice these things. If your accessories have meaning for your clientele, they can be great conversation openers. People would tend to reminisce and share important details with you about their lives that you might not otherwise have known. If you have a limited budget, spend time in secondhand or antique stores, flea markets, and garage sales. You could purchase a curio cabinet and fill it with artifacts such as rainbow glass or World War II memorabilia. You would be amazed at the memories clients will share with you when they spot a piece that evokes a memory. Remember to frame your pictures with nonglare glass.

The office of Dennis M. Gurtz and Associates, American Express Financial Advisors, in Washington, DC, is a good example of how effective well-selected art can be. The Gurtz office is very simple, but clients will almost always start a conversation about the pictures on the walls. The partners of the firm very prudently selected old prints of Washington in the early days before the massive development in the mid-20th century. Native Washingtonians love to reminisce about the lovely old buildings and the businesses they housed, as well as the old roadways and automobiles. Newer members of the community enjoy seeing how the city used to look. The nice thing is that all generations seem to take an interest in the pictures. Art such as this can be a conversation opener and a rapport builder.

Items Requiring Dexterity and Hand Grip

Use special care in selecting eating utensils, writing instruments, and other furnishings, keeping in mind that hand grip decreases as we age. Ergonomically designed products, which are suitable for all generations, are best so you don't appear to be appealing only to the older client. Thicker pens, or those that resemble an upside down triangle, and easy-to-grip eating utensils are recommended. Please see Further Reading for practical references to save you time in locating the most practical and brightly colored, visually appealing products currently on the market.

If your rest rooms are a part of your office, remember to decorate and furnish them with special care. Choose fixtures carefully, just like you would any piece of furniture. Select faucets with a handle to grab on to, rather than the round ones that slip in the older hand. The "hot" and "cold" labels on faucets should be in large easy-to-read letters. Sensor faucets are ideal. When the user places his hands under the faucet, they pick up his body temperature through infrared signals. The water comes on automatically matching the user's body temperature, decreasing the likelihood of scalding. Create an atmosphere of privacy by placing the facilities away from conference rooms and other meeting rooms. Wooden water closets, which are becoming very popular in restaurants, are ideal. They are attractive, nostalgic, and create more privacy. Textured wallpaper and acoustical ceilings can add an atmosphere of privacy. A tray of conveniences such as tissues, mouth wash, and hand lotion is a nice touch. Carry through your art accessories and wall coverings as well.

BUSINESS COMMUNICATIONS

Stationery, Business Cards, and Other Business Communications

Design your stationery , business cards, and other business communications with special care from the selection of the paper weight, style, and color to the type style, design, and color. Many financial businesses and practices do have a logo, slogan, or other identifiable artwork, which helps to create an image in your client's mind about what you do or how you do it. For instance, Prudential's logo, the Rock of Gibralter, has been known for over a century. For over five generations, this graphic has helped to position the company as one that is solid, stable, and dependable. John Hancock's logo is a mere signature of one of the most respected statesmen in our country's history, creating an image of stability, vision, and wisdom. You do not have to be a financial giant to position yourself using graphics, slogans, or other artwork.

Although I do not have a slogan for my practice, I do have a logo designed just for my practice and business (Figure 8–1). I worked with a designer who spent some time getting to know what aging meant to me. I gave him a basic idea of the concept that I wished to convey. Aging for me is a time in our lives when we are awakened about our own personal meaning about life. I see aging as a time of birth of the self and of new and creative ideas, and that is what the rising sun in my logo represents. The flower is a lotus blossom, which is the symbol in eastern religions for awakening. I was adamant that light show through the rising sun. Admittedly, creating that effect can give a printer fits, but the artist works with the printer to get the right effect every time we order stationery, business cards, and other marketing pieces. I selected blue for my color, but other colors would be just as appropriate. In my slides for presentations, we use the same blue-and-white logo, adding yellow for the sun. It makes for a striking color combination. We did not use yellow in the stationery for two reasons. The older eye does not see yellow very well, especially on white or off-white paper. And, two-color stationery, business cards and other pieces would be expensive. Yellow is acceptable for the slides since the audiences for those presentations are usually corporate personnel who are generally younger.

FIGURE 8–1

A byline that describes what you do or how you do it can help to better position you in the marketplace. Since I work both with individuals as their financial planner and with financial service professionals as a consultant, it was a bit of a challenge to find one byline to position my expertise with both markets. The artist who designed the logo came up with "Senior's Market Consultant," which we later changed to "Maturity Market Consultant". As long as I am a registered investment adviser or a registered representative with a securities brokerage firm, which must be disclosed on all marketing material, it is clear that my expertise is in financial services.

If you are a member of a large firm, the temptation is to include the names of all the partners or members of the firm down the left side of the page. I discourage this as it only confuses the aging eye. You could list this information elsewhere, such as in a brochure.

Newsletter

How you present information in your printed material is just as important as the message itself. Take the time to select the right title, masthead, layout, colors, and overall design. Carry the colors in your stationery, business cards, and other printed material through to your newsletter. Ask the opinion of a few of your clients before proceeding with the final design. For instance, during the design stages, my newsletter was called "Soit Sage" which is a French idiom for "be wise." I really liked it, especially because visually it was very attractive in the various type styles.

But the feedback was, "Why have a title with a byline explaining what it means. Why not just call it 'Wisdom'?" And so we did. When I thought about it, the *s* sounds were not a good idea given what we know about the aging ear. Besides, "wisdom" has a safe, solid, grounded feeling about it. Clients and others who read the newsletter seem to really like the name. (See Figure 8–2.)

FIGURE 8–2

VOLUME 1   NUMBER 2   SUMMER 1995

JOAN M. GRUBER, CFP
Certified Financial Planner
Maturity Market Strategist
3010 LBJ Freeway, Suite 1240
Dallas, Texas 75234
214-888-6045

© 1995 JOAN M. GRUBER, CFP

WISDOM

All powers of attorney are not created equal

DEAR CLIENTS & COLLEAGUES,

THE POWER OF ATTORNEY IS PROBABLY THE MOST ESSENTIAL LEGAL DOCUMENT YOU CAN HAVE. WHO NEEDS IT? YOU DO!

You do if you are of majority and are legally competent ("capacity", in some states). But the basic power of attorney document is useless if you become incapacitated unless it *specifically* states that it survives your incapacitation or disability.

That basic provision clearly makes the document more useful, and more valuable, especially in a crisis situation. Hence the name *Durable Power of Attorney*. It survives your incapacitation if it includes such language. It is this specific document which we will discuss in this article. We will also discuss provisions you might wish to include when having your own Durable Power of Attorney drafted.

Keep in mind that state law determines what must be included in your document (statutory language), what may not be included, and the interpretation of the various provisions. Always have your document drafted by an estate planning attorney who practices in the state where you live and execute it per his or her instructions. Have your financial planner review the document before executing it to be certain that all your investment spon-

sors would act upon it if need be. (Banks and mutual funds often insist that you execute their own document, regardless of the language in your own document.) Consider executing a document in each state (drawn up by an attorney in that state), where you spend time and where you own property. If you own assets outside your home state, consult an estate planning attorney in that state. Real estate transactions, especially, might not be able to be completed without specific instructions in the document.

POWERS GIVEN TO THE AGENT (ATTORNEY-IN FACT)

The agent, or attorney-in-fact, is the person to whom you are giving the power to act on your behalf. State exactly what it is you want him or her to be able to do. If it is likely that your agent may need to seek financial advice from a professional or to delegate certain money management powers to a private money manager, this should be stated. Otherwise, your agent might not be able to retain the appropriate financial advisory services when needed.

(CONTINUED PAGE 2)

Thank you so much for the response to our last newsletter. We hope you will continue to communicate your thoughts and feelings to us.

One frequent question regards what we actually do here. To put it succinctly: *We create awareness about the issues of aging and money (read abundance) and help people develop strategies and implement solutions.*

This includes writing, speaking, one-to-one counseling, consulting, strategic planning, and training.

I address issues of post-retirement planning, public policy, and marketing. We give individuals advice in the areas of investments, estate planning, long term care, and charitable giving. We accept no up-front commissions. Our individual clients include members of the mature generation and their concerned adult children. If you are interested in any of these services, or you know someone who might be, we would be very happy to send you a fee schedule. Our mission is to assist as many people as possible. Thank you for your interest. Have a great Summer.

Be Wise!   Joan

Once again, I had some difficulty conveying to the artist my concern about the readability of the colors, type sizes, type styles, and that the paper be nonglare. I was concerned that his recommendations for design did not offer enough contrast between the written material and the other colors in the piece, and that the paper was too shiny for the older eye. But when I showed it to clients, they thought it was acceptable.

Clients seem to like the newsletter, which they photocopy and give to their friends. I am not certain if they like the message or the artwork more. I have chosen to take an educational approach, with a touch of humor to maintain some levity. Your newsletter is your opportunity to tell your clients and professional network what you would say if you were face to face with them. It is your time to share important information that will cause them to think about an issue, tell them something they did not already know, tell them more about something about which they know very little, and perhaps motivate them to take action. I have decided not to include recipes, travel tips, health care tips, or the like. I might eventually, but for now I need the space for issues that are currently on my mind that I want them to know about. I do include a section to let them know about my speaking engagements, published articles, and other information they can send for. I find that some of them will ask to receive audio- or videotapes, or copies of articles if I will send them for free, but few are willing to pay for even the postage. Some to whom I have sent a free audiotape from a radio or television show interview have sent me referrals. I think it is especially important to include a very personal message on the front page from you with your picture next to your message. This is the next best thing to speaking with them on the telephone, meeting with them in person, or dropping them a personal line. I take this opportunity to speak to them in the first person and tell them what I am doing professionally, a new direction of my practice, a holiday greeting, or whatever comes to mind as I write. Even if you have someone else write your newsletter, I feel that this personal message needs to be written by you, just as you would speak in person, although you might wish to have it edited. All of my marketing pieces to date have been designed by Martin Communications, Inc., in Hood River, Oregon.

Brochure

I recommend that you develop a brochure about yourself, your services, the products you sell, and your education and experience. Some large companies have designed a prototype for their sales associates, who then provide the printer with the information to be printed on their own personal brochure. This is an excellent idea. Try to demonstrate why you are unique. Give the prospect a reason to want to do business with you. Always include a recent, realistic photo of yourself. Regardless of what you include in the printed material, the reader might decide to contact you because you have an honest or sincere look about you. The picture you include in the brochure creates an image of who you are and how you might do business. Work with a photographer who specializes in business portraits rather than personal portraits, which tend to convey a much different image. Include a quote that demonstrates how you think and express yourself. Include appropriate testimonials if the person who made the statement will give you written permission to use it.

I particularly like the marketing pieces of Rona Bartelstone & Associates, Inc. The firm has two brochures, a business card, and a Rolodex card that are simple and straight to the point, and void of all technical jargon. The colors and design are not fancy, but they are effective. They are on white stock with magenta ink. The copy is non-threatening and gentle, but professional, clearly demonstrating Rona's understanding of her potential clients. She carries the colors of magenta ink on white stock throughout all her marketing pieces. See Figure 8–3.

Telephone System, Voice Mail, and Headsets

Invest in quality telephone equipment. Check it out from the caller's end of the line before purchasing or leasing it. My clients have become very indignant in the past if the telephone reception was not good quality. Because the hearing ability of many of our clients is, or probably will be, declining, we need to plan for the future when making this investment. Voice mail is here to stay, and we need to observe the same rules of etiquette with it that we always have with the telephone. But it represents high technology, and if not used properly tends to challenge and annoy our older callers. Make certain that instructions to the caller are clear, both in content and in voice quality, pace, volume, and pitch, observing all the guidelines we previously discussed. Avoid long involved instructions and no way to get out of the system, except to hang up and start all over again. Always give the caller the option to speak with a real person at any time during the recorded message.

Voice mail can be viewed as a giant time-saver or a very rude way to distance yourself from every caller. The mature caller might find it unacceptable to be greeted by voice mail every time he calls you with no way to connect with a human being. We have all experienced this frustration at one time or another.

FIGURE 8–3A

FIGURE 8–3B

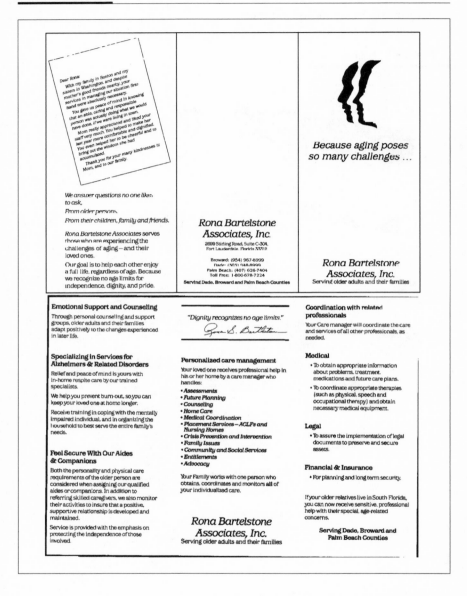

I use a headset every day. I recommend it for anyone who spends a great deal of time on the telephone. It adds about another hour to my day, since I can have my hands free to work while I am on hold. It also sets my hands free to locate what I need in a client's file as we speak. Unfortunately, the older person on the other end of the line sometimes has difficulty hearing since the reception is sometimes not as clear as it needs to be. I find it helpful to ask the person if I am speaking clearly enough, or if I need to speak louder. (Avoid asking if he can hear you, since it might sound like you are implying there is something wrong with his hearing.) I remove the headset immediately if he indicates that hearing me is at all a challenge.

Audio-Visual Equipment

When purchasing audio-visual equipment, keep your aging audience in mind. This is especially important if you plan to hold seminars in your office or use the equipment for client presentations. I am often asked to speak to groups of mature audiences. It is amazing how little thought often goes into such a purchase. If you are going to spend time preparing for a presentation, and expend a great deal of effort to assemble a roomful of prospects, it makes sense to use good-quality equipment to be certain that they can see and hear what you or your guest speaker is saying. Gather a group of mature individuals of all age groups, and test out equipment in your presentation room before making a purchase. Make note of their comments about the effectiveness of the equipment.

You will need to decide whether your presentations will be on overheads or on slides. Each has advantages and disadvantages. In order for the audience to be able to see slides, the room will need to be darkened. This usually does not work with an older audience. Overheads, on the other hand, have the advantage of being visible without the lights being lowered to the same extent. The drawback to overheads is that it is nearly impossible to create visually attractive graphics, and you are limited as to the amount of information you can fit onto an overhead and still have the text readable at a distance. The benefit of slides is that you can fit more information and creative graphics on them. The size of your room, the quality of the equipment, the lighting, and the type of information you are using will affect your decision.

Computer Hardware and Software

An abundance of quality software in all price ranges is available to help the pre-retiree plan for his retirement day. I mean that statement literally, because most software takes the pre-retiree right up to the day of retirement, and perhaps with some accuracy it shows him what his financial future will be a few years into retirement. If you are working with clients in the post-retirement phase, or those who want to see their financial future for the rest of their lives, in a very detailed way, you might need to develop your own spreadsheets. Out of frustration, I designed my own spreadsheet, which shows the client what his financial future looks like year-by-year to age 100, plugging in such options as long term care, the death of a spouse with any resulting loss of an annuity or pension benefits, and other calculations usually included in financial plans. I also can manipulate the inflation rate separately for various living expenses and for separate husband and wife's long term care costs; demonstrate the lost income stream from a retired note receivable; and explore numerous options that are particularly important to the post-retiree. This spreadsheet might be the biggest reason that I am able to convince clients that they need to purchase long term care insurance and equities. I include backup worksheets to support the numbers in the long term post-retirement spreadsheet. I also include extensive, but concise, comments and recommendations in my typical client reports. I keep these reports as simple as possible. I use no boilerplate text in the report. If the client wants more written information, I readily provide it. Overall, my goal is to keep the presentation of numerical and textual information as simple and easy to understand as possible. I also prepare the spreadsheets so they cover several pages so as to make them large enough to be readable.

When purchasing software, choose software that can easily be adapted for the post-retirement phase. This means that you will need to be able to omit all references to the client making annual investments or contributions to an IRA or 401(k). You will also need to be able to omit all references to "retirement date" and "beginning" Social Security date. These references are inappropriate for the client who has already retired and is already receiving Social Security or other retirement benefits. When clients see such references in their report, even if it does indicate a "zero" or other similar notation, they begin to wonder what other inapplicable calculations and assumptions the software automatically made. The result could be the beginning of loss of credibility for you. Invest in a high-quality laser-jet or inkjet printer to assure that your written material and client reports are readable to your clients as they age.

On-line Communication

I am convinced that we will be communicating with many of our clients on-line, although admittedly I have not yet discovered the applications, except for passing simple messages back and forth, setting up chat rooms, and having "client seminars." No doubt the baby boomers will be very comfortable with this mode of communication. But despite the misconception about the current maturity market, I think there are applications yet undiscovered for them as well. I have several older clients who work with various programs and on-line services daily. I am considering ways to communicate with them and to provide services on-line. I view on-line services as a way to not only provide information and advice but market our services to existing clients and prospects. I recommend that you ask every new customer or client what on-line service he currently uses, or is contemplating, and that you then become proficient in that on-line service.

SERVICES AND COMPENSATION

I deliberately saved this discussion for last, since for me, it is often the most challenging part of working with the already retired. Because this market is so diverse, a cookie-cutter approach to services and compensation will probably be ineffective. Here are some of the diversities you are dealing with:

1. Physiological.
2. Psychological.
3. Financial resources and income.
4. Level of personal attention they require.
5. Level of expectations about what you can and will do for them.
6. Level of sophistication about how businesses and practices work, including the costs to run them.
7. Level of sophistication about the information they need.
8. Perception about free information available.
9. Perception about the actual costs for financial products (especially commissions).

Add to the above list a proliferation of on-line information and written material available to educate them about everything from mutual fund performance to do-it-yourself legal documents, tables, charts, and easy college and retirement planning calculations. All of these will have a bearing on how willing the client is to compensate you, and how much he thinks your service is worth. Recent studies indicate that people in general want to pay low or no-load commissions, opting to pay fees instead. Several financial service giants are moving into the fee-for-service area. In addition, strong evidence suggests that financial planners, who have traditionally been compensated by fee and commission, are moving away from compensation by commissions in favor of fees.

It has been my experience that most retired people do not wish to pay commissions for the purchase of products, especially securities. They might feel the same way about commissions for purchases of insurance if they were aware of the commissions involved. Since insurance commissions need not be disclosed to the customer, they might not be objecting simply because they are not aware of them. Many of these people profess that they would rather pay fees for advice than a commission. In fact, most are adamant about not paying commissions. However, even though some might be willing to pay a reasonable fee at the beginning of retirement, or at the beginning of the relationship, I have found that the enthusiasm diminishes after they are a few years into retirement, and many eventually resist paying fees altogether, except for occasional meetings billed at an hourly rate. Many are not willing to pay a reasonable fee, even at the beginning of the relationship. The profile of the client I am referring to here has been a reasonably good client during his working years with an invested net worth (exclusive of home equity and personal possessions, and other assets not available to invest) of $300,000 to a few million. By the time these people reach their early 70s, their need for nonproduct information increases. This is about the time they are often not willing to pay a reasonable fee for sound advice. The question then becomes, who will assist them with their financial affairs, and how?

In a study done by Doran Levy and Carol Morgan of the 50-plus market, only 8 to 12 percent of those over 50 live in households where someone has paid to have a retirement plan written. Because an overwhelming majority of those surveyed over age 50 seek financial advice from their banker, stockbroker, insurance agent, and accountant, Levy and Morgan see this as an untapped opportunity for financial planners. Nearly twice as many of those surveyed now pay a commission for advice than those paying a fee.[2] For planners to be able to command the kind of fees that reflect their expertise, risk, and cost to do business, they will need to demonstrate that their services are absolutely necessary, that the planner's involvement is indispensable, and that these services and counsel are not available from another source or for "free."

Regardless of how the financial advisor or salesperson is compensated, most older people desire the following services and information:

1. Periodic written and/or verbal reports about the status of their investments.
2. How to make gifts to their children, grandchildren, and to charities.
3. Whether or not they need long term care insurance, and if so, what to purchase.
4. Whether they can afford to retire now and take the early-out package offered by their company.
5. What distribution options to elect for their retirement plans.
6. Where to invest their retirement plan "rollover."
7. How to reduce their estate taxes or pay for them (even if they are uninsurable).
8. Whether they should drop Medicare and join a Medicare HMO, and if so, which one.
9. Whether they should set up trusts and if so, what provisions to include.
10. Telephone consultations and in-person meetings a few times per year.

Your challenge is how to provide meaningful services at a price the client can live with and one that will justly compensate you for your time and expertise. The following is a list of strategies I recommend, some of the pitfalls you can avoid, and the future as I see it if you wish to continue to work with your clients well into the later years.

Recommendations

1. Be willing to negotiate with the client about your compensation, offering to be compensated by fees, commissions, or a combination of the two.
2. If you offer yourself as fee-only, quote a fee that is equal to the hourly rate for the better law firms in town. You will stand a better chance of attracting the most lucrative clients. If you are compensated by fee only, establish a relationship with licensed insurance salespeople who will share their commission with you when the client implements your insurance recommendations. (The typical share of the commission for you is 30 to 50 percent, depending upon

how well prepared the client is to purchase the insurance when the referral is made.)

3. Whether or not you are fee only, make establishing private management of individual issues or mutual fund portfolios a priority where appropriate.

4. When meeting with a new prospect, be prepared to offer him a choice between a set fee, package price, or an hourly rate.

5. Always put your engagement agreement in writing, signed by all, accompanied by a deposit for 30 to 50 percent of the estimated or set fee.

6. Be clear from the start how you will charge him once the initial work is completed for items such as telephone calls, calls from his other professional advisors or family members, or correspondence he initiates.

7. Charge an annual retainer to cover items such as incidental telephone calls and maintaining his files such as filing mutual fund statements, straightening out incorrect statements, etc., especially if you do not receive fees related to private money management.

8. Make it a priority to establish a relationship with an adult child and his other professional advisors as quickly as possible.

9. If you are compensated by fee only for the initial report, projections, etc., charge a percentage of the amount of the proposed investment portfolio, and a smaller percentage of other assets to be considered in the allocation but not to be invested.

10. Charge a fee for a portion or all of the initial interview, payable at the end of that meeting.

The Pitfalls

I have made mistakes along the way. Here are some pitfalls you can avoid:

1. Think twice about accepting clients for an hourly rate and no other form of ongoing compensation.

2. If you do work for a fee, make certain it approaches your total compensation as if you were also accepting commissions.

3. Set your compensation high enough so that you can afford to hire an extra full-time staff person to screen calls, and provide service. Keep in mind that the older client generally will demand more staff time than the younger client.

4. If you charge an hourly fee, provide a detailed invoice for all time devoted to that client, including travel time.

5. Have a provision in your ADV Part II that permits you to increase your fees by up to a stated percentage, such as 5 percent, automatically on January 1 every year.

6. Indicate in your ADV Part II that you charge separately for travel time, (such as 50 percent of your hourly rate), word processing, administrative, faxing, long distance calls, messenger, and other hard costs.

The Future

Investments, income tax, entitlement programs, and other issues that affect our aging population have become so complicated that older people need assistance in dealing with them. Many younger family members, though, lack the time and expertise to help their aging parents and relatives. I am not referring to the indigent here, but rather the middle class. These are the people who could end up indigent without competent assistance with their financial affairs. Many of their needs have nothing to do with the purchase of a product, nor can they afford to pay what I would consider to be a reasonable fee for sound financial advice. What I mean by "reasonable" is a fee that adequately compensates the professional for his time, expertise, risk, costs associated with compliance, marketing expense, and a profit commensurate with his level of expertise, experience, credentials, effort, risk, and goodwill. The question remains, who will assist this enormous, growing segment of the population? Many of us do pro bono work, but there are so many who need help, and so few helpers. Financial service professionals and companies have an opportunity to provide a valuable service, and public relations that money could not buy.

CHAPTER 8 ENDNOTES

1. Carol Musket, Callier Center for Communications Disorders, The University of Texas at Dallas, interview by author, January 30, 1996, Dallas, Texas.
2. Doran J. Levy and Carol M. Morgan, *Segmenting the Maturity Market* (Chicago: Probus Publishing, 1993), chapter 7.

CHAPTER 8 REFERENCES

Ambrosius, Richard, president, Phoenix Systems, Inc., interview by author, Sioux Falls, South Dakota, February 13, 1996.

Bagley, Martha, specialist to older adults at the Helen Keller National Center for Deaf-Blind Youth, interview by author, Dallas, Texas, February 8, 1996.

Bagley, Martha, "The Americans with Disabilities Act: A Revolution of Opportunity," *Sand & Video Contractor* (January 20, 1993), p. 10.

Bagley, Martha, Steven E. Boone, and Douglas Watson, eds. "Facilitating Oral Communication: Assistive Listening Devices," *The Challenge to Independence— Vision and Hearing Loss among Older Adults* (1994).

Bakker, Rosemary, Rosemary Bakker Design, interview by author, New York, New York, March 26, 1996. This interior designer for the mature market provided information about products mentioned in the text including the following:

- RCA Rubber Company: 216-784-1291
- Altro Floors: 1-800-382-0333
- R.C. Musson Rubber Company: 1-800-321-2381
- Enrichment (ergonomically designed products): 1-800-323-5547
- Lighthouse Low Vision Products: 1-800-829-0500

Bartelstone, Rona, president, Rona Bartelstone Associates, Inc., interview by author, Ft. Lauderdale, Florida, January 11, 1996.

Gaunt, Jan, Advanced Planner Group, senior financial advisor, American Express Financial Advisors, Dallas, Texas, February 19, 1996.

Wakefield, Doug, Gold Team financial advisor, American Express Financial Advisors, interview by author, Dallas, Texas, January 26, 1996.

9

CHAPTER

Adult Children: An Overlooked Market

A MARKET WAITING TO HAPPEN

Adult children of aging parents and relatives form a vast market that has been virtually ignored by financial services.

There are three ways to view adult children:

1. As family members of your existing older clientele.
2. As your current clients whose aging parents are potential clients.
3. As potential clients who are dealing with aging parents, but who could themselves become your clients.

If the members of the maturity market have not sought your advice, their adult children might contact you even if they are not currently your clients. Or, your existing clients, who could be anywhere between 30 and 60, could eventually seek your advice on issues related to caring for an aging parent or relative. Their call for help might start out as a casual comment, a request for information, or an explanation about anything from Medicare HMOs, Social Security, and long term care insurance to where to look for someone to watch over Mom a few days a week. You might have already brushed aside such requests for information, not realizing that the question was more than an aberration or a quirk. It is the beginning of a major phenomenon unprecedented in this country.

Corporations Feel the Effects

I have seen many contradictory statistics about the number of adult children who are currently dealing with aging parents and relatives, but the trend is apparent. According to a study conducted by the Families and Work Institute (1991), 8 percent of all workers have major caregiving responsibilities for older relatives. However, other researchers estimate that the percentage of workers with caregiving responsibilities can be as high as 20 to 30 percent (Dana Kochiri, former Research Analyst, New York Conference Board). These statistics might vary because many workers fear that their employers will discover that they are caring for an aging parent or relative. Many prefer not to call attention to their unscheduled time off and company time and money spent on personal long-distance telephone calls to aging relatives, physicians, and other service providers.

I met recently with a major corporation's executive vice president and two of its corporate benefits policy personnel. I pointed out that employees' dealing with aging relatives was becoming a major problem for corporations. I asked the VP what programs his company had in place to assist the employees. He did not know what I was referring to, so I cited a few statistics about employees taking unscheduled time off and making telephone calls on company time. He reared back in his chair, pounded on the conference room table, and roared, "They're stealing money. They are stealing from the company." You can see why an employee might not wish to go to his employer or his human resources department for help. He is terrified of losing his job, especially at a time when he is staring at the enormous costs of caring for an aging relative.

Not all companies are as unenlightened as this one. In fact, many are now contracting with such companies as The Partnership Group and Work Family Directions to provide elder services to their employees. These and similar companies set up libraries that house videos, books, pamphlets, and other resources. They also provide on-site workshops and an 800 number for the employee to call when he needs to be referred to care providers in the aging parent's geographical location. I sometimes deliver workshops to their corporate client employees, who are desperate for information from quality, nonsolicitous sources. I have heard stories from them, as well as from my own clients, about the struggle they endure in caring for aging parents and relatives who are often hundreds or thousands of miles away. Many are either shuttling back and forth on weekends to visit an infirm parent while some have actually moved the parent many miles to come live with them. This is not ideal since the older person usually will resist moving from his home, often resulting in unhappiness or failing health.

Adult Children Will Pay

According to two studies by AARP, one in 1989 and the second in 1992,[1] 84 percent of all those over age 55 plan never to move from their homes. I can verify that older people insist on remaining in their homes even when they are way beyond being able to care for themselves much less maintain their home. That same study revealed that 26 percent of those surveyed expected their children to care for them if they could not care for themselves. I conclude from this that aging parents often expect adult children to make it possible for them to "age in place." This usually results in the adult child not only arranging for and supervising in-home care, but quite often providing the financial means as well.

In-home care is quite expensive, especially since Medicare benefits are limited. The cost varies widely across the country, but here are a few figures to give you an idea of what your aging client or adult child is facing. In areas where institutionalized care costs $35,000 to $40,000 annually, in-home care, provided by a nonmedical professional, is typically $12.50 per hour or $125 per day. (In the Northeast, these costs are two or three times as high.) These fees are higher for professionals licensed to dispense medication and perform tasks other than basic homemaker and companion services, when services are provided by non-Medicare agencies, and for weekend care. I share this so you will begin to see what adult children are dealing with now and what they might face in the future. Given the increasing longevity of their parents' and grandparents' generation, you will begin to see that their fears are not entirely unfounded. Caring for aging parents could very well be the greatest financial risk they will ever face, not to mention the health risks resulting from stress. It could destroy all your years of planning for their financial independence.

I once had a client, an only child, whose 80-year-old mother, a widow, was unable to care for herself. His late father had once been a prosperous business owner, but after his death, all the money had gone to pay for his wife's care. She, like most older people I have known, insisted on remaining in her home and had made her son, an only child, promise never to place her in a nursing home. The son, divorced with two children in college, struggled to provide for his mother, who had long since run out of money. All that remained of her assets was a valuable piece of land she had inherited many years before. Due to its low cost basis, a sale would result in an enormous capital gains tax. The devoted son was paying over $80,000 per year for round-the-clock care for his mother, hoping to restore his own nest egg upon her passing with the proceeds from the sale of the land. (The land would receive a stepped-up basis at her death.) There were other options to pay for her care such as a charitable remainder trust, but the son could not bear to give away the land. He eventually sold it, paid the tax, and continues to pay for her care, which by now costs well over $100,000 per year. This story is not unique. I hear it every day.

The Media Is Hooked

The media is beginning to carry stories about the challenges adult children are facing. *The Wall Street Journal* has a regular column called "Work and Family" by Sue Shullenbarger, which depicts human-interest stories about the challenges adult children are facing. The *New York Times* recently ran an article about executives who are turning down promotions since it is less stressful to live close to an ailing parent than to shuttle back and forth on weekends to deal with emergencies and assist them and supervise their care. As we discussed in Chapter 7, even the financial service giants are recognizing that providing information to help adult children deal with aging parents is a value-added strategy to secure their business.

If your client does not work for a large corporation that offers elder services, you could very well be the first person the adult child calls when the situation with his parent reaches a crisis. At that point, your client will be seeking more than casual information. He will need immediate, specific information, either from you or from someone to whom you refer him. I currently receive numerous referrals from other financial service professionals who claim to know little about the issues of the aging. Although corporate elder referral services are doing a terrific job of assisting their corporate client employees, there is a tremendous need for financial service professionals who can be a resource for related services and give more than general advice to the families of aging elders.

Any financial service professional who professes to be an expert in the maturity market had better be prepared to accept telephone calls from adult children of aging parents and relatives. Many calls will come from a distance, often from outside your state. It is not uncommon for me to receive a call from an adult child who lives in another state, but whose parent lives in my state, or in yet another state. That is how desperate adult children are for quality advice. (This raises some compliance issues we will deal with later on.)

Although the caller might be aware of a parent's decreasing ability to function, he frequently has difficulty obtaining the full cooperation of his siblings or the other parent. He sees a crisis brewing and is attempting to deal with it now. Be prepared to hear about the family secrets. You will be privy to stories about the alcoholic sister who has taken control of Mom's assets and is spending all her money. You might hear tales about Dad's new, young wife who is taking advantage of Dad whose capacity is in serious question. Then there is the client or caller who is in the middle of a crisis. The crisis usually involves a parent's injury, acute illness, or the death of a family member.

ADULT CHILDREN NEED YOUR HELP

Your client or caller will want three things from you:

1. Expert advice about the questions he is raising as well as the ones he never thought to ask.

2. How to solicit the help of his siblings and the parent (if available).

3. Reassurance from you that he is handling the situation well.

Dealing with an aging relative can be like having a part-time, or in some cases, a full-time job. It is time-consuming and often gut-wrenching. Your client wants to feel better about himself after he speaks with you; he wants to know what to do next and whom to call. Even if you have no desire to become an expert in dealing with the issues of the aging, you can still be of service to him by referring him to someone else who is. I receive referrals quite often from other financial planners who would rather not deal with these issues. In fact, I often function as a consultant to other financial planners and product salespeople whose clients are aging or are requesting assistance with their aging relatives.

Once you begin to establish a reputation of expertise in dealing with aging adults and concerned adult children, you will become aware of how little the public knows about this enormous issue. Sometimes I've wondered if a telephone call was a gag. For instance, I received a call a while back from an attorney who I think it is safe to assume does not deal with the issues of the aging. He had been referred to me by a financial planner. His question was this: He was an only child of a 68-year-old parent who had been in a nursing home for almost three years. Fortunately she had a quality long term care insurance policy, but the three-year benefit would be terminating soon. He wanted to know how he could obtain another policy, since it appeared that she would be in the nursing home for the rest of her life. At first I thought the call was a joke (fortunately I played along), but when I realized that it was not, I was reminded of the terror the adult child faces when the parent is out of money long before the end of life, when there is no insurance, and government programs are disappearing. This man, like most people in his situation, was not yet able to face the situation logically.

Many adult children assume there is a government program to pay for their parent's care. They will look to you to explain the Medicaid rules and to help them rearrange assets or place them in trusts so the parent can qualify for benefits. This strategy might have worked had they addressed the issue sooner. In many cases they are working under old, vaguely understood rules that rarely work in their favor. In that case, perhaps the best thing you can do is to refer them to an elder law attorney in the state where the parent lives to assure that they are getting the best advice available. You might be shocked that I am talking about a welfare program that might not seem to fit the profile of your clients. Many of these people started out their retirement years financially independent, but the cost of care has drained their assets. The saddest story is when the parents are out of money, but by some quirk in Medicaid rules, they do not qualify for benefits. This can happen if they are disqualified medically. Your client might then have to start liquidating his retirement plan, children's college education fund, or other assets to pay for his parent's care. At any rate, you are often the bearer of bad news. Be prepared to deal with your client's anger and disappointment.

ESTABLISH A RELATIONSHIP WITH THE ADULT CHILD OF YOUR CLIENT

If you are currently the financial advisor for the older person, you will want his adult child to call you for help if his parent has a crisis. This is an excellent reason to be introduced now to the adult children. You do not want to be meeting the adult child for the first time when there is a crisis. This is a very stressful time, and not the ideal condition in which to establish a relationship of trust. Quite often you will need to get right to the point about what needs to be done, especially if the parent's capacity is on the wane and you need to move quickly to get legal documents signed. Under those circumstances, there is no time to establish a relationship. If they do not already know you and have confidence in you, their first reaction might be to take control of the situation, which for them might mean removing you from the account and replacing you with their own financial advisors. The new advisors may not know any more than you do about the issues of the aging, but the adult child will seek comfort by taking control, prudently or otherwise.

I recommend that you take steps to allow your client's family members to get to know you and to trust you. Make it clear to your client that this does not mean that you will divulge his personal financial affairs beyond what, if anything, he authorizes. I urge you to get to know the adult child long before your client loses capacity, or it might be too late. All your hard work to develop a trusting relationship with the aging parent will be lost if you lose the account.

Having lost accounts when aging clients became ill, I can assure you that it is sad to watch a good client for no apparent reason go out the door. I had a client until very recently with whom I had worked for nearly 10 years. I had designed and implemented a little-known strategy that saved her over $100,000 in capital gains tax, and had worked with her to implement other estate-planning and investment-planning techniques. I was very fond of this woman and had met with and spoken with her only child on the telephone several times. We had a good relationship, but like most adult children, she was probably suspicious. The client had a stroke and a heart attack a few days apart about two years ago at the age of 76, from which she made a remarkable recovery. The daughter did not call me when her mother became ill. I was distraught when I found out, for several reasons. The daughter had not read the long term care insurance policy prior to making major posthospital care decisions. My client had an older policy, which required that she first receive nursing care in a nursing home (or nursing care wing of a hospital) before in-home care would be covered. The daughter, despite the physician's recommendation, took the mother into her home to recover. Fortunately my client recovered. But had she required extensive long-term care, the claim probably would not have been paid. After her recovery, it became increasingly difficult to communicate with her, since she was not quite as sharp as she had been prior to her illnesses. I stayed in touch with the daughter, which, before her illness, the mother had encouraged. Unfortunately, my client ended the relationship for reasons I will never know. I assume that she is now working with her son-in-law's financial advisors, which I know would not please her. Older clients can be very loyal, but once they are no longer in control of their accounts, you could lose them as clients.

SERVICES TO OFFER ADULT CHILDREN

There are several basic services the adult child finds valuable. The services he needs will depend upon several things, such as whether or not his parent is currently declining or is totally incapacitated.

Here are some of the questions that will motivate the adult child to seek your help, even if the parent is not your client, especially if the family is not in a crisis situation:

1. Are my dad's investments appropriate? All he has are Treasuries and bonds. Shouldn't he have some stocks? I'm afraid he will run out of money.

2. Should my parents have long term care insurance? Where do I find out about it and who should I buy from?

3. What is a Medicare HMO? Should my mom become a member? Where do I go for more information?

4. Is the government going to reduce or take away my parents' Social Security benefits?

5. I worry about my dad living alone, but he won't move. How can I find someone to help him live independently?

6. My mom is thinking about selling her home and moving to a retirement community. Can you recommend someone to sell her house and show her what options are available for retirement housing?

7. My dad has an old will. Where do we go to have it reviewed and to find out what other legal documents he needs?

8. My parent needs income, but it would cost too much in taxes to sell and reinvest the current investments. Do you have any suggestions?

9. My parents have more assets than they will ever need and they want to give some to me. Can you help us work out a plan so that the income and estate taxes for both of us are minimized?

These are the typical questions the adult child asks if there is no crisis and there is time to do some planning. Most of them will revolve around how to keep the parent independent and how to preserve assets for both the parent and for your adult child client. Notice all the opportunities for a product sale.

If the adult child is in a crisis, his needs are a bit different and the level of urgency is noticeably higher. Here is a list of his needs if he is in a crisis:

1. How do I find a nursing home or someone to care for my mom in her home?

2. How do I take charge of the assets so I can pay bills and make other financial decisions?

3. How do I find out what my mom's house is worth, or what it would rent for? How long would it take to sell the house? Will selling or renting out the house disqualify her for Medicaid? Are there tax implications to renting or selling?

4. How do I find handyman services and carpenters to make changes to the house so my dad can stay there when he comes out of the hospital rather than go to a nursing home?

5. Where can I find someone to open mail, pay the bills, and make sure the medical bills are paid, or not paid twice?

6. Is my mom going to run out of money? How can we make it last longer?

As you can see, the adult child in a crisis has more urgency and needs answers quickly. But whether he is in a crisis or not, he still needs the same information. The difference is that there is less time to take action and less opportunity for a product sale. It would be worth your time to develop services to cater to this sector of the market. At least for now, you will have very little competition, and attracting this market could be a way to secure the adult child's own business as well as helping him deal with his parent's affairs.

Here are some basic services to offer to the adult child:

1. Referrals to experts on issues of the aging in the area where the aging parent lives such as elder law attorneys; geriatric care managers (they might not be familiar with this service); financial planners, stockbrokers, insurance agents (especially long term care insurance and Medicare HMOs); area agencies on aging; real estate agents; handyman services; and bill-payer services.

2. A detailed financial analysis of the parent's current and proposed financial condition, which includes detailed lifetime annual cash flow projections with all the variables appropriate for their older relative's situation

3. Personal interviews and screening of the other professionals to whom you are referring them.

4. Specific recommendations about how to extend the life of the portfolio.

5. Ongoing assistance with implementation of the recommendations, which might or might not include a product sale, and follow-up phone calls.

6. Marshaling assets at death and providing values six months after death.

7. Portfolio analysis during estate administration to determine the best assets to liquidate to pay bills and settle the estate.

8. Analysis of the costs and benefits of moving a parent long distance with your client's job relocation versus shuttling back and forth to care for aging parents left behind.

9. Analysis of the costs and benefits of providing for a parent's care in the parent's own home, remodeling your client's home and having the parent live with him, or settling the parent in a nursing home.

The list of services you can provide for the adult child is nearly endless. You will need to decide how involved you wish to become, and where a service or a prospecting strategy becomes social work, or pro bono. An entire business could be developed around providing services for adult children.

BENEFITS OF WORKING WITH ADULT CHILDREN

There are numerous benefits to working with the adult children of your aging clients and soliciting the business of adult children whose parents are not your clients. Our clients' money is a family affair and will remain so as long as the government taxes preceding generations when passing assets during their lifetime and at their death to succeeding generations, and so long as the government continues with its current trend to make the family responsible for the care of its aging members. Some of the benefits of working with adult children include: urgency, prospecting opportunities, client retention, and compensation opportunities.

Urgency

By the time the adult child becomes involved, there is usually some urgency that did not exist before. He often needs information on a timely basis and is prepared to take action. He is more likely than was the parent to act on your recommendations either because the options have narrowed now that the parent is declining or the situation is acute.

Although you might find him to be more cautious than he has been in dealing with his own financial affairs, he probably will not be as cautious as his parent is or was, nor will he take as long to make decisions. Making financial decisions for another person, especially one with whom he has an emotional attachment, can be a sobering experience, but he will usually proceed more quickly than the parent did, if only because he is often better prepared to understand the options. This could be due to a higher level of sophistication about financial affairs, physiological or cognitive abilities, or his familiarity with taking charge of a situation that demands quick decisions. The greatest challenge to you will be to have the information he needs on a timely basis. There will often be little time to do research, to locate qualified professionals to whom you can refer him with any level of confidence, or to become familiar with the jargon and the issues.

Prospecting Opportunities

Financial services have generally not done as well as one would hope in penetrating the maturity market, especially in the post-retirement market. Working with adult children is one way to reach this elusive group, although admittedly, marketing is a challenge. We will discuss the marketing aspect below. If the adult child came to you originally seeking help with his aging relatives, it is an opportunity for you to demonstrate your expertise. The adult child could himself become a client. I have addressed several groups of concerned adult children who came to hear about how to deal with the issues of aging parents and relatives only to learn that they ought to be considering many of the same issues for themselves. Many had not done any retirement planning, but having heard the facts as they pertained to their parents were willing to begin planning for their own future.

Client Retention

Generally, you will stand a better chance of retaining your aging clientele if you develop a relationship of trust with the adult child. This is more likely to happen if you can at least meet one or more adult children of your client. I explain to prospective clients during our first meeting that I find it beneficial to them if at least one family member knows me, knows how to reach me, and feels comfortable working with me if the client should ever be unavailable to make important decisions.

Compensation Opportunities

Although some older people might not be willing to pay reasonable fees for quality advice, it has been my experience that adult children are more realistic about what constitutes a reasonable fee. There will often be one dissenting sibling who thinks your fee is unreasonable, or who perceives that he can obtain all the information he needs for free from other sources. But there will usually be one sibling who is willing to make the decision to retain your services, even if he has to pay out of his own pocket. The adult child is usually still in the workforce, travels for business, runs a company, or has other family responsibilities. He will be willing to pay you since your service represents a necessary timesaving, stress-reducing convenience.

If you are compensated by commissions, you will usually meet with less resistance from the adult child than you would from the older person. If you are an expert, you will be able to do whatever needs to be done in a fraction of the time it would take him. If assets need to be reallocated, you might earn commissions. If the account is sizable and requires active management, private money management might be entirely appropriate provided you have determined that it will not be necessary to reduce capital rapidly to pay for the parent's living expenses.

I am convinced that all aging professionals could be doing a better job at identifying the mature adult who would benefit from long term care insurance. This includes just about everyone. Unless he will qualify for benefits under the new Medicaid rules, and no one knows what they will be, we need to be talking to the adult child as though his parent's long term care expense will be his responsibility, because it probably will. If the client is healthy enough to qualify and if the adult child can find the money to pay for the coverage, we need to be raising the issue, whether or not we are insurance salespeople. Even if you are not in the insurance business, you can make referrals to other licensed individuals and accept a commission as long as you are licensed to sell long term care insurance.

You can earn commissions and provide a valuable service in other areas. Viatical settlements are a little explored area where advisors could be advising adult children of terminally ill relatives and receiving commissions in return for a valuable service provided. Check to be sure you have the required licensing.

If you are in a position to make referrals to Realtors regarding the purchase or sale of housing, it might be prudent to obtain a real estate license. If you are a licensed professional, you can earn additional compensation by making referrals to other real estate-licensed salespeople. As an advisor to the adult child and the family, you can include assistance with the real estate transaction as an additional service.

HOW TO HANDLE EMERGENCIES

Over the last few years, I have received numerous telephone calls from adult children or other relatives of older adults who are in an acute situation. Some had already called their attorney, CPA, stockbroker, or insurance agent, none of whom had enough knowledge in the area of aging to feel comfortable giving information or advice. By the time they reached me they were desperate for quality information and advice. In fact, some, en route to an ailing loved one in another state, have called me from car phones, the airport, or the airplane. In cases like this, it did not seem appropriate to focus on my usual first meeting overview of the services I provide and how I am compensated. Like many geriatric care managers, I have never been able to turn away the adult child when in a crisis. I have counseled as many as three unrelated adult children in one day by telephone. I have given them the names of geriatric care managers, elder law attorneys, real estate agents, and anyone else who could assist them in the state where the parent lived, as well as basic information they needed to get them through the crisis. Many of those I have counseled are an only child upon whose shoulders often falls the administrative as well as the caregiving responsibilities.

I share this information because you will need to decide ahead of time how you will provide this service and how you will be compensated. I have investigated everything from taking credit cards over the telephone for my fee to establishing special services just for adult children and families of aging relatives.

COMPLIANCE ISSUES

If you give financial advice across state lines to adult children or aging adults for any compensation such as a fee or commission, you need to know the laws regarding registered investment advisers in those states where your customer or client resides. This brings us to the next question: Who is the client? Let's take a look at one example. I received a call last year from a young woman in San Antonio, Texas, who wanted assistance with her mother's finances. Her mother lived in Orlando, Florida, as did her three brothers. I could have been retained by the daughter, or I could have been retained by her mother. My decision about who my client is will to a great extent be determined by the state where the parent and the adult child resides and the rules in those states regarding registered investment advisers. Generally, I accept the older person as my client, since his money and financial affairs are at issue, but admittedly, this is not always the case. If the older adult lacks capacity and the adult child does not have a durable power of attorney to sign for the parent, I might accept the adult child as the client. Admittedly, before being retained by the adult child, I would need to have his goals and objectives clearly stated in our engagement agreement. I would not be inclined to accept an adult child as a client whose goal was to maximize his own inheritance, regardless of any other circumstances. If the adult child's objective was to preserve assets for his parent, I might be inclined to accept him as the client if the parent lacked the capacity to sign and there was not a durable power of attorney.

In interviewing other professionals, I have discovered one prominent elder law attorney who nearly always accepts the adult child as the client, while another considers the family to be the client. You need to make this determination for yourself, with counsel, or at the direction of the principal of your firm or company. Because this could be a major area of litigation, you need to give a great deal of thought to how you will work with adult children and whom you will represent. There are many unknowns and uncertainties about the adult child market, but one thing is certain: This market is not going to go away. If anything it will become an enormous segment of our aging society as we struggle to deal with our aging parents and relatives.

CHAPTER 9 ENDNOTES

1. "Understanding Senior Housing for the 90s," *AARP Survey of Consumer Preferences, Concerns, and Needs* (Washington, DC, 1992).

CHAPTER 9 REFERENCES

Guy, Heidi, account manager, The Partnership Group, Blue Bell, Pennsylvania, interviewed by author, April 25, 1996.

Hardman, Robin, Families and Work Institute, New York, New York, interviewed by author, April 25, 1996

10 CHAPTER

The Boomers Are Coming: Are You Ready?

A Drum Roll, Please

Ladies and gentlemen, may I have your attention, please. This is the moment we have all been waiting for: On January 1,1996, the first baby boomer turned 50 and for the next 18 years, a boomer will turn 50 every eight seconds. I present to you the baby boomers, all 76 million of them, born between 1946 and 1964.

The boomers have finally arrived at what is traditionally a worker's peak earning years and, hopefully, will now start to save and plan seriously for their future. AARP and all financial services that stand to benefit from this tremendous influx of cash into products and services have been waiting for this moment with great anticipation and excitement. At no point in history have so many people entered this phase of life in such a short period of time. They could enrich many corporations and systems, and impoverish others.

Everything They Touch Turns to Gold

From the moment of their birth, this post–World War II generation has created a demand for products and services like no other generation before them. Hospitals, baby food, grade schools, clothes, the music industry, colleges and universities, automobiles, housing, home furnishings, publications and communications, and entitlement coffers are just a few areas where their presence as a group has been felt. And now as they turn the corner of their working years, the big question is, will they now wave their magic wand over the financial services industry and create explosive growth just as they have with every other industry and product they touched in the past?

WHO ARE THE BOOMERS?

The oldest of this generation were born at the end of World War II, or during the Korean conflict. They lived their childhood in fear of the Communists. Throughout grade school they practiced diving under desks to protect themselves during air raid attacks, wondering all the while how a small desk could protect them from such a fierce enemy. Their very early experience also included attacks on Hollywood celebrities by Joseph McCarthy, the beginnings of rock and roll, "modern" kitchen appliances for Mom who cooked and baked all day, big shiny cars with tailfins, and Dad who worked at the same company for most of his career.

In the 60s, some fought against the Vietnam War at home as fiercely as those who actually went into battle. They let their hair grow long and vowed to change the world so all could live in peace. John Lennon was one of their heroes whose tune "Imagine" captured their passion to stop the fighting, the prejudice, the glorification of material wealth, and anything else that separated people from each other. Their leaders whose mission was to make these dreams a reality were all shot down—John Kennedy, Martin Luther King, Robert Kennedy, and even Lennon himself.

They are highly educated, late to marry, late to parent, and quick to divorce. They love to spend money, they love to indulge themselves and their children, and they are demanding social change. In fact, charities that make a sociological or political statement, such as AIDS and the environment, are attracting their dollars. When they were graduated from college, not surprisingly many with degrees in social sciences and humanities, they set out to change the world. But they soon discovered that to pay the bills, they needed to conform to the values of those still in charge. And even though many were seduced by material trappings and became known as the "yuppies," the early value system for many remains intact even today.

They purchase biodegradable products to protect the environment. They exercise to avoid the ravages of heart attacks, strokes, dimentia, and the loss of youth. They participate in self-help programs, read self-help books, and take time for solitary contemplation in an attempt to live consciously and to discover their purpose.

The younger the boomers, the more likely they are to have been latchkey kids. Many were raised by moms who worked either out of desire or out of a need to maintain a lifestyle created by post–World War II materialism, increased income taxation, and the overextension of government for entitlements, wars, and peacekeeping efforts. The younger boomers were raised with high-tech computers, communications, and entertainment equipment. While the older boomers might have had a vision to bring the world together, the younger boomers were raised on increased technology that made it happen.

The entire boomer generation is known as the "me generation," although a more accurate description might be the "can-do" generation. Going against the tide is their hallmark. They are fiercely independent and determined to make their visions a reality. They are not afraid to step out of the box to state their viewpoint. Family life is important to them, although that might not appear to be the case. To them, family does not necessarily mean a mommy, a daddy, and their children. Their idea of family can include any group of two or more people sharing their lives. Family for them can be any combination of ages, generations, cultures, religions, and genders who might not necessarily be related by blood. A family "couple" might be the same sex, live in separate cities, or be members of different generations. It can include one another's children, adopted children, "adopted" grandchildren, or children from other races and cultures. Their idea of career differs from that of previous generations as well. They recognize that the opportunities and demand for their skills and abilities are constantly changing and that it is unrealistic, if not undesirable, to remain in the same profession or with the same company for a lifetime.

Challenges They Face

The boomers are facing enormous challenges that will inhibit their ability to prepare financially for retirement. They are sandwiched between raising children, caring for aging parents, and dealing with massive public policy changes that could adversely impact their financial future.

Aging Parents, Grandparents, and Other Relatives

We discussed the phenomenon of adult children dealing with aging parents in a previous chapter. Between the ages of 40 and 54, 30 percent

of adult children will experience the death of their father, and 21 percent will experience the death of their mother.[1] For some, this passing
will be quick, while for others a long-term illness might precede death.

Since our elders are now able to live with maladies that in years
past would have ended their lives, dealing with an aging or dying parent can be a drain on the boomers' finances for many reasons. A boomer
might experience reduced work hours, early retirement, reduced pension benefits, and increased telephone and travel costs if a parent becomes
ill. Add home remodeling costs to the list of expenses if a parent comes
to live with him. These expenses can continue for many years, especially if the parent has dimentia such as Alzheimer's disease, which
generally does not result in a decreased lifespan. If the parent needs to
be institutionalized, or requires care in his own home, the adult child
might share in these costs. One way or another, the adult child might
need to contribute his time or money, or both, to care for an aging parent. Either way, it could seriously inhibit his ability to save for his own
retirement.

Up to this point, we have focused on the care of aging parents
with only a casual mention of aging relatives other than the boomer's
parents. There is a trend of aging elders, especially women, who have
no living spouses, no adult children, or none who are available to provide care. According to the U.S. Bureau of Census, the percentage of
those living alone has risen from 7.3 percent to 30.3 percent between
1960 and 1990. This is attributable to an aging population of women
who are outliving their spouses by an average of 6.8 years, the rise in
divorce rates, and an increasing number of people choosing not to
marry, or not to remarry after becoming widowed or divorced. I often
receive calls from nieces and nephews of aging elders seeking advice
about how to handle their loved one's financial affairs and how to pay
for their care.

It is not uncommon for the boomers to have living generations
who are older than their own parents. Until a few months ago, we had
five living generations in my own family. My grandmother passed on
recently at the age of 105. Fortunately, she lived independently until
103. The boomers will most likely be called upon to care for not only
their own parents, but their aging stepparents, in-laws, grandparents,
aunts, and uncles as well. I once had a client, a woman in her 40s, who
was divorced with children. She had three older spinster aunts for whom
she provided care all at the same time. They all passed on within the
same year. She spent that entire year caring for her aunts and settling
their estates, requiring that she take a leave of absence from work.

Unlaunched Children

According to the U.S. Census Bureau,[2] in 1994, 23 percent of householders age 45 to 54 had offspring age 18 and over living at home, up from only 5 percent of those age 35 to 44, and rising to 24 percent for those age 54 to 65. Clearly, the boomers could have dependent children living with them well into their later years. Although not all adult children living with a parent are financially dependent on them, most are to a certain extent. On the other hand, many adult children who have moved out remain both financially and emotionally dependent on their parents. Often an adult child will move back in with the parent when he loses a job or a marriage does not work out. Frequently, he brings his own young child or children to live with him at Grandma's. I have seen the effects dependent adult children can have on a retiree's and pre-retiree's finances. In my own practice, I have worked with retirees who pick up the tab when their adult children are unable to pay their rent, credit card bills, moving costs, auto, clothing, child care, and other expenses. Many either try to bury these expenses in their cash flow statements or deny that they are helping out a dependent adult child. Some older parents even sell their own assets to help the adult child pay his bills or to buy him adult "toys." The boomers could be facing this same issue of providing financial support for an adult child even after he is graduated from college. Given the boomers' financial unpreparedness for retirement, this phenomenon could add to their challenge.

College Funding

If their children are currently in college, many boomers are paying these expenses out of their current earnings or borrowing the funds. If their children are not yet in college, they are putting money away to fund that expense. Since many started their families later than did previous generations, it is very likely that their children will still be in college long after they retire, or when they are well into their 60s. This means that earnings that could have been saved for retirement might be used to pay for their children's college education.

Public Policy: Friend or Foe?

At first, it would appear that reduced Medicare, Medicaid, and other federal programs would ease the financial burden on the baby boomers by reducing taxes. In addition, a national sales tax, a flat tax, or taxation-free savings could also increase the take-home pay of the baby boomer, leaving more money for him to save for his retirement. But the reality is that someone has to pay for health care and long term care for the elderly. At this time, government programs pay for health care for the elderly, and long term care and housing for the indigent elderly. If the government does away with these programs, the burden will likely fall on the family. This means that the baby boomer will probably have to add health care, long term care, and housing costs for his aging parents and relatives to his own budget. In addition, reductions in aid for college funding from the federal government are already adding another burden to the boomer's budget.

Are the Boomers Preparing for Retirement?

Time is getting short for the boomers if they are serious about retirement. While most expect to retire as early as age 55,[3] others see no need, nor have the desire, to quit working at any particular age. The latter group is contemplating an extended work life well into their 70s and 80s, with a career change or two along the way.

Others expect to retire at age 65, anticipating that they will live as well or better in retirement than they did during their working years. But they have no idea how much money they will need, nor have they begun to save seriously for the later years when they will no longer have a paycheck. Some boomers who are planning to retire at age 65 are very serious about retirement and want to be certain that they will live comfortably. This group takes advantage of every opportunity to learn how to save and invest.

There seems to be some confusion about whether the boomers are financially on track to retire at age 65. The contradictory information seems to result from various studies, with their differing methodologies, and occasional misinterpretation by the media. It is helpful to be aware of the contradictory information and the underlying assumptions that lead to the wide disparity in the survey results.

U.S. Congressional Budget Office Study (September 1993)[4]
According to this study, the baby boomers will be at least as comfortable in retirement as their parents, leading the reader to assume that all is well. However, the study assumes several things:

1. The boomers will be able and willing to use home equity to provide needed income during their retirement.
2. The boomers would be willing to accept the same standard of living their parents currently enjoy.

3. There will be no changes in Social Security, income taxation, and other government programs.

THE MERRILL LYNCH STUDIES

The 1994 Merrill Lynch Baby Boom Retirement Index™[5] is based on two separate studies conducted by Dr. B. Douglas Bernheim at Stanford University. It portrays the boomers in an entirely different light. In the second study, "The Implications of Fiscal Realism," Dr. Bernheim recalculated the 1993 Baby Boom Index, incorporating the impact Social Security cuts or income tax increases could have on the baby boomers' financial independence in retirement. The Merrill Lynch study measured individual categories of assets and distinguished between assets available to fund retirement and those slated for other purposes. Based on this study (1994) of 2,015 respondents born between 1946 and 1964:

1. The boomers will have saved only 35.9 percent of what they will need to support their lifestyle in retirement. Unless they increase their savings rate and asset mix, they will have to either continue to work or reduce their lifestyle considerably.

2. If there is a 35 percent decrease in Social Security benefits, the boomers will have saved only 18.2 percent of what they will need to retire comfortably.

According to the 1995 Merrill Lynch Baby Boom Retirement Index™[6] conducted at Stanford University, workers are still woefully underpreparing for retirement. Their preparedness for retirement now stands at 38.2 percent, compared to baby boomers' preparedness of 35.9 percent in the 1994 study. This study included 2,055 respondents ages 30 to 48.

Another study, the Seventh Annual 1995 Merrill Lynch Retirement and Financial Planning Survey™[7] revealed some interesting facts about workers' attitudes and level of awareness about financial planning. The study, which was conducted in April and May 1995, included 395 45- to 64-year olds and 414 25- to 44-year olds. It revealed the following:

1. 98 percent believe that having a financial plan is the best way to reach financial goals.

2. Approximately 66 percent do their own financial planning.

3. Of those who save, 43 percent said they do their own calculations to determine the savings needed for retirement; 33 percent simply guess to determine savings needed for retirement.

4. 5 percent turn to their employer for retirement planning.

5. 8 percent turn to a professional for financial advice.

6. 27 percent of 55- to 64-year-olds seek the advice of a financial advisor, compared to 25 percent of 45- to 54-year-olds, and 19 percent of 35- to 44-year-olds.

7. 86 percent believe the federal government eventually will cut Social Security and Medicare.

8. 54 percent do not consider themselves informed about the Social Security benefits they will receive at retirement.

9. 85 percent say the federal government does not do enough to encourage Americans to save.

10. When asked what the government should do to promote saving, respondents said: reduce taxes on savings (23 percent); and provide education on financial planning (23 percent).

U.S. Trust Survey of Affluent Americans VIII[8]

This study, one of a series of eight studies of affluent Americans prepared for the United States Trust Company (July 1995), portrayed the boomer as wealthy and on track for a comfortable retirement. However, the survey included only respondents whose income and net worth fell within the top 1 percent of U.S. households. Unfortunately, this feature of the survey is sometimes overlooked by the media, which inaccurately portrays the baby boomer as much more prepared for retirement than he actually is. In fact, given the reported lifestyle of the study's respondents, it appears that despite their wealth, those respondents might be no better prepared for retirement than others in their age group with less income and net worth.

Will Social Security Be There for Them?

Many have serious doubts about whether the current pay-as-you-go Social Security system will be available to pay retirement benefits to the boomers throughout their retirement.

Since the boomers will need to depend on Social Security benefits to a much greater extent than do the current older generations, it is important for financial service professionals to understand how the system works and whether it will be there for the boomers. A quick look at the system will help us focus on the enormity of the problem.

At this time, a worker's Social Security contributions go into the Social Security Trust Fund, which pays out benefits to current beneficiaries. Most of the balance of the trust fund assets are used to purchase U.S. notes that fund other government programs. These notes, over $400 billion at this writing, will start to come due just about the time the oldest baby boomers reach age 65. In order for the federal government to continue to pay out benefits to the boomers, federal income tax as well as Social Security payroll tax will need to be increased substantially. In the year 2040 (when the boomers are age 77 to 95), the *effective* tax rate for workers will be at least 82 percent.[9] Since most workers would find this tax burden unacceptable, the boomers' Social Security benefits could be in jeopardy.

Most boomers are vaguely aware of this issue, although they might not understand how Social Security works, nor the cause of the problems. (Most think that fraud and abuse are the cause of problems with the system.) And even though 82 percent of all Americans surveyed believe that working Americans are beginning to lose faith that Social Security benefits will be available when they retire,[10] most are not saving enough for their retirement years, even if Social Security benefits were to be available.

Changes currently being contemplated in the Social Security system could change the boomers' preparedness for retirement. The Cato Institute, a think tank in Washington, DC, and other groups are studying possibilities for redesign of the system. At this writing, several proposals have been made by various legislators that would allow the worker to put all or part of his contributions in growth investments. This would give the boomers an opportunity to invest in stocks and bonds, which would be more appropriate for a young person saving for retirement than the current system, which invests Social Security dollars in U.S. debt issues.

Will Inheritance Bail Them Out?

According to a study done by Robert B. Avery and Michael S. Rendall at Cornell University in 1990, $10 trillion dollars will pass from the current older generation to their offspring between 1990 and 2040. The average bequest will be $90,000, although only one-fourth will inherit more than $50,000. This indicates that three-fourths of all beneficiaries will receive a paltry $50,000 or less. The transfer of wealth will be concentrated on very few legatees. Very little will pass to those in need of funds to sustain them in retirement. This study did not take into consideration the administrative expenses and estate taxes involved in passing assets, nor the final medical and long term care expenses of decedents. According to demographer Jeffrey Rosenfeld,[11] President of Plan-Wise, Inc., when speaking of the passing of wealth to the Boomers, there are other considerations:

1. The trend among the older generation is to leave significant assets to their new friends and acquaintances. As much as 33 percent of the estates of those who have moved to retirement housing or nursing homes is left to "fictive kin," or those not related by blood to the deceased.

2. Even if the decedent bequeaths assets to his adult children in his will, there is no guarantee that the children will actually receive the intended gift. This is due to an increase in litigation against probated wills, which has increased from 2 percent to 8 percent over the last 10 years.

3. Boomers are likely to receive less from deceased parents due to changing family patterns, remarriages, and an increased number of stepchildren.

4. Wealthy older adults often leave assets to charitable institutions, perceiving that their adult children are affluent and do not need their assets.

It would appear that the boomers' long anticipated inheritance might not be enough to add significantly to their net worth. However, the already wealthy boomer, who is not dependent on inherited wealth for his financial independence, might receive significant assets from his deceased parents or relatives.

How Will They Differ from the Current Maturity Market?

This is the question product and service developers and marketers are asking. Even if we learn how to attract and sell to the current maturity market, will these newly honed skills and strategies work for the enormous baby boom cohort? Will the boomers be like their parents?

In many respects, the boomers will resemble their parents. Certainly, physiologically they will experience the effects of aging, despite their herculean efforts to preserve youth with plastic surgery, face creams, PRK eye surgery, exercise, healthy diets, hair transplants, and tooth whiteners. But in many respects they will not bear the slightest resemblance to their aging relatives.

Education

The boomers differ from their elders in educational level. While 75 percent of the older generation lacked a high school diploma in 1950, 87 percent of the boomers today have a high school diploma, 25 percent have a college degree, and 50 percent have attended college.[12] Not only are the boomers better educated and more widely traveled, but they have had opportunities in their youth to learn more about the rest of the world through communications such as television, print media, and computers. Because of an abundance of differing experiences and their broad exposure to the rest of the world, the boomers will be far more sophisticated and demanding than the current older generations, and will be far more diverse as a group than previous generations. Their attitudes toward work and retirement will be different, especially between the various socioeconomic levels.

Attitude toward Work and Play

Even though many of them are hoping for an early retirement, their vision of retirement differs from that of their parents. Most plan to do consulting, or take on another line of work, working when and where they want and not at the demand of an employer. Some plan to combine work with play. Many who in their youth were aware of the threat of nuclear attack adopted an attitude that there might be no tomorrow, so let's live for today. Others see increasing longevity as a message that we could live a long, long time, so we might as well enjoy the journey and not spend our adulthood in slavery to a job, only to retire, or to die. This generation wants to live with vigor and purpose. Whatever their reasoning, they work and play equally hard. The boomers want more leisure and playtime in their lives. And because of this, the distinction between work and play and work and retirement is beginning to blur. This group is not satisfied to sacrifice family, friends, and hobbies for work. This might be the biggest difference between the generations.

Tolerance for Differences

The boomers do not see the world in black and white as some of their parents do. And as a result, they tend not to draw lines in the sand about work and enjoyment, definition of family, and right and wrong concerning cultural and religious belief systems. Theirs has always been a more permissive value system than that of previous generations.

Individual versus Community

The boomer places a high value on personal achievement, goals, and values. Unlike his parents and generations before him, he is not willing to follow the pack. Many male boomers refused to fight a war they did not believe in. Unlike their mothers, and generations of women before them, female boomers chose to marry later and delayed having children, if they had them at all, as they pursued their personal goals and financial indpendence. They are the first generation of "free agents," as demographer Cheryl Russell calls them. And at midlife, their individuality is clashing with community responsibilities.[13] Nowhere is this more evident than in the drama being played out on Capitol Hill over the role of government and its purpose in the lives of individuals where the leaders of both sides, President Clinton and Speaker of the House Newt Gingrich, are both baby boomers.

HOW TO ATTRACT THE BOOMERS' ATTENTION

If our goal is to motivate the boomers to seek our help as they prepare for their future, we will first need to attract their attention. Your message, packaging, and advertising need to display empathy, humor, creativity, information, youthfulness, "global" awareness and oneness, and "family" values. Position your message in church, health club, child care, recreational, and the arts publications, in "hometown" newspapers, and on-line . The larger financial services companies will need to advertise on television, radio, and in magazines as well. All advertising needs to be generation- and age-neutral. Market to families and lifestyles, including "life stages," "life phases," and "segments" rather than to age-related stereotypes. Address the issues. Allow them to determine whether or not the message speaks to them and their issues. Your product or service needs to exemplify integrity. Avoid overstating its capabilities. Pull a disappointing product off the market at the first sign of a problem. Be honest when a product fails to perform. Coverups as acceptable public relations strategy went out of fashion with Watergate. Demographer Faith Popcorn calls this "Truth in Consumerism".[14]

How to Market to the Boomers

If the boomers are serious about retiring or reducing work hours sometime in the next few decades, they need to get down to the business of planning and saving. The financial services that can make saving and investing easy and fun while addressing their concerns will capture their dollars.

How you present yourself in the marketplace and the image you project will determine your success at capturing their attention. Marketing to the boomers will be a tremendous challenge. They are bright, savvy, worldly, and demanding. One size fits all does not work for the current maturity market, and it surely will not work for the boomers. Some prefer an informational or educational approach, while others prefer to be entertained. Regardless of your approach, fear tactics will most likely be ineffective with all boomers. They want to know that everything will be all right, even if as professionals we have good reason to believe otherwise. All we can do is alert them to the issues and provide possible solutions. Each boomer needs to feel as though he is special, because that is how he is accustomed to being treated. We need to create an atmosphere in which talking about financial issues and his future is nonthreatening, informational, fun, and most importantly, interactive. Every customer and client needs to leave your office feeling better than when he walked in. He needs to feel safe, informed, secure knowing that he has a plan, and ready to act upon a plan he helped to create.

Levels of Service to Offer the Boomers

The financial future for many boomers is not as bright as it could be. Resist the temptation to use scare tactics in an attempt to motivate them to take action or purchase your product or service. You will have more success if working with you is easy and fun. This approach will be facilitated by evolving technology.

Boomers as Financial Service Consumers

I have observed four categories of baby boomers as financial service consumers, although there are probably many more. Here are the four I have identified so far:

1. Upscale
2. Do-it-yourself
3. Freebie
4. Needy

Upscale

The upscale boomer is very sophisticated and willing to pay a fee for professional advice. He is accustomed to working with other professionals who charge for their services. He demands the better things in life and is willing to pay for them. Although he might express a desire to purchase no-load products, he might not object to paying commissions. He will work with stockbrokers and financial planners.

Do-It-Yourself
Many boomers are computer-literate and prefer to do their own financial planning and investing in no-load products. For the do-it-yourself planners, there will be no shortage of information on-line, on television, on the radio, and in the print media. Even the resources commonly used by financial service professionals are now available at the library and on-line. Still, the user often seeks reassurance that his information, assumptions, or conclusions are correct. This boomer will seek out a professional to give him advice based on the work he has done on his own. He will seek the advice of a fee-only advisor, and demand no-load products. This client is looking for a bargain, even though he could easily afford to pay a reasonable fee for professional financial planning.

Freebie
This boomer lacks the time, expertise, or desire to do his own financial planning, but he still needs help. He is not willing to pay a reasonable fee for a very personalized, detailed financial plan. This customer has a need for products, and does not mind paying a commission as long as it is in line with the market, or better yet, if it is camouflaged or somehow disguised inside the product he is purchasing. He really does want to believe that the advice he receives is "free," even though he knows that he is paying for it somehow.

Needy
Many boomers lack the expertise, time, and sophistication to do their own financial planning. They also lack the resources to pay a fee for advice, although they might have some need for product, and do not mind paying a commission. This group is often in desperate need for information and advice in areas that have nothing to do with a product sale, such as planning for long term care for aging elders.

How to Engage the Boomers

Use your imagination when creating an atmosphere of convenience and entertainment to motivate the boomer to take action. Here's a list of items

I have developed. Some items are more appropriate for the upscale boomers, while some might work for all of them.

HOW TO PRESENT PRODUCTS AND SERVICES TO THE BOOMER

Market Retail Products in a Special Area of Your Reception Room

- Audio- and videotapes about financial information.
- Product information.
- Financial planning software.
- Free sample computer demo disks: Have a computer set up so he can try them out.
- Flyers about upcoming seminars, on-line meetings, and audio- and videotapes available from radio and TV shows and other events where you have been a guest speaker, or tapes of product education sessions.
- Resources such as other professionals and businesses you work with.
- Books and articles you have written or that you produce.
- Reprints of articles in which you were quoted.
- A "suggestion box" where he can let you know what other information he needs.

More Marketing Ideas

- Make presentations at the boomer's place of work, even to blue-collar workers. (Even they could become more valuable clients if Social Security is privatized.)
- Decorate your office with 50s, 60s, and 70s memorabilia. Decorate the walls with attractively framed pictures of rock stars from that era such as Buddy Holly, Jerry Lee Lewis, Fats Domino, Chubby Checker, Smokey Robinson, Dick Clark, the Beatles; or the "hippy" era such as Joan Baez and Judy Collins, and scenes from Woodstock. Put a jukebox in your reception area. It could be a great conversation opener.
- Offer on-line financial planning so the client can interact with you from the convenience of his home or office. Eventually, you will be able to see each other as you communicate.

- Set up teleconferencing so that the client can take advantage of your seminars and those offered from home office sites.

- Include a room for kids where they can entertain themselves while Mom and Dad meet with you. Stock it with snacks and soft drinks, VCRs, videos, computer games, books, toys, and a comfy couch with big fluffy pillows. Create a family room atmosphere. You might need to provide a babysitter and a limo driver to pick up the kids from school. (Check with your attorney about potential liabilities before implementing these ideas.)

- Retain a limo service to pick up and return your busy client for meetings in your office. Be sure to furnish the limo with a telephone (in case he forgets his), snacks, soft drinks, *The Wall Street Journal*, a television, pad and paper, and any other convenience to make his travel time to your office productive or relaxing. Include other conveniences such as a selection of tapes or CDs that would appeal to a boomer, such as "oldies" from the 50s, 60s, and 70s.

Show Him a Picture of His Ideal Future

The upscale client can afford to pay a fee or purchase considerable investments or insurance products, so you can provide services that really appeal to his need to feel special. When presenting your recommendations, especially about retirement planning, create an atmosphere of entertainment, or "edutainment,"[15] a term used frequently by interactive designer, "Digital Shaman" Chas Martin. Instead of focusing on numbers, charts, and prospectuses on a flat page, make your client's future come alive by demonstrating on CD-ROM projected on a big screen what his future will be like if he implements your recommendations. Show him a story about his future. Show him with his kids on their graduation day. Show him with his own parents playing with his kids in their home or in a retirement community. Show him running on a sandy beach, doing volunteer work on the other side of the world, or whatever it is he tells you he wants to do when he "retires." Someday we might be able to recreate your client's voice and his own image in his Picture Story, but for now we might have to settle for cartoon characters or models, using lots of humor, graphics, colors, and animation. Make sure the room is comfortable with lots of ambiance. Seat him in a big comfortable chair, or on a couch. Create an atmosphere of a home entertainment center. Let him control the images and sound with his own set of controls. This experience needs to be as interactive as possible. Show him a movie where he is the star. The focal point needs to be his own future Picture Story, not you, and not the financials.

Have a "make it happen" screen where all he has to do is hit a few buttons to automatically debit his accounts to invest, gift, or spend allowing him to implement your recommendations immediately. Soon the entire implementation process, and payment of your fee, can be paperless, but for now the client will probably need to sign the paperwork. The purpose here is to inform, entertain, and motivate, so we need to make certain that the client stays involved in the presentation as well as the implementation. The Picture Story can include information about the investments, insurance, housing, or charitable gift you are recommending as a solution to make his dream come true.

Give him a CD-ROM version of his Picture Story as well as the hard copy of the numbers to take home with him. You can still make an interactive high-tech presentation if you meet with the client in his home. Although you cannot create the same atmosphere, at least not at this time, you can make his story come alive with interactive CD-ROM Picture Stories. Work with computer and marketing students at the local university. Many are now experimenting with new ideas and applications for interactive technologies. They might be willing to work with you to try out new high-tech ideas using your business application.

No-Frills Financial Services

You will find many boomers who are either not affluent or are not appropriate for the "kid glove" treatment described above. They still need financial advice, but you will need to be creative in designing services and compensation when serving their needs. Stock brokerage firms are doing a remarkable job of providing services to meet the needs of all boomers, although those of lesser means will pose a bigger challenge for financial service professionals.

As long as the stock brokerage firms are set up as registered investment advisors, they will be in a position to give fee-based advice to all three groups of baby boomers as well as the upscale boomer. But they will need to capture more of the "Upscale" and the "Freebie" boomers to cover the costs of serving the "Do-It-Yourself" and the "Needy" boomers. Since some of these groups could come to their own conclusions if they had the correct information, it might be more efficient to establish no-frills information centers to provide both product and nonproduct information only, without advice, and let it be known that the information center is underwritten by a certain insurance company or a stock brokerage firm, or perhaps a group of such underwriters. Any product could be implemented by the sponsoring financial services companies. This could be an effective public relations strategy.

Products and Services They Seek

The boomers' resources are not unlimited, but their needs are great. They will be attracted to financial products that create value, or the illusion of value. Many who are afraid of losing their jobs due to downsizing will also be attracted to products that offer liquidity, or stable, nonfluctuating balances. At the same time they need growth and protection of their assets and income. Products that offer a solution to more than one need will be popular. Here are some product scenarios that might appeal to the boomers:

- Hybrid products that combine any of the following: equities, long term care insurance, disability insurance, life insurance.

- Disability and long term care insurance with return of premium or cash value buildup, especially with equities they chose.

- Reverse mortgages with increasing income tied to equities.

- Equities with a guaranteed "bailout" downside.

- Securities with tax-favored growth.

- Social consciousness investments.

- Investments with planned giving proto-types.

Services

Regardless of their socioeconomic level, all boomers will want and need services that address the same basic issues. Whether or not they plan to continue working, they want to know that they can afford to "retire," if only temporarily. They seek the following services or answers to the following questions:

- How much money will I need?

- How much do I need to save?

- Where should I invest?

- How do I protect my savings and income?

- How do I deal with the challenges in my life such as unlaunched children, college funding, and aging parent responsibilities?
- How do I access convenient high-tech services.

The boomer will want you to be his partner as he plans for and lives out his future. Unlike previous generations, he is extraordinarily independent. He knows what he wants and he wants you to be his partner as he creates his own reality. He will be looking for professionals who can help him make magic.

CHAPTER 10 ENDNOTES

1. Cheryl Russell, "The Baby Boom Turns 50," *American Demographics*, quote from 1994 General Social Survey (December 1995), p. 22.

2. Ibid.

3. Pamela Mergenbagen, "Retirement Rethinking," *American Demographics*, quote from April 1991 *The Gallup Poll Monthly* (June 1994), p. 28.

4. U.S. Congressional Budget Office, "Baby Boomers in Retirement: An Early Perspective" (September 1993).

5. B. Douglas Bernheim, "The 1994 Merrill Lynch Baby Boom Retirement Index" (Stanford University, July 1994).

6. B. Douglas Bernheim, "The 1995 Merrill Lynch Baby Boom Retirement Index" (Stanford University, 1995).

7. Merrill Lynch, "The Seventh Annual Merrill Lynch Retirement and Financial Planning Survey" (1995).

8. U.S. Trust, "Survey of Affluent Americans VIII" (United States Trust Company, July 1995).

9. Peter G. Peterson, *Facing Up* (New York: Simon & Schuster, 1994).

10. Employee Benefits Research Institute, "Public Attitudes on Social Security" (Gallup Organization, EBRI Report #G-62, 1995).

11. Jeffrey P. Rosenfeld, president, Plan Wise, Bayside, New York, interview by author, February 2, 1996.

12. Russell, "The Baby Boom Turns 50."

13. Cheryl Russell, *The Master Trend: How the Baby Boom Generation Is Remaking America* (New York: Plenum Press, 1993), Chapter 5.

14. Faith Popcorn, *The Popcorn Report* (New York: Harper Business, 1992), Part Five.

15. Charles Martin, president, Martin Communications, Inc. Hood River, Oregon, interview by author, February 15, 1996: *Edutainment* is "educational content imbedded in a format that holds the viewer's attention. Call the viewer, 'an interviewer.'"

Further Reading

CHAPTER ONE

Ackerman, Robert J., Ph.D. *Perfect Daughters*. Deerfield Beach, Florida: Health Communications, Inc. Ackerman takes a look at women who are daughters of alcoholics, but this book is helpful for anyone who comes from a dysfunctional family.

Bach, Richard. *Illusions*. New York: Delacorte Press, 1977. For an entertaining and lighthearted approach to life's lessons, read anything by Richard Bach.

———. *One*. New York: Dell Publishing, 1988.

———. *The Bridge Across Forever*. New York: Dell Publishing, 1984.

Bailey, Alice A. *From Intellect to Intuition*. New York: Lucius Publishing Company, 1960. An excellent discussion of the workings of the western mind from a logical, left-brained approach as contrasted with the eastern mind which experiences a more feeling, right-brained approach. Bailey, who writes from a metaphysical perspective, points out the limitations of the purely intellectual approach. I recommend anything written by Bailey for further insight into the challenges to attainment of full maturity.

Bessant, Annie. *Death—and After?* Madras: The Theosophical Publishing House, 1977. A philosophical and very thought-provoking treatment of the subject of death.

Borensenko, Joan. *Fire in the Soul*. New York: Warner Books, Inc., 1993. This book is about the process of transformation, which every mature person has experienced or understands as an ongoing reality. It is filled with anecdotes of those who have lived through the process.

Bradshaw, John. *Creating Love*. New York: Bantam Books, 1992. Bradshaw talks about what comes after dealing with the challenging issues of breaking loose from the family mythologies—creating love. Highly recommendable.

————. *Home Coming*. New York: Bantam, 1990. I have found Bradshaw's work invaluable in learning how to understand people and their motivations. His work is especially helpful when dealing with the less mature adult.

Chopra, Deepak. *The Seven Spiritual Laws of Success*. San Rafael: Amber-Allen Publishing/New World Library, 1994. An abbreviated version of Chopra's beliefs on abundance and how to create it. This is a must read for every baby boomer who will need to know how to create abundance. It also includes one of the best explanations of "detachment" I have ever read.

Collins, Mabel. *Light on the Path*. Madras: The Theosophical University Press, 1976. A concise discussion of the human transformational process, and the aspects of detachment. After listening to this tape (or reading it in book form), you will have a clear understanding of why so few pass on to the highest levels of human maturity.

A Course in Miracles. Glen Ellen, CA: Foundation For Inner Peace, 1992. This is the text used by students of A Course in Miracles. It is probably one of the best curricula for those who are ready to confront and deal with fear, often manifested as anger, judgment, and other self-defeating behaviors. Terrific reading for anyone who is serious about moving to a new level of maturity.

Covey, Stephen R. *The 7 Habits of Highly Effective People*. New York: Simon & Schuster, Inc., 1989. Adapted for audio by Sound Ideas. An easy-to-understand version of some of the more philosophical and psychological concepts regarding maturity and adult-level communication, especially as it applies to the business world.

De Laszlo, Violet Staub, ed. *The Basic Writings of C. G. Jung*. New York: The Modern Library, 1993. This is a surprisingly easy-to-understand overview of Carl Jung and his theories.

Dyer, Wayne W., Ph.D. *You'll See It When You Believe It*. New York: Avon Books, 1990. This is a touching account of Dyer's own personal transformation and how we can create our own reality.

Eadie, Betty J. *Embraced by the Light*. Placerville, CA: Gold Leaf Press, 1992. An engaging autobiographical account of Eadie's near death experience and how it changed her outlook on life and death.

Ford, Betty. *The Times of My Life*. New York: Ballantine Books, 1979. Former First Lady Betty Ford reveals how she struggled to grow out of denial and into acceptance of herself. A very candid and touching account of her determination to confront and deal with alcoholism.

Hendrix, Harville, Ph.D., *Getting the Love You Want—A Guide for Couples*. New York: Henry Holt & Company, 1988. A must read for anyone who seeks to have an adult relationship of any kind, but between mates especially. It demonstrates the real meaning of adult relationships and what it means to take personal responsibility in an intimate relationship.

Hubbard, Barbara Marx. *The Book of Co-Creation: The Revelation Our Crisis Is a Birth*. Novato, California: Nataraj Publishing, 1993. This is an autobiographical account of Hubbard's process of maturation. She looks at it from several different viewpoints, including a religious one.

Humbert, Elie. *C. G. Jung: The Fundamentals of Theory and Practice*. Wilmette: Chiron Publications, 1993. This small book makes Jung's basic concepts simple and easy to understand for those not familiar with his work. Humbert's treatment of Jung's Individuation Process is valuable reading for anyone attempting to get a grasp on the maturation process.

Jampolski, Gerald G. *Good-Bye to Guilt*. New York: Bantam Books, 1985. Jampolski has the keen ability to take profound concepts and express them in simple, lighthearted terms. In this work he shows us how there is no need for guilt and the destructive role guilt plays when it lingers.

———. *Love Is Letting Go of Fear*. Toronto: Bantam Books, 1970. You can read this book in an hour, but its lessons will last you a lifetime. A simple, unpretentious treatment of a baffling, often misunderstood subject: the relationship of love and fear. This is required reading for anyone who is trying to see things in a different, more constructive way.

Lee, John. *The Flying Boy*. Deerfield Beach, Florida: Health Communications, Inc., 1951. Excellent reading for anyone who has difficulty committing to anything.

Lerner, Harriet Goldhor, Ph.D. *The Dance of Anger*. New York: Harper & Row, 1985. An insightful treatment of anger and the role it plays in our ability to relate to others, including its insidious goal to hurt and to destroy, often covertly.

Maslow, A. H. *The Farther Reaches of Human Nature*. New York: Penguin Books, 1971. This work was published after Maslow's death. It explores among other things, "metamotivations," or the motivations of those whose lower needs are already gratified. This is excellent reading for anyone who wishes to understand the mature consumer.

May, Rollo. *Man's Search for Himself*. New York: Dell Publishing, 1953. I particularly enjoy May's discussion of time and the transcendence of it which we experience by living in the moment. This book will help you understand the concept of "timelessness" in the mature person.

Melody, Pia. *Facing Codependency*. San Francisco: Harper, 1989. Pia Melody's work is indispensable if you want to understand people and what motivates them to act the way they do.

Moyers, Bill. *The Power of Myth*. New York: Doubleday, 1988. Any conversation between Joseph Campbell and Bill Moyers is well worth your time to read or view. This particular book is fascinating reading about the various myths throughout history which still influence our thinking.

Parrish-Harra, Carol W. *The New Age Handbook on Death and Dying*. Santa Monica: IBS Press, 1982. A practical nonintellectual approach to the various aspects of death including how to relate to those who are dying and some possible reasons why some have difficulty dealing with death.

Pearce, Joseph Chilton. *The Crack in the Cosmic Egg*. New York: Washington Square Press, Pocket Books, 1971. Pierce, an educator, takes a look at the transformational process, especially the aspects which appear when the process begins.

Peck, M. Scott, Ph.D. *The Road Less Traveled*. New York: Simon and Schuster, 1978. This is one of the best books, and most widely read, on taking personal responsibility.

Redfield, James. *The Celestine Prophecy*. New York: Warner Books, Inc., 1993. This little book, although fiction, provides thoughtful insight into what life is all about from Redfield's point of view. It offers another way of looking at life from the point of view of the more mature adult.

Sanford, John A. *Between People*. New York: Paulist Press, 1982. Sanford explains how when we communicate, the male or female parts of ourselves are actually communicating with the male or female aspects of the other person. An interesting treatment of a Jungian concept.

———. *The Invisible Partners*. New York: Paulist Press, 1989. There is more to a relationship than meets the eye. According to Sanford, each male has a female side and each female has a male side. He points out how often we are having a conversation with an aspect of the other which is not obvious.

Satir, Virginia. *Your Money Faces*. Milibrae: Celestial Arts, 1978. Beautifully written, and not at all heady. Satir confronts us with our self-imprisonment, which keeps us bound to old, self-destructive thought patterns and belief systems.

Sheehy, Gail. *New Passages*. New York: Random House, Inc., 1995. An engaging audio version of Sheehy's book, which discusses how we can grow as a result of life's most challenging experiences. This work in particular is important reading for the baby boomer who is nearing, or already in a midlife crisis.

Singer, June. *Androgyny—Toward a New Theory of Sexuality*. Garden City: Anchor Books, 1977. Singer has invested a great deal of her career as a Jungian psychologist studying the roles the female and male sides of us play and how our undeveloped male and female aspects result in a less than fully developed adult.

———. *Boundaries of the Soul*. Garden City, New York: Anchor Books, 1973. Singer offers an expansive view of human development based on the work of Carl Jung.

———. *Energies of Love Sexuality Revisited*. Garden City, New York: Anchor Press/Doubleday, 1983. Singer discusses the inner workings of male- and femaleness and how they interact between people as well as within ourselves.

Viorst, Judith. *Necessary Losses*. New York: Fawcett Gold Medal, 1986. A popular book that brings fresh insight into the meaning of losses we experience in our lives.

Watts, Alan. *The Book*. New York: Vintage Books, 1972. Alan Watts was a man of few words, but what he wrote was profound. This book includes his ideas about life, its meaning, and where we fit in.

Woititz, Janet G. *Struggle for Intimacy*. Deerfield Beach, Florida: Health Communications, Inc., 1985. Offers valuable insight into our need to be intimate with ourselves as well as with others, and that the ability to be intimate (not necessarily sexually) is one aspect of maturity.

Woodman, Marion. "Holding the Tension of the Opposites," an audio tape. Sounds True, 1991. Includes an easy-to-understand explanation about integration of the spirit and body, and the role played by addictions during the struggle. Addictions can include any behaviors which are self-defeating such as inappropriate outdated belief systems and behaviors.

———. *Leaving My Father's House*. Boston: Shambhala, 1993. If you wish to understand the process of the transformation of human experiences, and all its terrors, as you grow into full maturity, read everything written by Woodman. In this work, she takes a look at three women who share their stories about their own personal transformation. This is great reading for women as well as men whose female side is undeveloped.

———. *The Pregnant Virgin*. Toronto: Inner City Books, 1985. Excellent reading for women in particular and men as they strive to integrate the more receptive, female aspects of their personalities.

———. *The Ravaged Bridegroom*. Toronto: Inner City Books, 1990. More great reading by a gifted writer and Jungian psychologist on the struggle for wholeness.

The book explores her analysands' dreams, which reflect the collective unconscious of humanity struggling to integrate and become whole human beings.

Young-Sowers, Meridith L. *Spiritual Crisis*. Walpole, New Hampshire: Stillpoint Publishing, 1993. The path to maturity is no easy road as most of our older clients will tell us. Sowers discusses the benefits to be derived from life's challenges.

Zukov, Gary. *The Seat Of The Soul*. New York: Simon & Schuster, 1989. A very engaging book which pulls together many seemingly disparate concepts such as science, philosophy, and evolution of the human. And yet, it is easy reading.

CHAPTER TWO

Damasio, Antonio R. *Descartes' Error*. New York: Avon Books, 1994. Demasio discusses the brain, the emotions, and the body in one book, demonstrating how science and philosophy coexist in the human. A fascinating book written for the layman.

Chopra, Deepak. *Ageless Body–Timeless Mind*. New York: Harmony Books, 1993. Chopra shares his extensive knowledge of the relationship between how we think and our physical vitality using his background as medical practitioner and his belief in eastern philosophies. The book includes several anecdotes.

———. *Creating Health*. Boston: Houghton Mifflin Company, 1991. An enlightened physician and philosopher, Chopra shares in all his writings how the mind and the body are connected and how we can improve our health by creating a healthy mental outlook.

Hochanadel, Gail Susan, Ph.D. diss. "Neuropsychological Changes in Aging: A Process-Oriented Error Analysis." Clark University, 1991.

Martin-Halpine, Loretta A., Ph.D. diss. "Decision-Making and Older Adults: Accurate Decision-Making as a Demonstration of Practical Wisdom." Indiana University, 1990.

Moyers, Bill. *Healing and the Mind*. New York: Doubleday, 1993. Moyers interviews healers who view the human systems as a unit: mind, body, and spirit. If you think that growing old means falling apart, this book will change your mind. The wisdom of the mind will prevail if we will allow it.

Pollack, Richard David, Ph.D. diss. "Deductive Reasoning in Late Adulthood." Temple University, 1992.

Spence, Brenda A., Ph.D. diss. "Determinants of Cognitive Functioning in the Aging: A Hierarchical Linear Analysis." University of Notre Dame, 1990.

Williams, Mark E. *The American Geriatric Society's Complete Guide to Aging and Health*. New York: Harmony Books, 1995. This is a good basic book about health care issues in the later years.

CHAPTER THREE

Hopkins, Tom. *How to Master the Art of Selling*. Scottsdale, AZ: Tom Hopkins International, 1982. Never pass up an opportunity to hear Tom Hopkins speak. When with him, I always got the feeling that it was not so much what he said but the warmth and compassion with which he said it that really mattered to people. But it was his sales techniques to which I attribute much of my success as a Realtor in the 1970s. If you cannot arrange to attend his seminars, read this book.

CHAPTER EIGHT

Pirkl, James. *Transgenerational Design: Products for an Aging Population*. New York: Van Nostrand Rhinehold, 1994. This book discusses ergonomically designed products appropriate for *all* generations, not just the aging.

CHAPTER NINE

Gruber, Joan M. *Your Money: It's a Family Affair*. Dallas: Odenwald Press, 1996. A collection of articles originally written for senior citizen newspapers on the basic financial planning issues, including how the older person and his family will be affected by changing public policy. A concise and informative book for the adult child who wants to know about how to deal with the financial issues of aging parents and relatives.

Weltman, Barbara. *Your Parent's Financial Security*. New York: John Wiley & Sons, 1992. A practical book about the financial issues of aging parents written by an attorney.

CHAPTER TEN

Borden, Karl. "Social Security Privatization–Dismantling the Pyramid: The Why and How of Privatizing Social Security." Washington, D.C.: Cato Institute (August 14, 1995). This is one of the most credible pieces about the various proposals to privatize Social Security.

Braus, Patricia. "Will Boomers Give Generously?" *American Demographics*. July 1994, 48. This article looks into how baby boomers feel about charitable giving and their favorite causes.

Dychtwald, Ken. *Age Wave*. New York: Bantam Books, 1990. This is a must read if you are not familiar with the demographics of our aging society.

Employee Benefits Research Institute. "Are Workers Kidding Themselves." Washington, D.C.: Results of the 1995 Retirement Confidence Survey, EBRI Issue Brief Number 168 (December 1995).

_____. "Baby Boomers in Retirement: What Are Their Prospects?" Baltimore, Maryland: Johns Hopkins University Press. SR-23, EBRI Issue Brief Number 151 July 1994. Read anything from EBRI to find out about retirement economics. This report, like most others, points out the challenges the boomers are facing.

_____. "Public Attitudes on Social Security." Washington, D.C.: Full Report based on the survey conducted by Gallup Organization, Inc. (1995). This is another report that points out how uninformed the public is about Social Security and its ambivalence about what to do regarding any perceived problems. Not surprisingly, it reveals the public's overwhelming belief that Social Security will not be there when they retire.

The Equitable Life Assurance Society. "The Equitable Nest Egg Study." May 10, 1994. An interesting study about the investment habits of those nearing retirement. The study includes surprising statistics about the boomers and the current older generation's attitudes about their perceived investment knowledge, including how men and women in the different generations view their abilities.

Farnham, Alan. "The Windfall Awaiting the New Inheritors." *Fortune*. (May 7, 1990). This article dispels the myth that the boomers stand to inherit wealth. Whatever they do inherit will not be enough to make up for what they have not saved for retirement.

Francese, Peter. "How to Target the Baby Boom." *American Demographics*. American Demographics, Inc., 1993. This is a composite of articles which have appeared in *American Demographics* about how to market to the baby boomers.

Friedland, Robert. "When Support and Confidence Are at Odds: The Public's Understanding of the Social Security Program." National Academy of Social Insurance, May 1994. This shocking report reveals the ignorance of the public regarding how Social Security works and the current problems of the system.

Goodman, John C. "Health Care After Retirement: Who Will Pay?" Dallas: National Center For Policy Analysis, NCPA Policy Report N. 139 (June 1989). This is a shocking report about the realities of the future of Medicare and the crisis our country is facing regarding health care entitlements.

Kemper Investments. "Kemper Pre-Retirement Research Home Office Report." (December 1995). This extensive report is about the Silent Generation, currently age 50–64. It is worthwhile reading and packed with valuable information.

Kemper Investments. "Pre-Retirement Research Wholesaler Report." (December 1995). This report summarizes the Kemper Pre-Retirement Research Home Office Report.

Kotlikoff, Laurence J. *Generational Accounting*. New York: The Free Press, 1992. This book by a well-known economist is written in an easy-to-read, jargon-free style. In his tell-all fashion, Kotlikoff makes it clear that the current system of entitlements will bankrupt our children and grandchildren. Kotlikoff keeps no secrets.

Lash, Joseph P. *Eleanor and Franklin*. New York: The New American Library, 1971. This is the story about the life and times of Eleanor and Franklin Roosevelt. It provides a rare insight into the circumstances that surrounded the creation of the concept of entitlements, Social Security in particular, and other government programs.

Peterson, Peter G. *Facing Up*. New York: Simon & Schuster, 1994. This is a factual, yet passionate, discussion of current public policy, how we got here, and why the old paradigms will no longer work. A startling account of what the future holds if we fail to make dramatic changes in entitlements now.

Scholen, Ken. *Retirement Income on the House*. Marshall, Minnesota: National Center for Home Equity Conversion, 1982. This book outlines the basics of reverse mortgages, who makes such loans, and the benefits and drawbacks.

———. *Your New Retirement Nestegg*. Apple Valley, Minnesota: NCHEC Press, 1995.

Stockman, Larry V. and Cynthia S. Graves. *Grown-Up Children Who Won't Grow Up*. Rocklin, California: Prima Publishing, 1990. The number of unlaunched children is reaching epidemic proportions. Supporting adult children well into adulthood is often a deterrent to the parents' financial independence in retirement. Psychologist Larry Stockman offers a practical way to help both parents and children live independently.

Toffler, Alvin and Heidi. *Creating a New Civilization*. Atlanta: Turner Publishing, Inc., 1994. This is a lively and entertaining account of the transformation our society is experiencing as we move into the "Third Wave" civilization, which features information as its central resource and smaller marketing segments that target increasingly "demassified media."

INDEX

A

Adult children
  benefits of client relationships,
    200–201
  compensation for services,
    202–203
  corporations and, 192–194
  emergencies, 203
  market defined, 191–194
  media and, 194–195
  needs of, 195–200
  prospecting, 201
Advertising, 50–51
  audience analysis, 118
  comparative advertising, 116
  consumer needs and values,
    112–113
  John Nuveen Human Bond
    campaign, 122–129
  Kemper Funds Nest Egg
    campaign, 129–131
  marketing message, 110–112
  maturity market and, 112–113,
    116, 130, 133–134
  packaging, 111–112
  purpose of, 110–111
  tributes to aging, 132–133
  TV and radio advertising, 51, 119
Age Wave Communications
  Corporation, 152–153
Aging
  attention span and, 33

Aging *(cont.)*
  brain changes, 32
  cognitive functions, 31–32,
    36–38
  equilibrium (balance), 29–30
  hearing, 27–29
  incontinence, 30
  language comprehension,
    34–36
  muscular changes, 30
  physiological aspects, 25–26
  response time, 33–34
  sleep patterns, 28, 30–31
  vision, 26–27, 32–33
Altgelt and Korge Advertising
  Agency, 119
Alzheimer's disease, 32, 36
A.M. Best, 146
American Association of Retired
  People (AARP), 62, 66, 116,
  133–136, 193
    AARP Scudder Funds, 149
    Women's Financial Information
    Program, 66
The American College, 62
American Express Financial
  Advisors, 145, 153–154
American Funds, 147
American Institute of Certified
  Public Accountants, 62
American Skandia Life Assurance
  Corp., 160
    Advisors Portfolio, 144–146
American Society on Aging, 62

U

V

W

Asset Allocation—Roger C. Gibson
Balancing Financial Risk

Second Edition

Noted expert Roger Gibson provides a thorough review to the capital market behind asset allocation, plus step-by-step guidelines for designing and implementing appropriate investment strategies.
250 pp. ISBN: 1-55623-164-4 $50.00

Charitable Remainder Trusts—Peter J. Fagan
A Proven Strategy For Reducing Estate and Income Taxes Through Charitable Giving

Since the 1980s, several Internal Revenue tax code changes have severely restricted the number of individual income tax deductions available to American taxpayers. Although these changes continue today, one area has survived the onslaught of the new and increased activity, the charitable deduction. In *Charitable Remainder Trusts*, author Peter Fagan outlines the information that enables you to make clear decisions about your wealth.
200 pp. ISBN: 0-7863-0229-1 $50.00

The Financial Advisor's Guide to Divorce Settlement— Carol Ann Wilson
Helping Your Clients Make Sound Financial Decisions

Divorce is both an emotional event and an economic event, forever affecting the finances of both members of a former economic unit. With divorce continuing to divide half of all marriages, financial advisors must understand the issues surrounding divorce to help clients reduce the financial devastation often created by this common event.
225 pp. ISBN: 0-7863-0851-6 $45.00

The New Life Insurance Investment Advisor— Ben G. Baldwin
Achieving Financial Security for You and Your Family Through Today's Insurance Products

This completely updated best-seller provides professionals and savvy investors with a solid understanding of the dazzling array of insurance products on the market today. Insurance products such as life insurance and annuities can provide balance and long-term benefits to a profitable investment portfolio. *New Life Insurance Investment Advisor* shows just how to use insurance products to obtain the best overall return on an investment.
350 pp. ISBN: 1-55738-512-2 $24.95

The Wealth Management Index—Ross Levin
The Financial Advisor's System for Assessing & Managing Your Client's Plans & Goals

In this landmark book, Ross Levin presents the Wealth Management Index™, an innovative tool for financial advisors to quantify their clients' success in financial planning. The index helps financial advisors establish rational goals with their clients and measure their progress toward achieving goals.
200 pp. ISBN: 07863-1020-0 $50.00

Wealth Management—**Harold R. Evensky**

The Financial Advisor's Guide to Investing and Managing
Your Client's Assets

Wealth Management lays out all the secrets for attracting new clients, managing their expectations and establishing workable investment plans. It provides financial professionals with the tools and information to effectively run a financial advisory/asset management business as part of the overall financial advisory practice.

375 pp. ISBN: 0-7863-0478-2 $50.00